THE PLAYS

Applications for permission to perform these plays should be addressed
to the author, care of Dalkey Archive Press.

Library of Congress Cataloging-in-Publication Data

Reed, Ishmael, 1938-
[Plays. Selections]
Ishmael Reed: the plays / by Ishmael Reed. -- 1st ed.
p. cm.
ISBN 978-1-56478-551-0 (pbk. : alk. paper)
1. African Americans--Drama. I. Title.
PS3568.E365A6 2009
812'.54--dc22
                                                2009018674

Partially funded by a grant from the Illinois Arts Council, a state agency, and by the
University of Illinois at Urbana-Champaign

www.dalkeyarchive.com

Design by Danielle Dutton
Photograph of Ishmael Reed by Ed Lawrence
Printed on permanent/durable acid-free paper and bound in the
United States of America

Ishmael Reed
THE PLAYS

DALKEY ARCHIVE PRESS
CHAMPAIGN AND LONDON

For Adrienne Kennedy, Nora Vaughn, Mona Vaughn Scott,
Sean Vaughn Scott, Rome Neal, Miguel Algarin,
Carla Blank, Vern Henderson, Ed Bullins,
Carman Moore, and Bill Cook

Table of Contents

9   INTRODUCTION

23   MOTHER HUBBARD

101   SAVAGE WILDS

163   HUBBA CITY

225   THE PREACHER AND THE RAPPER

281   THE C ABOVE C ABOVE HIGH C

337   BODY PARTS

Introduction

When I was a kid in grammar school, I holed up in my room reading stories about the doings of royal families in European countries. In these stories, ordinary people with pluck and luck could go far and some might work their way into the castle. In second grade, I started a play about a young man seeking his fortune.

I was considered a discipline problem by most of my teachers. Two viewed me differently. One was Fred Bartholomew, a music instructor who traveled from school to school teaching kids how to play the violin. He thought that I had an exceptional talent and when I performed for him, he ran from the classroom and called my mother and alerted the principal. I studied violin for about two years with Fred Bartholomew and resumed playing with a string quartet in high school. Though I get called an angry black arts militant from time to time, I once played Schubert's "Death and the Maiden," something that the majority of Eurocentrics can't claim. (Of course, black male writers have been considered a discipline problem, bitter, angry, unruly, and crazy ("paranoid") for over a hundred years, and even a man with the grace of James Baldwin was called "antagonistic.")

The other teacher was a black teacher, Hortense Nash, member of one of Buffalo's historic old families, who gave me tickets to concerts. The closest I got to a professional theater person in high school was Nanette Lancaster, who claimed to have some connection to actor Franchot Tone through a 1920s Buffalo theater stock company known as the McGarry Players. She really looked out for me and encouraged me to seek a career in the theater. When Ms. Lancaster was going over theater techniques in the classroom she sometimes interrupted her lectures, telling the class that she wanted "Ishmael to learn this." I wasn't used to receiving this kind of individual attention. She was a fierce right-winger and tried to indoctrinate me with America First pamphlets. I'd read them at breakfast and would return them to her covered with spots of syrup. She never complained.

In the late '50s, Ray Smith, then a roommate, Fred Clifton, whom I met at The University at Buffalo, and NBA winner, Lucille Clifton, and I began The Buffalo Community Dramatic Workshop at the Michigan Avenue YMCA. Our producer was Dr. Joe Byron, who once secured the auditorium at Roswell Hospital where he then worked for a performance of *Raisin in the Sun* by Lorraine Hansberry. I played Beneatha's gentleman caller, George Murchison.

At the Y, I appeared as Creon in Jean Anouilh's *Antigone* and in Tennessee Williams's *Moony's Kid Don't Cry*. Lucille and her late husband Fred's performance in *A Streetcar Named Desire* was called "poetic" and " sensitive" by The Buffalo Evening News.

In 1960, I auditioned for a role in Edward Albee's *The Death of Bessie Smith* and got the role of the orderly. It was staged at the Jewish Center's theater-in-the-round, and directed by Neal Du Brock, a director who premiered Edward Albee's *Box* and Lanford Wilson's *Lemon Sky*. Well-known director José Quintero came up from New York to attend one of the performances.

While writing for a local black newspaper and living in Buffalo's Talbot Mall projects, named for the black abolitionist, I was reading plays by England's "Angry Young Men." These plays spoke to my condition. I was young, married, and a father. We were poor and my job paid eighty-eight dollars every two weeks. I decided to try my hand at a play.

The result was "Ethan Booker," a play about clashes between Christians and members of the Nation of Islam at a historical black college. The play was lost when a car driven by Bart Farmer, an art critic, broke down on the way to New York during my attempt to leave town. His car was never recovered. I lost all of the documents having to do with the first twenty-two years of my life, including my high-school diploma, and newspaper clippings.

During an earlier weekend trip to New York, a screenwriter had read parts of the play at Chumley's, a bar located on Bedford Street in Greenwich Village. I was introduced to him by Dave Sharpe, an Irish-American poet with whom I shared an apartment briefly after arriving in New York. That was enough to convince me to leave Buffalo for New York.

In New York, I wrote poetry, prose, and finally a novel, *The Free-Lance Pallbearers*, which was published in 1967. New York cultural life offered many temptations and I was being showered with praise and fame. Before my novel was published, however, I left for Los Angeles with my partner Carla Blank, whose *Wall Street Journal* (1966), performed at the Judson Church, featured classical Japanese dancer Suzushi Hanayagi and Carla. *Wall Street Journal* was among the first artistic responses to the Vietnam War. Instead of remaining in the New York limelight, she operated a Berkeley community theater school (1978–1992) with her business partner Jody Roberts and co-authored a book with Jody that introduced new techniques of teaching theater to middle school kids. Their book *Live On Stage!* was adopted by four states and school districts in the U.S. and Canada. She also continued her career as a choreographer. Carla returned to the dance world big time when she collaborated with Robert Wilson in a work called *Kool*, which began its run at the Guggenheim Museum in April 2009.

I hadn't thought about writing a play again until the late '70s when the Actors Studio organized a staged reading for my play *Hell Hath No Fury*, which was directed by Jason Buzas. Clarence Williams III, who was to gain fame as an actor on *Mod Squad*, played the lead. It was presented in 1980. When I entered the theater and heard actors actually speaking my lines, I was hooked. In 1981, Bill Cook, Dartmouth's legendary professor directed a version while I was Professor in Residence at Dartmouth. Ed Bullins directed a scene from the play that was presented at the Julia Morgan Theater in Berkeley on January 8, 1988.

The great playwright Adrienne Kennedy, who was teaching at UC Berkeley at the time, told me that Nora Vaughn, the late founder of Berkeley's The Black Repertory Group, wanted me to write about the crack epidemic that had hit Oakland and other cities in the 1980s. I had also been invited to become Writer in Residence for *The San Francisco Examiner* at the invitation of Willie Hearst III. Part of this deal was a nice apartment in Pacific Heights, where I wrote an article about the apathetic response to the crisis by officials in downtown Oakland, and mentioned that the City Manager, when a neighbor and I met with him, had been more interested in talking about his trip to England than dealing with the crack operation on my block. The City Manager made an angry call to my house and requested that I go to the police and take a lie detector test. I refused. The leading Oakland developer arranged for me to have dinner with the then-Mayor Lionel Wilson. But nothing happened and the crack operation was ended by what might be called light vigilantism. All of this entered into the work *Hubba City*, which premiered at The Black Rep in 1988 and later played at The Nuyorican Poets Café to good reviews in the *New York Times* and *New York Post*, the latter by the late Clive Barnes.

Bizarre incidents occurred during the first full production of a play of mine. During the second performance, the leading lady collapsed on stage and had to be rushed to the hospital. Our director, Vern Henderson, who, against my advice, used real guns to give the scenes more authenticity (they lacked cartridges), got into an altercation with a drunken San Francisco cop on the way home from a rehearsal. The cops converged upon him like gangbusters and demanded that he open the trunk of his car. They found the guns.

He tried to explain that the guns were used as props and showed the fake stage money, which he thought would convince them that he wasn't a drug dealer. They reasoned that the stage money was going to be used to deceive his clients. He went to trial, was convicted, lost his job and his apartment, and had to return to Mississippi. He returned a year or so later and directed another production of *Hubba City* that took place in San Francisco at the Potrero Hill Neighborhood House. A few years later he was dead. Vern Henderson's talent for a gritty dark theater has gone without recognition. In fact, one local reviewer thought that his arrest and conviction arising from a misunderstanding was funny. But with his skillful direction, our message about the complexity of the drug problem got through.

Though the media and Hollywood, in order to protect their target audience, white consumers, stereotype drug use and sales—another media hoax—as a black problem, I was aware that cocaine was the drug of choice among Washington's political and media elite. Even on Wall Street. Joseph Jett, an African-American bond trader and author of the memoir, *Black and White on Wall Street: The Untold Story of the Man Wrongly Accused of Bringing Down Kidder Peabody*, writes that such was the cocaine problem on The Street that waiters employed by restaurants located there had to clean up the coke residue left by diners in order to prepare for new patrons.

Journalist Liz Trotta says that her friend Craig Spence, who had connections with the Bush I White House and the Pentagon, was a crack addict. Col. North's secretary Fawn Hall said that she did coke on weekends in Georgetown, and in a book called *The Senator: My Ten Years with Ted Kennedy* by Richard E. Burke and William and Marilyn Hoffer, the authors report how widespread the use of cocaine was in official Washington:

> . . . although once you're even partly familiar with the drug's use, you sometimes pick up a sixth sense about who else is a user, even if the signs are no more overt than sim-

ply a runny nose. And in the Capitol, I noticed, there seemed to be a number of young people—and even some well-known congressmen and senators—who had a disproportionate series of 'colds' and runny noses, even out of season. There were also a number of lawmakers who were conservative Republicans by day, railing on the Senate floor about stiffer drug laws and the ills of drug users, who were coke users by night. This I knew from my own connection, who was more amused by the hypocrisy than anything else. I chalked it up to all the pressures we were under and the emerging, more lenient times.

Another report indicated the length to which the Justice Department went to use a black woman who was on welfare and food stamps to entrap Marion Barry, the black mayor of Washington, D.C. They paid her $1,700 per month.

African Americans have complained for decades about how they're treated differently by the criminal justice system than whites, and how black politicians seem more likely to be placed under surveillance than white politicians. In 1967, I produced a book about Adam Clayton Powell, Jr. in which I pointed out that white congressmen were guilty of the same practices that Powell was being hammered for. News stories about the Barry case exposed the lengths to which the government sought to entrap Barry:

> She kept calling him up to come to the room, and he resisted it because he had a sense: 'too many nosy rosies,' as he said, literally. But she said, 'look, I just got some takeout food from downstairs, they're delivering it to my room, why don't you come up here and have a bite to eat with me.' And that became the reason that Marion Barry actually came to the room, 'cause he didn't want to do that.
>
> He kept saying, 'I'll meet you downstairs.' He came to the room, and then it was a matter of Rasheeda Moore

actually getting Marion Barry to smoke some crack, and it took a lot of convincing, which I think was one of the weakest parts of the federal government's case. Because if you view the videotape, it wasn't just Marion Barry toking on a pipe; it was the amount of time and the amount of cajoling and the amount of liquor, in the form of cognac, that it took to get Marion Barry to light that crack pipe. (*Booknotes* interview with Harold Jaffe, October 2, 1994.)

While the big bucks media used the Barry incident as comic relief—which, like the OJ case, was meant to humiliate black Americans by proxy—many black observers saw his entrapment as a deliberate attempt on the government's part to diminish the power of a public official and to apply a double standard to how black and white politicians are treated. For example, while white politicians lie all the time about their affairs and continue to serve, Kwame Kilpatrick and his mistress went to jail. Many agreed with William Safire commenting about the Barry entrapment. He said, "never has the United States government stooped so low."

Fearless Kitty Kelley exposed the hypocrisy of the Barry entrapment when she reported in her book, *The Family: The Real Story of the Bush Dynasty* that George Bush was using cocaine at Camp David while his father and his justice department were persecuting Barry.

Savage Wilds was performed at Ed Bullins's BMT, the Bullins Memorial Theatre, in 1990. This theater was housed in a rundown building located on San Pablo Avenue, a section of town that might qualify as a "skid row." The collaboration offered me an opportunity to work with Bullins, one of the great playwrights of the American theater.

Savage Wilds dramatized the government and the media's hypocrisy as well as the foolishness of the philandering Mayor. Black media feminists led by the distinguished journalist Phyllis Crockett paid for a staged reading at a Washington, D.C. theater.

Ms. Crockett was one of those black journalists who criticized a notorious NPR product called *Ghetto Life 101*, executive-produced by Ellen Weiss. This broadcast, produced by David Isay, they charged, exploited two black kids to prowl the ghetto of Chicago, where they were assigned by Isay to record the most sordid material they could uncover and, when not finding some, invent it. *Savage Wilds* received a good review in *The Sacramento Bee*, and *The Amsterdam News* when it was performed in New York. After I read from the play at a Washington, D.C. auditorium, a *Washington Post* reporter chastised the play in an article whose title was "The Writer and the Joys of Paranoia."

An amusing episode took place during my collaboration with Bullins. One day, I entered my classroom to find written on the blackboard, "Dinner with Professor Reed at 5:30 P.M. Bring Your Own Watermelon." I was cool about it. I'd been tested by white and black students over the years. Most of them have been respectful. But from time to time I ran into a racist smart aleck, usually someone who grew up in isolation from those of a different culture than they. I knew the identity of the scribbler and invited him into my office. I told him that I could either report his actions to the dean or he could work with Ed Bullins at the Black Repertory Group. He chose to work with Ed Bullins. After ten weeks of participating in a Bullins workshop the student performed in one of his plays. This was a transformative experience for this student.

In theater, publishing, and even the gallery world, feminist arts have dominated black culture since the 1970s. Some of it has taken the form of chick lit. Some of the leaders of this wave have made sometimes caustic criticism of black male personal behavior, but since the middle persons who push this product and its consumers know very little about ethnic culture, they tend to treat individual characters as representing all members belonging to a particular group—the kind of group blame to which ethnic groups have been subjected, historically. This is like blaming white women for Lady Macbeth, and white men for the incestuous violator in the movie, *Bastard Out Of Carolina.*

I have noticed that some of the most fervent enthusiasts for this material are those who are silent about the abuse of women taking place in the ethnic groups to which they belong.

How many women are suffering in silence because all of the finger-pointing about misogyny is directed at black men? One has to agree with bell hooks that white feminists have a double standard for the misogyny of black and white men. She said that she was told by white feminists that in order for her to succeed, she had to write for them. This seems to be the historic pattern. That in order for a minority writer, artist, filmmaker to get over, one has to appeal to a white audience. In the movie *Cadillac Records*, which retreads the old "white man's burden" theme, a happy ending means that Muddy Waters has crossed over to white fans. I have been fortunate to create a body of work that has appeal across racial and ethnic groups. The late Walter Bowart, with whom I founded an underground newspaper, once forwarded a postcard from a friend. He said that he was traveling across the Gobi Desert and found a kid sitting next to a camel. She was holding a copy of my first novel.

A black art historian has said that the same double standard is also present in the art world. That if one doesn't present Mammy works or works that invoke the sexual depravity of the ante bellum period, one has to take one's portfolios elsewhere. Plays that are welcomed by mainstream producers, whose ideas haven't changed since the late Lorraine Hansberry observed that white producers have it in for cerebral blacks, are those in which the problems of black Americans are self inflicted, an angle that fit the Reagan era. Plays and movies that offer stock portraits of black men as buffoons and the embodiment of male evil are much in demand. Currently, HBO is preparing a series about the careers of Oakland California pimps. The real pimps are the HBO executives who sell the most degrading aspects of black life for profit and stunt the growth of the black actors whom they hire.

When I criticized David Simon and his fellow white writers for their creation of *The Wire*, which locates all drug sales and consumption among African Americans (when a recent report published in the *New York Times* documents soaring cocaine use among white teens), he said that I was against the work because he was a white writer writing about blacks. My reply was that I was opposed to this HBO product because the subject was a cliché. I proposed that HBO do something fresh. Maybe the family life of one of those suburbanites who is responsible for the proliferation of illegal weapons that are pouring into inner-city neighborhoods like mine.

I tried to address the double standard that bell hooks wrote about and some of the excesses of radical white corporate feminism in my play *Mother Hubbard*. First I attempted to make a film of the play, which was ruined when a soundman whom we were required to use by a nonprofit film company damaged the sound. After the early readings of the play at the Actors Studio, at Dartmouth, and in Boston, the play lay dormant until my partner Carla Blank produced a version at a private school where she was drama instructor: the Arrowsmith Academy. This convinced Miguel Algarín, producer of the Nuyorican Poets Café, who was traveling through Berkeley at the time, to give *Mother Hubbard* a run at the Café. I added song lyrics and the music was composed by Ronald Lee McIntyre. Mary Wilson of the Supremes attended one performance and asked for the part of Margo, which was granted by director Rome Neal. Neal directed all of my plays at the Nuyorican Poets Café.

With little money and a lot of creativity and invention he was even able to stage the big-cast *Gethsemane Park* in that tiny space.

Gethsemane Park was an opera for which I wrote the libretto, and Carmen Moore composed the music.

This double standard that bell hooks mentioned also applies to the music business. While white heavy metal has become the theme music for international fascism—the kid who murdered the students at Virginia Tech was a heavy metal fan—the media have singled out hip-hop for its misogyny. Admittedly there is a corporate hip-hop that is poisonous, but hip-hop has become the means of expression by those who lack media power all over the world. There is a Palestinian hip-hop. I recently interviewed Susanna La Polla, Italian hip-hop star who told me that hip-hop is the mainstream music in Italy. I tackled the contradictions of the Christian church's criticism of hip-hop in my play, *The Preacher and the Rapper*, arguing that the Christian ministers who were critiquing hip-hop were wedded to a book that provided a handbook for misogynists.

While serious hip-hop is a subversive music and therefore rarely played on commercial radio, I discovered that Louis Armstrong was the most unlikely subversive. My generation viewed Louis Armstrong as a Tom. Our music was bebop. He was too hot and corny for our tastes. Years later, I read that Armstrong got into trouble with the FBI for criticizing President Eisenhower and making other statements that didn't endear him to the establishment. Also, listening closely to modern trumpeters, including our hero, Miles Davis, I could hear the influence of Armstrong and the early musicians of the bop generation. I was not surprised that some referred to music of the swing era as "orchestrated" Armstrong. The play which includes an imaginary scene between Armstrong and Eisenhower in the oval office was entitled *The C Above C Above High C*, which was taken from Wynton Marsalis's description of Armstrong's technical abilities.

My most recent play, *Body Parts*, was produced at the Nuyorican Poets Café in 2008. It took on the issues of exploitation of blacks and Africans by pharmaceutical companies who use these populations to test dangerous drugs.

The play also covered the awarding of considerable op-ed column and television space to a select group of commentators because they mimic the lines formulated by the right-wing think tanks that fund them. Some of them front for operations that are covers for the eugenics movement, a connection that's been neglected by the news media that employ them to run with the points-of-view of the media bosses. A number of reporters are left leaning, but those who own the news product are conservatives. One report has it that 95% of the views printed on the op-ed page of newspapers jell with those of the media owners.

With the mass buyouts and firings of black, Hispanic, Native-American, and Asian-American journalists, the arts, fiction, theater, music, etc. will be the only venues available to them to challenge a mainstream narrative that is often hostile to them.

As a poet, playwright, novelist, and songwriter, I have, since the 1960s, been fortunate to have had editors who advocated for my work, even though I have been what is regarded as a midrange writer whose sales have been modest. The Black Repertory Group and the Nuyorican Poets Café have presented my plays without my being required to tone them down. But my career as an author with books published by the big firms is drawing to a close.

Recently, a giant publisher asked for an outline for an autobiography that they wanted from me. They approached me. It was decided that a book by me would only appeal to a "cult" and win prizes and critical praise. This is a firm that publishes books about black life written by white authors. Like what they used to do with Native Americans. Have their stories told by anthropologists when the Natives were capable of telling their own stories.

But unlike Chester Himes and Richard Wright who in their final years found themselves left out in the cold when large publishers rejected their manuscripts (including Richard Wright's great novel, *Island of Hallucination*, which remains unpublished), the contemporary African-American author—whose works make "mainstream" audiences uncomfortable—has alternatives.

I've published the works of authors since the 1970s. There's the small press. And then there's Dalkey. Dalkey has kept six of my titles in print. And now, the plays.

MOTHER HUBBARD

A PLAY IN TWO ACTS

Mother Hubbard was first presented in 1979 as a staged reading, at the Actors Studio in New York City, with Jason Buzas as director and actor Clarence Williams III playing the part of Rudolph Greene. Its next stage of production was as a film, which was shot in Oakland, California in 1983, also directed by Jason Buzas, and produced by Ishmael Reed and the Reed and Cannon Communications Company. In December 1997, *Mother Hubbard* was rewritten during workshops with students at Arrowsmith Academy, a private high school in Berkeley California, where it received its first fully mounted stage production. Carla Blank was the director. After viewing that production, Miguel Algarín, Executive Producer at the Nuyorican Poets Café, 236 East Third Street, New York City, suggested making it into a musical. Six songs were added to the script, and the musical version of *Mother Hubbard* premiered October 16, 1998 at the Nuyorican Poets Café with Rome Neal as director. The original score and musical direction was by Ronald L. McIntyre.

This script is the musical version, with the six songs, plus other musical cues indicated.

CAST OF CHARACTERS

Newscaster #1
Olympia Greene, women's lightweight champion of the world
Koko, her trainer
Rudolph Greene, Olympia's husband
Bobbie Rat
Rabbit Protestors #1 and #2
King Rabbit
Hubbardite Assassin/Guard
Newscaster #2
Cameraperson
Manicurist
Model
Mother Hubbard
Yvonne Hawkins, Mother Hubbard's assistant
Margo Madison, another assistant
Male Prisoners: First Man, Second Man, Third Man, and Pete Wilson
Woman
Dad
Mr. Money
Jocko Bing, fight promoter
Rex, Mother Hubbard's dog
Detective
Sportscaster

ACT I

SCENE 1

(The apartment belonging to Olympia and Rudolph Greene. Sparsely furnished. Photo on the wall of Kid Chocolate. On the mantle are boxing trophies. RUDOLPH is sewing Olympia's boxing trunks. He is medium sized and slight. Dresses like a nerd, bow tie, glasses, etc. Interrupts his sewing long enough to rise and turn on the radio. In a spotlighted area onstage, the NEWSCASTER #1 appears, sitting on a stool.)
(Sound Up and then Fades Out as NEWSCASTER #1 speaks: News Signature.)

NEWSCASTER #1: And here once again are tonight's top stories. The Hubbardites, a group of women terrorists, have just captured Sacramento, California. The Governor has fled. They are demanding sovereignty for the state and that it be renamed Califia, after the ancient Amazon Queen. Mother Hubbard has given all men exactly sixty days to leave the state. Those found in the state after that will be sent to what were described as recreational retreats. As you know, Mother Hubbard came to national attention when she, having had her Social Security, food stamps, and rent subsidy terminated, went to the bank to obtain an equity loan on her little cottage in order to feed her dog a bone. Denied by the bank, Ms. Hubbard's dog perished from malnutrition. Angered by this incident, Mother Hubbard began knocking off banks left and right, and soon rallied many women to her cause. The Governor tried to enlist the aid of the federal government, but due to the states' rights trend of the 1990s, California hasn't heard from Washington in more than a decade. Most people here don't know who the president is and don't care. And now we turn to sports: Olympia Greene, women's lightweight champion of the world, in a unification bout with the men's division, has knocked out Luis Rodriguez and is the new undisputed lightweight champion of the world.

> (*Sound Up: Station Break.*)
> (RUDOLPH *rises from his sewing and turns the radio off.*
> (*Sound Out with gesture.*)
> (*Disgustedly,* OLYMPIA *and her trainer,* KOKO, *enter. They ignore him. He continues to sew.*)

KOKO: I thought we'd never get out of there. The crowds trying to get into the dressing room. The press. We're lucky that they had an underground exit.

> (KOKO *flops down in a chair.*)

OLYMPIA: (*To* RUDOLPH) Hey, you. Make yourself busy. Go and fetch my trainer a root beer.

> (RUDOLPH *puts down the sewing and goes to the refrigerator.*)

KOKO: Olympia, must you be so hard on him?

OLYMPIA: I'm tired of carrying him, Koko. Everything he's done has been a failure. First it was real estate, then computer school, and now sewing classes. His mother said that he kept his paper route until he was twenty-six. He's never going to get it right. He'll never grow up. He's either at the park feeding birds or at the movies or the beach. He lives in a dream world.

KOKO: But he does the housework, he cooks. I wish I had a man like that.

OLYMPIA: I'd be better off hiring help. Now that I've won the light-weight championship of the world, I can afford all of the help I need. I don't need him. He's not as exciting as my new friends.

KOKO: Are you sure about them, Olympia? I mean, I don't want to get into your business, but they're charging everything to you. One of them insisted that he have a three hundred dollar ringside seat for tonight's fight and another jerk rented a Lincoln Town Car for every member of his family and charged it to you. The sports writers and the bookies didn't give you a chance. But then, a knockout in the second round. You've shocked the sports world.

OLYMPIA: I just followed your instructions, Koko. Kept hitting them with the Mexican liver punches. That weakened him. And then when he dropped his hands in order to protect his body, he left his head unguarded and I knocked him out. Good idea of yours, having me watch those César Chávez tapes.

KOKO: They're already making excuses. They say that Rodriguez deliberately threw the fight. That his wife and mother told him not to return home if he beat up a woman. I'm telling you, Olympia. These men will never give you credit.

OLYMPIA: You can't expect a fair decision from men. The referee, the judges, the sports writers, the trainers, the commentators, even the hotdog salesmen.

OLYMPIA and KOKO: All men!
    (RUDOLPH *enters carrying a bottle of root beer.*)

OLYMPIA: (*Hostile*) What took you so long?

RUDOLPH: One of my plants looked a little droopy. I had to coax it a little. Fuss with it.

OLYMPIA: Oh, you think that playing with those plants is more important than serving my guests? I'm the one who brings money into this household. You and your self-righteous disdain for money. You're always recycling things. Joining those nutty people who are trying to save the redwood forests. Protesting nuclear energy. If it weren't for my fight purses, you'd be recycling your stomach growls.

KOKO: It's alright, Olympia. I wasn't really thirsty.

RUDOLPH: I wish you'd get off my case, Olympia. Awwww, baby.
> (*Tenderly. He approaches* OLYMPIA *and tries to embrace her. Folding her arms, she wriggles from his grip.*)

Don't you see what your career is doing to us? Why don't you quit this violent sport? Go back and teach physical education.

OLYMPIA: A lot of good that did me. Not only did they have me teach gym, but I had to fill in as a history teacher. Shows you the little regard they have for history.

RUDOLPH: You didn't set out to be a boxer, anyway. You wanted to lose some weight, and took up noncompetitive boxing for exercise. But now look at you. A pug. Your nose has been broken twice. And who knows what else.

OLYMPIA: You're just jealous. Jealous because I'm famous, but nobody's ever heard of Rudolph Greene.

RUDOLPH: You know that kind of thing doesn't impress me, Olympia. I just don't want to see you get your brains scrambled or for you to get cauliflower ears. You've been lucky so far, but one of these days your luck is going to run out. Won't it Koko?

KOKO: Look, I'd better go.

OLYMPIA: You can stay. He can go.
(*Softens*)
I don't want to hurt your feelings, Rudolph. I mean we had some good times since that day we met in graduate school. But things have changed. I have new interests. New friends.

RUDOLPH: (*Angry*) Gangsters, players, and party girls. I wish they'd stop dropping ashes on my rug. All they do is make bets and talk about money. They seem obsessed with money. Money this, money that. You'd think that money were alive or something. They have no cultural interests whatsoever. I'll bet that not one of them has read Proust, or meditated over Beethoven's last quartets. One of them came over here and made a long distance call to Tokyo on our bill.

OLYMPIA: Look Rudolph. I won't be needing you anymore. In fact, I'm giving up this apartment and buying a training camp up in Mendocino County.
(*Distant*)
A place where the air smells like champagne and where I can ride horses and chop wood and prepare for the first defense of the title.

RUDOLPH: Throw me out, huh.

OLYMPIA: Don't be angry, Rudolph. We've had our fun. But all you seem to want to do is go roller-skating and fly your kite in Venice with all of the other losers. Grown men like you, flying kites.

(*Both* OLYMPIA *and* KOKO *laugh.*)
How about me writing you a check? That'll get you by until my lawyer contacts you.

(*She begins to write a check.*)

RUDOLPH: I don't want your money. Just give me a loan, until I get
a job.

OLYMPIA: (*Vicious laughter*) A job? What do you know how to do?

RUDOLPH: I don't have to take these insults. I have my pride.

(RUDOLPH *exits.*)

KOKO: Look. Olympia. We'd better get going. You have to get over to
Burbank for the *Tonight Show.*

OLYMPIA: Oh my god. I forgot.

(*They exit.*)

(*Sound Up: Arthur Prysock: "Bring It On Home to Me."*)

ACT I

SCENE 2

(*A street. Spotlight on* RUDOLPH. *Wears shorts, Beanie cap. On roller skates. He holds a kite and a cellular phone. Fade Out Sound: Arthur Prysock "Bring It On Home to Me."*)

RUDOLPH: Mother's phone is busy . . . I'll call her later. I feel better already. Olympia never spent any time with me. All of the nights I'd wait for her to come home from the Great Western Forum in Inglewood and she'd be tired. She'll miss those western omelets I used to make. She won't find anything like that in her precious training camp.

(*Pause.* RUDOLPH *sings "I Can't Figure Women Out."*)

They told us that we were macho brutes
That we were insensitive,
And didn't know how to cry
They told us that we were truculent
And they were tired of our telling lies
They criticized our hitting on them
Said that we were disrespecting
And bidding on them
Every fresh remark would gain a fine
We couldn't even say
Baby, you so fine
I can't figure women out

So we became tender
Waxed the floors, cooked the supper
Studied foreplay
Stopped calling them broads
Cunts and bitches
Farragoes shrews cows
And witches
I can't figure women out
We bought Johnny Mathis instead of Arthur Prysock
Attended the ballet instead of the White Sox
We did everything we could to be a model man
And what did it get us
Some wrinkled and red dishpan hands
Now they're saying, "Why can't you be a man?"
I'm so frustrated that I want to shout
All because
I can't figure women out

(*Full Stage Lights Up. Street sign says "Hollywood Blvd." Beret-wearing* KING RABBIT *and his rat companion,* BOBBIE RAT, *are being chased around the stage by two other* RABBITS. *Half of* BOBBIE RAT's *face is disfigured.* RABBITS #1 & #2 *hold signs that read "King Rabbit Hates Own Kind." "King Rabbit is a butcher." They hit* KING RABBIT *with the signs until he is unconscious.* BOBBIE RAT *is unable to assist him.* RUDOLPH *intervenes and throws* RABBITS #1 & #2 *off* KING RABBIT. RABBITS #1 & #2 *flee the stage.* RUDOLPH *and* BOBBIE RAT *are standing over* KING RABBIT *as he comes to.*)

KING RABBIT: Where am I?

BOBBIE RAT: You should have seen this young man, King
        (BOBBIE RAT *points to* RUDOLPH.)

He sure knows how to handle his dukes.
>(KING RABBIT *rises and is brushed off by* BOBBIE.)

RUDOLPH: My wife is lightweight champion of the world. I've picked up a few points.
>(KING RABBIT *and* BOBBIE RAT *stare at each other, puzzled.*)

KING RABBIT: Seems that every time I try to accomplish something, I get stopped by my own kind. What handle do you go by, chum?
>(*Extends hand*)

RUDOLPH: Rudolph. Rudolph Greene. I'm the easiest guy in town to get along with.

BOBBIE RAT: Our customers are afraid to come down because of these protesters. Business is in a slump.

KING RABBIT: Instead of hating me, they should be proud.

BOBBIE RAT: They should honor you in the Rabbit Hall of Fame next to Peter, Harvey, the March Hare, Bugs, and Br'er Rabbit. You've improved their reputation.

RUDOLPH: I don't understand.

BOBBIE RAT: King Rabbit has discovered a way to transform Rabbit fur into mink. He has made thousands of rabbits rich. And he has made it so that even women of modest means can own mink. But there are those essentialists
>(*Said sarcastically*)
who believe that rabbits should remain rabbits.

KING RABBIT: A bunch of crybabies. Rudolph, I need a bodyguard.

I'm not only harassed by these protesters, those dreadful animal-rights people, but I'm also being stalked by obscure and dangerous forces.

RUDOLPH: I don't know, King Rabbit. I'm opposed to violence. You're asking me to become a goon.

KING RABBIT: You wouldn't be a goon, silly boy. Who ever heard of such a thing? Goons beat up people. You'd be beating up rabbits. What good is a rabbit? I can't think of a single purpose that they serve. Of course there are those who do succeed.
(KING RABBIT *puffs out his chest.*)
Get over. A sort of aristocracy. A talented tenth. But they're individuals. Not rabbits.

BOBBIE RAT: You should take the job, Rudolph. King Rabbit is a great boss. Why, he promised to give me a new face. He's hired a Beverly Hill's surgeon. I'm going to get Winston Churchill's face.
(*Slide projection showing Churchill. Or* BOBBIE RAT *displays photo taken out of his pocket.*)
You know, a face with a sort of bulldog prominence.
(*Mimics Churchill.*)

KING RABBIT: Bobbie's right, Rudolph. I treat my employees well. You won't regret it.

RUDOLPH: I am broke, and I guess if I beat up rabbits, nobody will get upset. Well, maybe Cleveland Amory. King Rabbit, you have yourself a new bodyguard.
(*They shake hands.*)
(*Sound Up: Paula Cole: "Where Have all the Cowboys Gone?"*)

ACT I

SCENE 3

(*The apartment of* KING RABBIT. *He is sitting on a chair, reading "Women's Wear Daily."* BOBBIE RAT *enters. He's bringing* KING RABBIT *a cup of tea.*)

KING RABBIT: Bobbie, listen to this: "King Rabbit has done it again. Taken all honors at the International Furrier's Exhibition." And this: "Another smashing show by King Rabbit. His competitors, those who haven't filed for bankruptcy, are furious. Because of his powers to transform rabbit fur into mink, some are accusing him of practicing black magic."

BOBBIE RAT: Oh, that's so over the top, K.R. They're just jealous of your success.

(KING RABBIT *sips some tea.*)

KING RABBIT: Well, they won't have to worry about King Rabbit for very long.

BOBBIE RAT: What do you mean, King?

KING RABBIT: Bobbie. You, my confidante, are the first to know. I'm taking early retirement.

BOBBIE RAT: Retirement? But K.R. you're at the zenith of your career. Besides, who could possibly take over the business?

KING RABBIT: Rudolph can handle the business. He's performed wonderfully as my bodyguard. Those rabbits and other protesters dast not show up with Rudolph around.

BOBBIE RAT: Are you sure, K.R.? And what about me? What's going to happen to me?

KING RABBIT: As a part of the deal for his becoming my successor, I have written in a clause that requires him not only to keep you on, but to see to it that the plastic surgeon I hired gives you Winston Churchill's face.

BOBBIE RAT: Oh thank you, K.R. Rudolph is a nice boy. He'll be so happy. He's finally succeeded at something. You know, this story about his wife being lightweight champion of the world is true.

KING RABBIT: Poor men and women. The world is in such turmoil. Must be some bad lingering star. There's such mistrust and suspicion between men and women. How is it going to end?

BOBBIE RAT: Maybe they've come to the end of the line. You know, some are saying that the earth is a dying planet. That is, if the human nations don't blow up each other first. Our people are the only ones who survived those nuclear tests. The rats living on those sites are thriving while the other animals have either perished or gotten their signals all mixed up.
     (*Sighs*)
It's such a responsibility. Wonder what kind of world we'll create?

KING RABBIT: Man is not finished yet. I've devoted my life to trying to communicate with them, to give them the benefit of thirty million years of experience. But they won't listen.

BOBBIE RAT: You shouldn't give up yet.

KING RABBIT: They come into my establishment. Buy my furs. They write me up in their glossy magazines. But sometimes, I think that I'm invisible to them.
> (*Offstage Sound Up: Buzzer.*)

BOBBIE RAT: That must be Rudolph.
> (BOBBIE RAT *exits.* KING RABBIT *rises. Sound Up as* KING RABBIT *puts on a recording of the last scene from the opera,* Salome, *and continues until the opera ends.* KING RABBIT *sings along. An* ASSASSIN, *from* MOTHER HUBBARD's *gang, enters. In black suit and black mask. Sneaks up on* KING RABBIT. *Sticks a dagger in him and then flees.* KING RABBIT *slumps to the floor, clutching his wound.* BOBBIE RAT *rushes in.*)

BOBBIE RAT: Boss!
> (RUDOLPH *enters.*)

RUDOLPH: King Rabbit!!
> (RUDOLPH *falls to the floor. Cradles* KING RABBIT's *head.*)
Bobbie! Go get help!
> (BOBBIE RAT *exits.*)
King Rabbit. Who did this to you?

KING RABBIT: I haven't much time, Rudolph. Listen to me, Rudolph. Listen as you've never listened before. First, lad, I'm turning over the business to you.

RUDOLPH: (*Surprised*) To me! But, King Rabbit. I'm . . . I've never run anything—I mean, but the formula, turning rabbit into mink?

KING RABBIT: Oh, there's nothing to that.
(*He begins to whisper.*)

RUDOLPH: Wait!
(RUDOLPH *removes a notebook from his pocket. Begins to take notes.*)
Okay, King Rabbit.
(KING RABBIT *whispers into* RUDOLPH's *ear.*)
That simple!
(KING RABBIT *nods and begins to cough.*)

KING RABBIT: (KING RABBIT *holds* RUDOLPH's *hand.*) When you get into trouble, accountants will help you out. Rudolph . . . Mother Hubbard had this done to me. The closer she's come to power, the more she's tried to eliminate me, because I know her secret.

RUDOLPH: That crazy woman who's asking all of the men to leave California within sixty days? You worried about her?

KING RABBIT: Don't underestimate her, Rudolph. She's armed and well organized. Remember those women who did all of the legwork for men seeking power. The ones who went from door to door, licked stamps, made the coffee, handled the phone banks, organized bake sales.

RUDOLPH: The den mothers, the chauffeurs, the ones who were always searching for a solution to dishpan hands?

KING RABBIT: They're with her now. And she's focused. Next to her General Schwarzkopf has an attention deficit disorder.

RUDOLPH: But what's this secret?

KING RABBIT: Look, Rudolph. I wasn't always rich and powerful. I was born and raised in the grasses located on Buffalo International Airport. Though of humble circumstances, I knew that some day, I would be able to fly. One day, some of us left the homestead and hopped our way to freedom. Almost immediately we suffered misfortune. One was smashed under the wheels of a truck. A few others were captured by some fiendish children, burned and tortured. One was eaten by a dog. There were only two of us left. A man told us that if we went with him and did what he said, he'd give us enough money to reach Chicago. He sweetened the deal by sharing his carrot juice with us. It was drugged. When I awoke, I found myself strapped to a table in a laboratory. I got loose during the night, and found my buddy dead, lying next to a half-empty bottle. It had some sort of liquid culture in it. You see, some doctor had gotten the notion that if a woman's liquid culture came in contact with a rabbit, and the rabbit died, then this would be proof of the woman's pregnancy. He saw it as a useful way to solve the rabbit overpopulation problem and contribute to science as well. The bottle had a name on it. After I escaped, I took it to a sailor and a sailor charged me fifty cents to read it. The name on the bottle was Mother Hubbard. You see, I'm a threat to Mother Hubbard because she's been able to draw adherents with her boast that she's never been with a man. She was with at least one man.

RUDOLPH: (*Indignant*) I have no respect whatsoever for a woman like that.

KING RABBIT: It's all part of human nature. Rudolph. Please look after Bobbie Rat. He's such a trusting, loyal creature. His face got that way because he tried to reason with the exterminator. And now, the poor thing is so hard pressed that he wants to be a man.

RUDOLPH: Now wait a minute, King Rabbit. What's wrong with being a man?

KING RABBIT: I'd rather be a dying rabbit than Bill Gates. What good is man? Not only does he kill his own, but any other species that happens to get in the way. He abandons his young. They're all up on Telegraph Avenue or the boardwalks of Venice or the beaches of Santa Barbara and La Jolla, smoking pot, engaging in promiscuous sex while their parents are out collecting assets like squirrels collect chestnuts. All of the runaways on Geary Boulevard and Hollywood Boulevard. Lost. Latchkey children. Unloved. Man is aesthetically unappealing, lacking the grace of the birds. He brags about these tools that he has created, but now these very tools threaten to wipe him out. You see Rudolph:

> (KING RABBIT *sings "Man Has Come To The End Of The Line."*)

Man has come to the end of the line
Every sign you see
Makes this very clear
His end is near and he's
Running out of time
It won't be long before the
End of his career
Of this green planet
He's made a big mess
As the caretaker of life
He's failed the test
It's time for nature to
Make a clean break
With a creature whose caused
Such colossal heartbreak

I've done my duty and
I've tried to do right
To warn him of his
Miserable plight
Now it's up to others
To make the fight
While I wander into
The celestial twilight

RUDOLPH: Don't sing, King Rabbit. Bobbie's gone to get help. They should be here at any minute.

KING RABBIT: (*Gazing, and pointing*) No. I'm ready to go. To a world of a million friendly buglike eyes. I go to a balmy land beyond of beautiful carrot fields, and palm trees . . .
    (KING RABBIT *dies.* BOBBIE RAT *enters.*)

BOBBIE RAT: I couldn't catch the killer. And do you know what? Oh, I could kick myself. I went to the human hospital! I should have gone to the vet.
    (*Sees* KING RABBIT. *Begins to sob. Embraces* RUDOLPH, *who is obviously uncomfortable.*)

ACT I

SCENE 4

(*Newsroom area in spotlight, with stool, where reporter sits to deliver the news.* NEWSCASTER #2 *wears pilot's outfit. Leather jacket, white scarf, goggles, etc.*)

(*Sound Up and then Fades Out as* NEWSCASTER #2 *speaks: News Signature.*)

NEWSCASTER #2: Freeways throughout the state are jammed with autos and trucks as men flee to Nevada, Oregon, and Mexico, in compliance with Mother Hubbard's ultimatum that all men leave the state within sixty days, a deadline that is rapidly approaching. Mother Hubbard has vowed that those men remaining will be sent to camps located in the Sierras where they will join the harassers, batterers, obscene phone-callers, and rapists already there.

(*Sound Up and then Fades Out: News Signature.*)

ACT I

SCENE 5

(KING RABBIT's *apartment.* RUDOLPH *is on the phone. A woman is manicuring his nails. And another one is modeling a mink coat.*)

RUDOLPH: Look, pal, either you book first class for every member of my party or we won't come to Rome. And we need more than three suites, we need two hotel floors.

(Pause)

Glad you see it my way. Good.

(Pause)

Nice doing business with you.

(Pause)

Well, Ciao to you, too.

(Hangs up. Phone rings again.)

People magazine? I told you to quit bothering me.

(Phone rings again.)

Tell David Rockefeller that I'm in conference.

(Phone rings again.)

Donald Trump wants to have lunch? Tell him my calendar is full.

(Hangs up. RUDOLPH *and the* WOMEN *sing:)*

RUDOLPH: I never thought that money could be so much fun

MANICURIST: When it's new, it's as crisp as fresh lettuce

MODEL: And when it's old, it's as soft as a baby's rump

RUDOLPH: All of the things that you can buy with it

MANICURIST: A dozen or so shiny Yamahas

MODEL: A villa in the sunny Bahamas

RUDOLPH: It can make all of your dreams come true.

MANICURIST: A franchise making linguine

MODEL: A brand new Lamborghini

RUDOLPH: I can go anywhere I want to go. Do what I want to do

MANICURIST: Flying first class to Katmandu

MODEL: And cruising the Mediterranean blue

RUDOLPH: I get all the perks that go with fame

MANICURIST: Invites to all of the best parties

MODEL: The very best table at Sardis

RUDOLPH: Versace, Bruno Magli, and Armani. I wear the best of threads

MANICURIST: No more Montgomery Wards

MODEL: And no more ghetto Keds.

RUDOLPH: Magazine covers carry my face

MANICURIST: Paparazzi stalk you from place to place

RUDOLPH: I'm marvelous, I'm charming, I'm wonderful, I'm cool

MODEL: You're eligible, you're saleable, you ain't no fool

RUDOLPH: My furs are worn by divas and queens

MANICURIST: You're motivated, intelligent, resourceful and keen

RUDOLPH: My forecasts are quoted on the floor of the market.

MODEL: Your brilliant career has taken off like a rocket.

RUDOLPH: Seems like everybody wants to press my flesh

MANICURIST, MODEL: You the best, Rudolph! You the best!
(BOBBIE RAT *enters.* WOMEN *scream.*)

RUDOLPH: Don't you know how to knock?

BOBBIE RAT: I'm sorry, Rudolph. This was King Rabbit's apartment. I'm used to coming and going as I please.

RUDOLPH: Well, get unused to it. Look at him, girls, a crippled rat with half his face gone.
(MODEL *and* MANICURIST *laugh.*)

BOBBIE RAT: Don't humiliate me, Rudolph, please, anything, but don't humiliate me.
(*The* MODEL *and* MANICURIST *begin to taunt* RAT.)

RUDOLPH: If it weren't for King Rabbit, you would be sliding up and down the ropes of ships.

MANICURIST: Or taking his meals in an alley.

MODEL: He'd be hobbling in and out of holes.

RUDOLPH: Anyway, what do you want? Make it quick.
>   (MODEL *taunts him. Pulls back* BOBBIE RAT*'s ears.*)

BOBBIE RAT: Ouch! Don't do that. Rudolph, can't we talk in private?

RUDOLPH: I keep no secrets from my girls.

BOBBIE RAT: King Rabbit said that he left a will guaranteeing that I would be taken care of.
>   (*Pauses, embarrassed*)
I'm being humiliated.

RUDOLPH: Did you hear him girls? He says that I should honor
>   (RUDOLPH *laughs.*)
a contract
>   (*Laugh*)
between a rabbit and
>   (*Laughs*)
a rat.
>   (MODEL *and* MANICURIST *break up with laughter.*)
Have you ever heard of such a thing?
>   (RUDOLPH *becomes serious.*)
That's the most ridiculous thing I've ever heard of.
>   (RUDOLPH *tears up the contract.*)

MODEL and MANICURIST: You smell bad.

BOBBIE RAT: You shut up! You trinkets . . . You wait . . . Mother Hubbard will take care of you, and you too Rudolph. You'd better not stay around after her deadline for all male humans to leave the state. She'll send you to those camps in the Sierras.

RUDOLPH: Mother Hubbard won't tangle with me. I know her secret. If her followers knew what I know, they'd turn on her.

BOBBIE RAT: Rudolph. What's come over you? Where's the nice young man who won the confidence of King Rabbit. Courteous, gentle, nimble with a needle.

RUDOLPH: If that's all you have to say, you can leave.

BOBBIE RAT: Please, Rudolph. I'm running out of cheese. Can't you give me some work? I'll do anything. I had to sleep in a gutter last night. The other rats shun me. They scorn my role as a mediator between humans and animals. They're saying that my experience proves that you can't make alliances without getting your fur singed. Don't you see, Rudolph? It's our task to prove them wrong.
    (RUDOLPH, MANICURIST, *and* MODEL *laugh.*)
I won't have you humiliate me. You'll pay. I'll see to it that you pay.
    (BOBBIE RAT *exits, shaking his fists, leaving* RUDOLPH *and the* GIRLS *laughing.*) (*Sound Up: Salt-N-Pepa, "Ain't Nuthin' but a She Thang."*)

ACT II

SCENE 1

(MOTHER HUBBARD's *headquarters. A desk, some hard-back chairs. Posters on the wall, of Harriet Tubman and Emma Goldman.* MOTHER HUBBARD *is looking at some blueprints with* MARGO, *an architect and Hubbardite. A Hubbardite* GUARD *stands sentry. They're wearing khaki or camouflage uniforms. Offstage screams are heard occasionally throughout their conversation, which the women appear not to notice.*)

MARGO: (*Pointing to blueprint*) And here Mother, at the end of this boulevard, will be a statue of Princess Diana surrounded by fountains. All along the Martyrs' Blvd. will be smaller statues dedicated to Pat Nixon and Dorothy Dandridge and others who've been undone by men.

(*A scratching sound is heard.* MARGO *motions to* GUARD *to check it out.* GUARD *exits.*)

MOTHER HUBBARD: What is that noise?

MARGO: What noise, Mother?

MOTHER HUBBARD: That scratching sound.

(MARGO *listens carefully. Scratching sound is still heard.*)

MARGO: I do hear a scratching sound. I'll have someone check it out.

(*Pause*)

Well, Mother. What do you think?

MOTHER HUBBARD: It's wonderful. When we enter the capitol next week, my first official duty will be to reward you for your work with the Hubbardites. You're my right hand, Margo. What would I do without you?

MARGO: The Hubbardites saved my life, Mother. I had tried everything. Zen, biofeedback, holistic medicine, dancercise, black power, EST, ESP, but it wasn't until I joined you that I found a purpose in life. An honor bestowed upon me by the Hubbardites will be the happiest occasion of my life.

(*They embrace.*)

MOTHER HUBBARD: Margo, do you think that a statue could be built to honor my dog, Rex?

(MARGO *looks at her, quizzically.*)

MARGO: A . . . sure Mother Hubbard. No problem.

MOTHER HUBBARD: Did they take care of that rabbit?

MARGO: One of the sisters did the job. Why did you want him out of the way, Mother?

MOTHER HUBBARD: It was something personal.

(*Scratching noise*)

There it is again. Margo would you go and see what you can do about this problem.

(MARGO *exits.* GUARD *enters with* FOUR MALE PRISONERS

wearing black masks, and their hands are bound. YVONNE
enters with them.)

MOTHER HUBBARD: Another hearing. This is becoming a round-the-clock procedure.

YVONNE: While you're asleep, the enemy is out causing mischief. They can't help themselves.
(MOTHER HUBBARD *pats down her hairdo, straightens her khaki uniform, sits down at her desk, and bangs a gavel.*)

MOTHER HUBBARD: Very well, Yvonne. Read the charges.

YVONNE: Mother Hubbard, from left to right. Well, the dude on the end enticed this young innocent freshman into his office and seduced her. He made her come back every week during his office hours and told her that if she didn't continue this arrangement he'd give her an *F.*
(MOTHER HUBBARD *and* YVONNE *glare at the* FIRST MAN.)

MOTHER HUBBARD: You worm!

YVONNE: Heel!

FIRST MAN: Mother Hubbard, please, let's be civilized about this. Please don't make a snap judgment, I . . .
(YVONNE *walks over to* FIRST MAN *and slaps him.*)

YVONNE: Get to the point, you prick.

FIRST MAN: She may have been a freshman, Mother Hubbard, but she had a body on her that would reduce a man to incoherence. Her nipples showed through her sweater, like brown pearls. They were elegant as green peas, and those thighs—thighs the color of strawberry yogurt—Mother Hubbard, I couldn't help myself.

(*Sobbing*)

Give a fellow a break.

MOTHER HUBBARD: You couldn't help yourself. You men have no control over your emotions, creatures of the flesh . . .

YVONNE: He even has a Ph.D.

FIRST MAN: But I'm only human. Born to make mistakes. What kind of person are you?

YVONNE: He's got a lot of lip.

MOTHER HUBBARD: You're going to have to learn. Next case.

FIRST MAN: But Mother Hubbard . . .

YVONNE: The next one's charged with reckless eyeballing, and whistling.

MOTHER HUBBARD: A bird, huh?

YVONNE: A woman can't walk down the street without him making some crude remark.

> (SECOND MAN *makes attempt to speak, making dumb sounds. Gestures frantically.*)

MOTHER HUBBARD: What's the matter with him?

YVONNE: He's also an obscene phone-caller, and, well, some of our women got to him before we arrested him. They cut out his tongue.

MOTHER HUBBARD: And the third one, what did he do?

YVONNE: Told his secretary he'd give her a promotion if she'd . . .
> (*Whispers into* MOTHER HUBBARD'*s ear.* MOTHER HUBBARD *expresses shock.*)

THIRD MAN: Oh, Mother Hubbard, give me a break. I'm not like these other men. I'm a pillar of the community, leader of the Boy Scout troop, and chairman of the Community Chest.

MOTHER HUBBARD: Spare me your wretched pleas.

THIRD MAN: (*Drops to his knees, pleading, carrying the rest of the* MALE PRISONERS *down with him.*) Please, Mother Hubbard, let's discuss this . . .

MOTHER HUBBARD: So that I have to listen to your lies?

YVONNE: The last one is Pete Wilson.
> (MOTHER HUBBARD *surprised. Rises from her chair walks over to where* WILSON *is standing. Is in his face.*)
Former Governor of California. We found him living in a cardboard box underneath the Santa Monica freeway.

MOTHER HUBBARD: You! It was the Draconian policies that you and your successors adopted that caused me to lose my cottage and my dog. How could you have been so heartless?
> (WILSON *looks down.*)

YVONNE: He endorsed that dreadful three-strikes bill that sent a welfare woman to prison for ten years for stealing a ham. Then he had the nerve to criticize the visiting President of China about human rights when, during his administration, California had incarcerated more people than any country outside of China.

MOTHER HUBBARD and other MALE PRISONERS: Hypocrite!

YVONNE: In 1996, he signed a welfare plan that reduced the benefits of 2.7 million California families . . .

MOTHER HUBBARD: Horrible! How many kids went hungry because of you?

YVONNE: And to really irritate the poor, he signed the bill on Thanksgiving.

MOTHER HUBBARD: A perverted fiend. What else?

YVONNE: He signed a bill preventing the state armories from being opened to the homeless during the El Niño winter of 1997.
(MOTHER HUBBARD *shakes her head in disgust.*)
And in 1995 he suspended the Endangered Species Act. This put a number of plants and animals in jeopardy.

MOTHER HUBBARD: Does your iniquity know no bounds?

FIRST MAN: He also cut off prenatal care for 70,000 immigrants with no advance notice or hearings. Can you cut me a little slack for giving you this information?

YVONNE: Shut up you. Nobody asked you.

WILSON: Now wait a minute, Mother, I was only exercising the will of the people.

MOTHER HUBBARD: The will of the people my eye. You were little more than a pawn for corporate interests. My dog died because of you. Get these men out of my sight.

WILSON: Hold on Mother. Why I'm a former governor, I deserve a little respect.

(YVONNE *and* MOTHER HUBBARD *laugh.*)

Look I know when I'm licked. I can read the tea leaves. You're right Mother, I should have known that I couldn't deceive you as I did the people of California for two elections. You can see right through me. I wouldn't have had clothes to wear or a place to sleep without the corporations paying the bills. They even provided me with a wife. You remember her? She used to ride on floats at the football games in Pasadena when she was young. She must have had thirty face-lifts since then. But Mother, my fortunes waned after I left office. My corporate sponsors abandoned me. As a budget saver, the public passed an initiative that denied me a pension. I lost my savings on the stock market. And before you knew it, I was getting a dose of my own medicine. Food stamps. Soup kitchens. The whole nine yards.

(*Tearfully*)

I understand the misery I caused Mother Hubbard, because of my suffering . . . I've changed. I'm sorry about the thousands of people who went hungry because of me, who had to sleep out in the cold, and I'm sorry for the long-toed salamander. I think of what I did to the little critters every night. Please, can't you give me a little slack?

(*Drops to knees and begs.*)

MOTHER HUBBARD: Does he look as though he's changed, Yvonne?

YVONNE: He just a lying politician if you ask me, Mother.

MOTHER HUBBARD: Get them out of here.
> (*The* FOUR MALE PRISONERS *begin sobbing and pleading for mercy as they're moved off stage. Distraught* WOMAN *rushes in, with* GUARD *following her. She wears mascara, short dress, lipstick, high heels. No screaming is heard while the* WOMAN *is in the room.*)

GUARD: (*All out of breath*) We tried to stop her, Mother.

MOTHER HUBBARD: It's okay. What can I do for you, child?

WOMAN: (*Gesturing wildly*) My husband . . . I made a complaint. I said that he sexually harassed me, Mother Hubbard. Please don't be mad at me, but . . . but, I made it up. He wasn't paying enough attention to me. I just wanted him to take me out to dinner.

MOTHER HUBBARD: What's your husband's name, child?

WOMAN: George. George Johnson.

MOTHER HUBBARD: Do you have anything on a George Johnson, Yvonne?
> (YVONNE *examines her clipboard.*)

YVONNE: (*With a sinister grin*) He went out yesterday, Mother.

MOTHER HUBBARD: Don't worry, my dear. We have these camps in the mountains. The men are safe there. There are twenty-four hour sports channels and an unlimited supply of Budweiser beer. We even built a meeting house for the Promise Keepers. They can hug each other and cry.

(YVONNE *and* GUARD *laugh.*)

WOMAN: (*Screaming*) I don't care about that, you crazy woman. I want my husband. I know all about you. You're ugly. You look like an owl. You hate men because they won't have you. You've never been with a man. A middle-aged virgin.

(GUARD *removes* WOMAN *from the room.*)

MOTHER HUBBARD: (*To* YVONNE) The young ones. They don't understand. Don't they understand that we're protecting them from a depraved beast? An animal. Look how rapidly the crime rate is declining since men have begun leaving California.

YVONNE: They'll be thankful one day, Mother. They'll honor you as a soldier and as a prophet.

MOTHER HUBBARD: Do you think that they'll finally realize that we don't need men? I've never had any use for one.

YVONNE: All of us admire your discipline, Mother.

(*Pause*)

Mother, the camp directors are beginning to complain about the overcrowding. Maybe we should send some of the overflow to camps in Wyoming.

MOTHER HUBBARD: Good idea, Yvonne. They can play cowboys and Indians.

(*They laugh. Scratching sound is heard again.* MARGO *returns.*)

MARGO: We tried to locate the source of the scratching sound.

MOTHER HUBBARD: We—

> (BOBBIE RAT *breaks through the wall from where the scratch-
> ing sound is heard.* MARGO *and* YVONNE *scream.* MOTHER
> HUBBARD *draws a pistol.*)

BOBBIE RAT: Ladies, ladies, please don't be alarmed. I know that my
appearance may repel you. But appearances are deceptive. I may
have the body of a rat, but I have the soul of a man. Why, I've read
every page of *Finnegans Wake*. Enjoyed every word. Please, Mother
Hubbard. I have important information for you.

MARGO: This had better be good, Rat.

MOTHER HUBBARD: What do you have to tell me?

BOBBIE RAT: Not so fast. In exchange for this information, you will
have to grant me a request.

YVONNE: We're not making any deals with a rat.

MOTHER HUBBARD: Hold on comrades. Let's hear what he has to say.

BOBBIE RAT: In exchange for this information, I want you to hire a
plastic surgeon to repair my face. I want Winston Churchill's face.
A face with bulldog prominence.

> (*They laugh.*)

Please don't laugh at me. Do anything, but don't laugh.

MOTHER HUBBARD: (*Still laughing*) We'll consider it. What's the information?

BOBBIE RAT: As you know, I was an assistant to King Rabbit.

MOTHER HUBBARD: Yes. I was sorry to hear about his unfortunate demise.

> (*Exchanges knowing glances with* MARGO *and* YVONNE.)

BOBBIE RAT: Thank you, Mother. He was a great rabbit. A genius who discovered the secret of converting rabbit fur to mink, allowing thousands of low income women to wear mink for the first time, and making many rabbits rich. He . . .

YVONNE: Get to the point, Rat.

BOBBIE RAT: Before he died, King Rabbit designated Rudolph Greene, a young househusband, to succeed him. He intervened when King Rabbit was being set upon by protesters. He was devoted to King Rabbit and would even substitute for some of the seamstresses when they were out sick. The lad really knows how to handle a needle.

YVONNE: I've never seen such a garrulous rat.

BOBBIE RAT: Now that he's taken over, Rudolph has undergone a change. He has these all-night parties in King Rabbit's apartment and plays that blaring hip-hop music around the clock. The lyrics are so distasteful. And he's become a real braggart. He says that your deadline doesn't apply to him because he knows your secret.

MOTHER HUBBARD: He what?

BOBBIE RAT: He says that if your followers knew what he did, they'd turn on you.

> (MARGO *and* YVONNE *study* MOTHER HUBBARD. *She glances at them nervously.*)

MOTHER HUBBARD: (*Nervously*) What on earth could he be talking about?

MARGO: I wouldn't be surprised at anything your enemies say about you, Mother. The hatred that men feel for us. The things that they call us: "Wenches, witches. Whores and bitches."

MOTHER HUBBARD: Next to them, a rat is dignified.

BOBBIE RAT: I return the compliment, Mother.
>   (MOTHER HUBBARD *and* MARGO *glare at him.*)

MOTHER HUBBARD: Thanks for the information, Rat.

YVONNE: You can leave now.

BOBBIE RAT: What about my deal?

YVONNE: Get out of here, Rat. We're not making any deal with you. A lowly vermin.

BOBBIE RAT: I'm not leaving here until I get my deal.
>   (YVONNE *drags him out.*)
But you promised. You promised.
>   (*They exit.*)

MARGO: What do you think that he knows, Mother? Do you think that he's bluffing?

MOTHER HUBBARD: There's one way to find out.

MARGO: How's that, Mother?

MOTHER HUBBARD: Give Rudolph a one-way ticket up here.

MARGO: Good idea, Mother. But we have to be careful. He's a sweet talker, I gather. Knows how to wield the jive. You know the kind. Talks such trash that you feel like submitting to him. But of course, how would you know? You've never been with a man.

(MOTHER *studies her.*)

MOTHER HUBBARD: (*Nervously*) Right!

(*Pause*)

I got it. I'll call him. Tell him that I want him to prepare a special mink that I can wear when we enter the capitol next week.

(*She pulls out a cellular phone and dials.*)

Hello, Rudolph Greene.

(*Pause*)

Yes, Rudolph, it's really me.

(*Winks at* MARGO.)

(*Sound Up: "Dangerous" or Too Short's "Big Thing."*)

ACT II

SCENE 2

(KING RABBIT's *apartment, which* RUDOLPH *has taken over.* RUDOLPH *is having a party with the* MANICURIST *and* MODEL. *There are drinks, food, and party decorations scattered everywhere. They are dancing to the music.* OFFSTAGE VOICE *is heard.*)

OFFSTAGE VOICE: Rudolph! Your father is on the way up.
(RUDOLPH *and* WOMEN *begin to clean up party debris quickly. The* WOMEN *put things in bags and exit.* RUDOLPH *prepares himself for his* DAD's *entrance.* DAD *enters. And the old man hobbles.*)

RUDOLPH: Dad!
(*They embrace.*)

DAD: Son, your mother and I are proud of you.
(RUDOLPH *fetches him a chair.* DAD *sits.*)
I guess I had you all wrong.

RUDOLPH: Wrong? I don't follow, Dad.

DAD: Well, you know, while the other lads were out tossing the ball and kissing the girls, you were always alone in your room, reading, playing solitary chess, and sewing. Now look at you. Successful. Wealthy. Your picture in the newspapers, dating the most glamorous of women. Mother Hubbard now asking you, my son, to design her inaugural mink. Major stuff.

RUDOLPH: Thanks, Dad. And you and Mom are invited to the ceremonies. Even though you adopted me, you treated me as though I were your natural son.

DAD: But what about the deadline? Your Mom and I were thinking about moving to Reno. Mother Hubbard gave all men sixty days to get out of the state.

RUDOLPH: That doesn't apply to you or me, Dad. Mother Hubbard won't bother us.

DAD: What do you mean, son?

RUDOLPH: Can't say, Dad. Just take my word for it.
    (*Pause*)

DAD: Son, your mother and I have been thinking.

RUDOLPH: About what, Dad?

DAD: We don't think that you should go up to Sacramento. Mother Hubbard . . . well, sometimes she doesn't make sense.

RUDOLPH: She's going to run California. I have to deal with whoever is in power. It's strictly business.
    (DAD *shakes his head in disgust.*)

DAD: You've changed, son. There was a time when I would have been thrilled to hear you talk that way. But now . . . it doesn't sound right.

RUDOLPH: But it was you who always chastised me for lacking ambition. You called me an idealist and a dreamer and worse. My wife put me out because I wasn't competitive and now that I've seen the light, you say that I shouldn't enter into what might be the greatest opportunity of my life.

DAD: I know son, but the older I get the more I realize that these earthly things are transitory. I'm more concerned with whether I can get enough oxygen to my brain or whether I can keep my cholesterol down than about making money. Now don't get me wrong. Me and your mom aren't trying to hold you back, we just want you to think about it. There's something about this Mother Hubbard that just ain't right.
(*Rises*)
Well, I guess I'll be going, Rudolph. Promised that I would take your mom to the opera.
(*They embrace.*)

RUDOLPH: What are you going to see?

DAD: An opera called *Salome*. It's about John the Baptist, who got beheaded because he knew the secret of a powerful woman.

RUDOLPH: (*Nervously*) Oh.

DAD: Take care of yourself, Rudolph.

RUDOLPH: Ciao.

(DAD *gives* RUDOLPH *a curious look*)

I mean, bye Dad.

(DAD *exits*)

(*Special Light and/or Sound Up to signal* MONEY *entrance from the opposite direction. He wears a green jumpsuit or is in a green spotlight.*)

MONEY: Don't listen to him, Rudolph.

(RUDOLPH *turns toward* MONEY.)

RUDOLPH: Who are you? And how did you get into my apartment?

MONEY: I'm the one who opens doors for people, and so no door is closed to me.

(*Sound Out*)

Allow me to introduce myself. My name is Mr. Money.

RUDOLPH: So it's true.

MONEY: What's true, son?

RUDOLPH: Money talks.

(BOBBIE RAT *enters from an upstage wing and positions himself behind the sofa.*)

What can I do for you, Mr. Money?

MONEY: Call me Change, son. That's the nickname I like the most. I change things. Rudolph. Your father is giving you the wrong advice. You need to go up to Mother Hubbard. You're just the guy to soften her up. She—well I don't have to tell you why she's so hard. You go up there and turn on the charm. This war she's waging against men is bad for my health. Any threat to the economy is a threat to me.

RUDOLPH: You'll have to explain, Mr. Money. I flunked economics.

MONEY: Look at it this way, Rudolph. Love is at the center of the capitalist system. Look at all of the products that are sold using images of romance. People are worried about bad breath, and whether they have sharp clothes, and a good-looking car, because they want to make an impression on the opposite sex. Why do you think there's a multibillion-dollar industry in keeping thin. Not to mention cosmetics, greeting cards, ballads, and the whole dining-out industry. Why would anybody want to sign up for ballroom dancing? And when people get married—look at all of the people who get paid: bridal consultants, tuxedo renters, limousine services, and then the people who bake those huge killer cakes. Roses, orchids, lilies. Whole countries will go out of business, lacking the revenue from honeymoons. Niagara Falls will have to shut down.
(*Pause*)
What's love got to do with it? Love has everything to do with it.

RUDOLPH: This is serious.

MONEY: Of course it is, Rudolph. But you can change it. This Mother Hubbard is telling women to remain chaste. This will cause a depression that will make the one of the '30s seem like a picnic. And do you know what else?

RUDOLPH: What, Mr. Money?

MONEY: Her scientists have come up with a plan to clone nothing but human females. Women can perpetuate themselves now. There ain't no need for men anymore.

RUDOLPH: What? What did you say?

MONEY: Men have outlived their usefulness.

RUDOLPH: So by me going up to Mother Hubbard's headquarters, I can save mankind.

MONEY: Rudolph. You're not as simple as you look. You go to Mother Hubbard's and men will praise your name forever. The economy will start cooking again.

RUDOLPH: Mr. Money. Thanks for helping me make a decision. You know, you're not so bad. All of my life, I've heard terrible things about you.

MONEY: All about me being the root of all evil. Just propaganda, Rudolph. I have a mellow disposition. Got a Sphinx on my cufflinks,
     (*Shows cufflinks*)
and an Egyptian eye on my tie clasp.
     (*Shows his tie clasp*)
Why, why the way I look at it, I'm pretty deep. And look how swell you're living now.

RUDOLPH: I am doing pretty well.

MONEY: You have ladies. Respect. You're a dashing young stud, Rudolph, otherwise I wouldn't be wasting my time on you. You do something for me and I'll do something for you. I'm a good friend. Sometimes, I'm a man's only friend. I mean, what would you rather have—money or a dog?
     (MONEY *sings* "Mr. Money.")
  When your wife or girl have left you blue
  Mr. Money is always there for you
  When they put you in the county jail

Mr. Money is the one who makes the bail
When you're at your wit's end
And you don't know what to do
Mr. Money is always there for you
When you're so down you
Don't have a place to stay
It's Mr. Money who
Saves the day, pays the way
Comes through for you
So let's give credit where
Credit is due
To Mr. Money
    (*Spoken*)
I will always be there for you, buddy.

RUDOLPH: (*Thoughtful*) Okay. I'm going. You've convinced me that there's a lot at stake. Besides I have to show Olympia and that Las Vegas fight crowd that I can deal and throw a little weight around with the rest of them.

MONEY: Now you're talking, Rudolph.
    (MONEY's *Sound Up*)
I get the impression that you and I are going to be great pals.
    (*They exit,* MONEY's *arm around* RUDOLPH's *shoulder. Sound Out.*)

BOBBIE RAT: (*Appears from behind the sofa*) I'll fix that Mother Hubbard for humiliating me and refusing to accede to my request for Winston Churchill's face. I'll go to Olympia's and tell her that Mother Hubbard is setting a trap for Rudolph. Let's see how the Hubbardites fare against Olympia Greene, undefeated lightweight champion of the world!

(BOBBIE RAT *sings "Getting Even."*)
I tried to be so reasonable and nice
Instead of a rat I became a little field mouse
I abandoned my nature
And swallowed my pride
And what did I get for it
A kick in the hide
I should have known from the very start
That communicating with man is not very smart
My brother rats warned me that
I couldn't make peace
With our two-legged cousins
Without getting fleeced
King Rabbit tried and paid the price
Instead of giving them advice
He should have given them lice

You can have your money power and fame
Your love your beauty they're all the same
What turns me on is greater than all
Getting even is my way of having a ball
I'll get respect and I'll win my prize
As man declines
We rats shall rise
        (*Raises fist*)

ACT II

SCENE 3

(*Sound Up: TLC, "Case of the Fake People."* OLYMPIA's *dressing room. She is lying on a massage table.* KOKO *is giving her a massage.* JOCKO, *wearing dark glasses and gesticulating with a cigar, is being interviewed by the* SPORTSCASTER, *who is accompanied by a* CAMERAPERSON *with video camera.*)

SPORTSCASTER: Ladies and Gentlemen we're broadcasting live from the dressing room of Olympia Greene, who has successfully defended her lightweight crown by knocking out Luis Rodriguez in the second round of their rematch. I have with me, Jocko Bing.

(JOCKO *is smiling all the while, waving and grandstanding.*) Jocko Bing as you know has been indicted many times but never convicted. Mr. Bing to what do you attribute Olympia's victory in the ring tonight?

JOCKO: Olympia is at the top of her game. She has the heart of Vinnie Panziano. She can dance like Roy Jones and Sugar Ray Leonard, and she knocked him out with the old Joe Louis one-two.

(*Gestures the old Joe Louis one-two: a left followed by a right.*)

SPORTSCASTER: What lies in the future for Olympia?

JOCKO: Olympia is going to move up in weight.

> (*Massaging stops. Both* KOKO *and* OLYMPIA *gaze, angrily, at* JOCKO.)

I wouldn't be surprised if, after taking the welterweight, middleweight, cruiserweight, and light heavyweight championships, Olympia will fight for the heavyweight championship of the world.

> (OLYMPIA *and* KOKO *are shocked.* SPORTSCASTER *turns to* OLYMPIA.)

SPORTSCASTER: How about that, Olympia? Are you ready to move up?

OLYMPIA: Whatever my promoter has in mind is fine with me.

SPORTSCASTER: Olympia, when did you know that you had Rodriguez in trouble?

OLYMPIA: I hit him with that overhand right in the first round
> (*Demonstrates*)

and his knees buckled. I knew that I'd take him out in the second.

SPORTSCASTER: Thanks. And now, ladies and gentlemen, back to our anchors for a summary of tonight's fights featuring the second-round knockout of Luis Rodriguez, proving that Olympia Greene's defeat of the boxer in their first bout was not a fluke.

> (SPORTSCASTER *signals to* CAMERAPERSON *as Sound Up on News Signature.* SPORTSCASTER *thanks the three and exits with* CAMERAPERSON. *Sound Out.*)

KOKO: (*To* JOCKO) What in the hell's wrong with you? Telling him that Olympia's going to move up in weight . . .

OLYMPIA: Do you know what that would do to my figure?

JOCKO: (*Oily charm*) But Olympia. I thought that you wanted to make some money. A fight between you and the male heavyweight champion would be the largest gate in history.

OLYMPIA: How much?

JOCKO: At least fifty million. Easy.

KOKO: You haven't paid her all of the money you owe from the last fight.

OLYMPIA: (*Menacing*) And the one before that—the check bounced.
> (OLYMPIA *gets down off the massage table and moves toward* JOCKO *threateningly.*)

JOCKO: Now hold off, Olympia—I can explain. Listen, I'll catch you next Thursday.
> (*Backing off the stage*)

OLYMPIA: You can skip that next Thursday jive. You pay me now.

JOCKO: Sure, Olympia. Sure. Uh, let me go and talk to the people at Caesars Palace before they close for the night. I'm sure that I can persuade them to advance a little cash.

OLYMPIA: You'd better or you're going to get what I gave to Rodriguez.
> (JOCKO *hurries off stage. Scratching sound is heard.*)

OLYMPIA: Did you hear that?

KOKO: Hear what, Olympia?

OLYMPIA: That scratching sound.

KOKO: I didn't hear anything. You all right, Olympia?

OLYMPIA: I'm sparring with more than sparring partners these days. Jocko is a crook, I have these camp followers annoying me day and night, charging me, flattering me, telling me how great I am, but I know that if I stopped paying their bills, they'd desert me—and if I started losing, Jocko would find some other fighter to rob. He'd be slapping somebody else on the back and flashing his upper and lower dentures. And the fight fans . . . Joe Dog and Nancy Bitch. They could hold a fight in the most elegant rooms in the country, at the Fairmont or the Plaza, and they'd still be demanding the same thing.

OLYMPIA and KOKO: Hotdogs and beer.

OLYMPIA: All they want to see is fighters giving each other brain concussions. Blood. All of those people breathing heavily. Aching to see blood gushing from our wounds.
        (*Scratching sound*)

KOKO: I heard it that time. What could it be?

OLYMPIA: Maybe it's harmless.
        (*Pause*)
You know, Koko, my love life is the pits. Who wants to date the lightweight champion of the world? They're afraid that if they get

fresh, I might punch them out. Suppose I get old. I'll be thirty-two next year. I'll be over the hill. Oh damn it. I miss Rudolph so much, Koko.

(OLYMPIA *begins to sob.* KOKO *comforts her.*)

KOKO: If you're talking about a reconciliation, that may not be easy, girl. Rudolph is as famous as you are now.

OLYMPIA: Oh, I know. I was so nasty to him and he was so sweet and kind. I miss those apple pies and the roller-skating and his flying those kites. I didn't know how well off I was. His smile . . . it was a smile like . . . like butter.

(*Picks up championship belt and flings it across the room.*)
(*Scratching sound is heard.*)

KOKO: This is getting weird.

OLYMPIA: What good is the championship belt if you don't have a sweet sensible man to come home to. Someone to tell you when you're wrong. What good is a fawning entourage? I need someone to stand up to me, to tell me when I'm wrong.

(OLYMPIA *sings* "A Good Sweet Man.")

I've climbed to the top of my profession
I know how to deal a concussion
In so many ways, I can hurt someone
When my rivals see me, they turn and run
I have cash, cars, jewels, and plenty of fans
But what I miss is a good sweet man
Somebody to stand up to me
Somebody to tell me when I'm wrong

I party with the in-crowd
With Calvin, Madonna, and Naomi
Giuliani takes me out to lunch
And the President attends my
 testimony
I own a private jet
Prime stocks and bonds
And a lavish suite at the Sands
But the one thing I lack
Is a good sweet man
Somebody to stand up to me
Somebody to tell me when I'm wrong

I can walk a man down
I can shake a man up
I can bob and weave in a crunch
and throw a sucker punch
I can do an uppercut
I can deliver deep cuts
I know all the smart moves
I have power in both hands
But all of this don't mean nothin'
If you ain't got a good man
Somebody to stand up to me
Somebody to tell me when I'm wrong

> (BOBBIE RAT *jumps out from where the scratching sound has been heard. He's all out of breath. The women scream.*)

OLYMPIA: (*Jumping behind* KOKO *for protection.*) Koko. Don't let him bite me.

KOKO: A rat! A rat!

BOBBIE RAT: (*Looks around*) Where?

KOKO: What's the big idea bursting into our dressing room?

BOBBIE RAT: Rudolph is in great danger. I was up at Mother Hubbard and she finked out on my deal and, and . . .

KOKO: Slow down, Rat. Take it from the top.

BOBBIE RAT: I used to work for King Rabbit. He discovered the secret for converting rabbit fur to mink. He was killed by unknown assassins, but before he died he had turned the business over to your husband.

OLYMPIA: Even a rabbit had more confidence in Rudolph than I. What a fool I've been.
(KOKO *comforts her.*)

BOBBIE RAT: He's changed, Olympia. He doesn't have the refined tastes that he once had. He listens to Ice T and Too Short now and has private showings of noir movies. He treated me so nasty that I went to Mother Hubbard—

OLYMPIA: Mother who?

KOKO: She's that woman who wants all of the men to leave the state in sixty days.

OLYMPIA: What? I've been traveling so much that I haven't had a chance to read the newspapers.

BOBBIE RAT: We're wasting time. We have to get to Sacramento. Mother Hubbard has given him a one-way ticket up there.

(OLYMPIA *and* KOKO *begin to follow* BOBBIE RAT *to exit when* JOCKO *appears.*

JOCKO: (*Carrying cash*) Olympia they gave me some of your money—

KOKO: Don't have time, Jocko. We have to go and rescue Rudolph. Come on.

(*They all exit.*)
(*Sound Up: Salt-N-Pepa, "Whatta Man."*)

ACT II

SCENE 4

(MOTHER HUBBARD's *headquarters.* MOTHER HUBBARD *is seated.* YVONNE *and* MARGO *are standing. Sound Out.*)

YVONNE: (*Announces*) The poor misguided fool is here, Mother.

MARGO: We have to watch this one, Mother. Don't let him sugar you up. He's a slick devil. He'll have you submitting to him.

YVONNE: I hear that can be nice.
     (MARGO *and* MOTHER HUBBARD *are shocked.*)

MARGO: What can be nice?

YVONNE: You know. Submitting to a man . . . a man rubbing your breasts, your thighs, putting his finger into intimate places.
     (MOTHER HUBBARD *and* YVONNE *are horrified.*)

MARGO: Girl! What's wrong with you! You gettin' weak, child. Let me school you
     (*To audience*)
and all the rest of you women who want to give up the fight.
     (*Song:* "World Without Men," *a slow rhythm and blues number of the sort that's done in night clubs. The singer,*

MARGO, *takes the audience into her confidence. While she's performing* YVONNE *and* MOTHER HUBBARD *hum in the background, "Do-Do-Bee-Do-Bee-Do," like James Brown's backup singers.)*

MARGO: Now, I know all of you women out there
  Have had some pleading guy
  Promise you the moon
  And promise you the sky
  Tell you that you're the only one
  To set his soul aflame
  Get on his hands and knees and beg
  To get between your legs
  It's all a game

  The best thing that could happen
  To we women
  Is a world that don't have
  No men

MARGO, YVONNE, MOTHER HUBBARD: (*Chorus*) A world without men
  Is a world without pain
  A world without men
  Is a world without sin
  A world without men
  Is a world that is sane
  A world without men
  Let's start over again

MARGO: You can trust a man
  As far as you can throw him
  Some of you give up your treasure
  Before you even know them

A man lives only for pleasure
And when the good times with you
Are gone
He moves on to another sucker
Like a dog, to another bone
There's only one solution
To the contemporary scene
Let's bring about a new world
A world that's without men
    (*Repeat Chorus*)

MARGO: These men nowadays?
    Shoot, honey, let me tell you about it.
    They take you out for dinner
    You end up paying the check
    You run through a series of losers
    And end up marrying a wreck
    All that men want to do
    Is lay up and give you orders
    And when you come up with their babies
    They headin' for the border
        (*Repeat Chorus*)

MARGO: So, you heard wrong, child. How can some man putting paws on you feel nice? It's a perfectly disgusting sensation. Isn't that right, Mother Hubbard?

MOTHER HUBBARD: Yes.
    (*They both glare at her.*)
I mean, what I mean to say is that I wouldn't know one way or the other. I mean—look girls, let's stop bickering. We must be united in the face of the enemy. Bring him in.
    (GUARD *brings in* RUDOLPH, *dressed in a business suit, tie,*

shined shoes. RUDOLPH *hands* MOTHER HUBBARD *a bouquet of flowers.*)

MOTHER HUBBARD: (*Rises and shakes* RUDOLPH's *hand*) Oh, thank you, Rudolph. So nice of you to come up here. I've heard so much about you.

> (YVONNE *and* MARGO *exchange glances.* MARGO *throws down flowers from* RUDOLPH, *as* MOTHER HUBBARD *passes them to her.*)

This is Margo, second in command, and Yvonne, the chief of my paramilitary forces.

> (RUDOLPH *smiles. Extends his hand. They refuse to shake it.* YVONNE *turns her back and* MARGO *glares at him.*)

RUDOLPH: Mother Hubbard. I have a sketch here of your inaugural outfit. Your combat boots will have a mink lining and your two-piece suit will be made of silk. Then this mink jacket with your initials in a secret place.

> (*Hands* MOTHER HUBBARD *the sketch.*)

MOTHER HUBBARD: (*Examines the sketch*) I love it, Rudolph. You are a genius, as they say you are. And very handsome too, isn't he, girls?

> (*They fold their arms and glare.*)

RUDOLPH: Thank you, Mother. Alistair Cooke and I have the same tailor. And you know, I am more righteous than the other men. I am very sensitive to the needs of women. When E.R.A. failed, I went around sulking for months.

> (MOTHER HUBBARD, YVONNE, *and* MARGO *exchange suspicious glances.*)

Why, my wife is lightweight champion of the world. I let her do her own thing.

MARGO: (*Whispers to* MOTHER HUBBARD) Watch him, Mother. He's a slippery seductive scoundrel. He'll be having you eating out of his hand.

MOTHER HUBBARD: Rudolph. Bobbie Rat was up here.

RUDOLPH: (*Panics*) Look, Mother Hubbard, Bobbie Rat was fired. He went away mad. I thought that since I was the new boss, I should have the right to hire my own people. You wouldn't take a rat's word over mine.

MOTHER HUBBARD: He said that you know my secret. What might that be, Rudolph?
   (*She rises.* YVONNE *and* MARGO *move toward him.*)

RUDOLPH: What secret? Mother Hubbard, I don't know any secret. The rat's crazy, Mother Hubbard. He has a host of identity problems.
   (*Laughs nervously*)

YVONNE: (*To* MOTHER HUBBARD) Don't let him wiggle out of the situation with his blandishments, Mother.

MARGO: (*To* MOTHER HUBBARD) He's a sly one, Mother. Keep your wits.

RUDOLPH: I mean this thing that he has about Winston Churchill. That's got to be one demented obsession. This rat wants to be given the face of one of the 20th century's great leaders, a renowned statesman who led the Allies to victory in World War II.
   (MARGO *and* YVONNE *move toward him.*)

MOTHER HUBBARD: Take him downstairs and put him with the incorrigibles. Men for whom there is no hope of redemption.

(MARGO *and* YVONNE *grab* RUDOLPH. *Screaming is heard in the outer office.* BOBBIE RAT, OLYMPIA, KOKO, *and* JOCKO *charge in.* OLYMPIA *knocks the women down and rescues* RUDOLPH. MOTHER HUBBARD *tries to flee but is retained by* JOCKO, BOBBIE RAT, *and* KOKO. RUDOLPH *and* OLYMPIA *embrace.*)

OLYMPIA: Oh, Rudolph, I was so mean to you. Please forgive me.

BOBBIE RAT: Are you sure that you want to have a reconciliation with him Olympia? He's not the same person. He's been living in the fast lane with the decadent fashion crowd—those degenerates who gave us heroin chic. King Rabbit hated those people. Rudolph and his girl friends ridiculed my face, he's—

KOKO: Bobbie, can't you keep your trap shut sometimes.

BOBBIE RAT: I'm just looking out for Olympia.

OLYMPIA: Is he telling the truth, Rudolph?

RUDOLPH: (*Shakes his head*) After you threw me out, Olympia, and I got the job with King Rabbit, I decided that I should change my image. I thought that if I would behave like those friends of yours in the prizefighting business, you know, add a little panache and flash to my style, that you would realize the mistake that you made. I wanted to get even with you. Make you jealous.

OLYMPIA: I was wrong about those people, Rudolph. Gangsters and parasites. Just like you said. They didn't care anything about me. They were just using me.

(*She glares at* JOCKO *with disgust.* OLYMPIA *and* RUDOLPH *embrace.*)

RUDOLPH: Why don't we get away for a while. I have some travel brochures about Vancouver, British Columbia. It sounds exciting there.

OLYMPIA: Rudy, you're so sweet. As for you, Mother Hubbard . . . what a hypocrite you are! Telling your followers all of these years that you were without a man.
> (MOTHER HUBBARD *shrinks*.)

You've known at least one man.

MARGO: What?

YVONNE: Mother say it isn't so. Please Mother say it isn't so.

MOTHER HUBBARD: (*Pause*) She's right. I was in love once.

YVONNE and MARGO: Oh no, Mother Hubbard. Don't shatter the dream.
> (MOTHER HUBBARD *sings "Lament."*)

I'm sorry my darlings
But I can't continue this lie
Somebody held me tight
Somebody made me sigh
Somebody whispered
Naughty nothings into my ear
I've known bliss and joy
And ecstasy, my dears
I tried to keep my secret
I tried to save my face
But the word is out
My future in doubt
And I'm ready to accept

My fate
Let this be a lesson
To all who will hear me
Out
When you fall in hate
Instead of love
You'll burn your insides
Out
I say
When you fall in hate
Instead of love
You'll burn your insides
Out

MOTHER HUBBARD: It's an old story. I was a librarian. He too was a librarian. On the slow days, we would read Browning to one another. His favorite passage was Browning's advice to painters in the poem, "Fra Lippo Lippi":

    "Give us no more of body than shows soul!
    Here's Giotto, with his Saint a-praising God,
    That sets us praising—why not stop with him?
    Why put all thoughts of praise out of our head
    With wonder at lines, colors, and what not?
    Paint the soul, never mind the legs and arms!
    Rub all out, try at it a second time.
    Oh, that white smallish female with the breasts
    She's just my niece . . . Herodias, I would say—
    Who went and danced and got men's heads cut off!"

You know those beautiful words. He would tell me how uncultured his wife was and how she'd wander about the house in a nasty bathrobe and talked with food in her mouth. He was miserable. One day we were reading a sensual poem there beneath the stacks and I permitted him to have his way. He promised me that he was going to leave her and run off with me. He said that it was I who made him happy.

(MOTHER HUBBARD *begins to cry.*)

OLYMPIA: Don't cry Mother, take your time.

JOCKO: Mother Hubbard you have a lot of heart, confessing like this.

MOTHER HUBBARD: Thank you. I didn't get your name.

JOCKO: Jocko. Jocko Bing.

MOTHER HUBBARD: Well, as I was saying. One day I went to work and discovered that he'd been transferred. I never heard from him after that. Oh, did I resent that man. How I would curse his name. Before my doctor died, an old friend of the family, he told me that one of the rabbits who was going to be used in pregnancy tests had escaped from the laboratory and had seen my name on a sample bottle. After the passing of Proposition 13, I was laid off from my job. I devoted all of my attention to my dog, Rex. I was broke and didn't have the funds to feed myself, let alone a dog. I went to the bank and they wouldn't give me a second mortgage. And a few days later, my dog died of hunger.

(*Begins to sob again.*)

BOBBIE RAT: Oh, darn it. Here!
(*Hands* MOTHER HUBBARD *a handkerchief. She examines it for a moment. Blows her nose.*)

MOTHER HUBBARD: I really lost it. I thought that I had been deserted. That nobody loved me. I refused to believe that my dog was dead. I treated him as though he were still alive. I saw him dancing and playing the fiddle. And then my dog came to me in a vision.

(*Sound Up: "Façades" by Philip Glass and Spotlight Up on dog,* REX.)

REX: Get a grip, Mother. Sitting in your cottage, wallowing in victimization.

MOTHER HUBBARD: Is that you Rex? Are you all right?

REX: I'm fine Mother. Not a care in the world. I spend my time romping around the golden meadows and there are plenty of cooperative fire hydrants. I'm in the VIP section and dine with Fala, all the Lassies, Checkers, and Rin Tin Tin.

MOTHER HUBBARD: Oh, Rex that's so nice, but if everything is so grand where you are, what are you doing here?

REX: Mother, I know that you'd do anything for me. You've proven that countless times. But your rage is misplaced. There are millions of women in the country like you. Deserted. Beaten down. Going hungry. Without a shoulder to cry on. All over California women and children are living on park benches and in cars. The rich are getting richer and the poor are getting poorer, and most of those people are women, Mother Hubbard.

MOTHER HUBBARD: I see Rex. But what can I do, Rex?

REX: You have to figure that out for yourself, Mother. But whatever you do, Mother, do something. Don't just sit in the house worrying about me. Worry about the widows, the single mothers, the bad diets of adolescent girls, the abuse, the assaults, their smoking, their abuse of drugs. Mother, you can do it. Just reach all the way down inside yourself and summon the energy that will emancipate the women of California.

(REX *vanishes and Light and Sound Fade Out.*)

MOTHER HUBBARD: Well, after that vision, I tried to follow Rex's instructions, but I went about it the wrong way. I conflated my rage against the father of my child with my need to help my sisters. And so I turned against the institution that had most recently humiliated me. The banks. But then I began to read feminist theory and decided that what I was really upset with was the dominant patriarchal discourse. With my loot I built an organization. We raided the Bohemian Club. We kidnapped the Oakland Raiders. And then there was the battle of Pacific Highway when we captured Hollywood scriptwriters, directors, and producers who had been promoting sexist images in film. I began to believe my own speeches that a good man is hard to find. All of the turmoil that followed. Broken homes. Mothers and daughters versus fathers and sons. Search-and-destroy missions in our living rooms. Shootouts in the bathrooms. A cold war at the dinner table. And King Rabbit. Poor King Rabbit. Why didn't someone stop me? Like that Indian Goddess. What's her name? Skulls protruding from her bosom, sword between her lips, she came to a halt when her gentle husband thrust himself into her path of destruction. Rudolph. Thank you for delivering the secret. It was a burden that I could no longer bear.

(*Sirens are heard in the distance. Sound continues intermittently, getting progressively louder, until it is abruptly cut off, shortly before entrance of the* DETECTIVE.)

RUDOLPH: It was a pleasure, Mother.

(YVONNE *and* MARGO *embrace* MOTHER HUBBARD.)

MOTHER HUBBARD: Forgive me, girls. I didn't want to tell my secret. I thought that you, my new friends, would abandon me if I told the truth.

YVONNE and MARGO: We love you, Mother.

JOCKO: I've got the perfect solution, Mother. You know these mouth-pieces who are always getting me these hung juries and mistrials? I'll hire them for you. You can plead diminished capacity. Tell the judge that you ate too many doughnuts. That you were on a sugar high and couldn't think.

KOKO: Jocko, you can be so disgusting sometimes.

JOCKO: (*Shrugs shoulders*) Just trying to help.

MOTHER HUBBARD: It's all over girls. I'm willing to pay my retribution.

RUDOLPH: I'll vouch for your character, Mother.

OLYMPIA: I'll fight a benefit fight and all of the proceeds will go to your defense committee.

KOKO: I'll teach the prison inmates how to do the Philadelphia Left Hook.
　　(*Hooks*)

JOCKO: Hey, Mother. You didn't tell what happened to the baby?
　　(*All murmur "Yeah, what happened?" etc.*)

MOTHER HUBBARD: I left the child on the porch of a little cottage in Berkeley, California. I think that it was on Cedar Street. Cedar near Rose.

RUDOLPH: Cedar and Rose? Was it a little Italianate house?

MOTHER HUBBARD: Yes, now that you mention it. It was.

RUDOLPH: Did it have petunias and daisies growing in the front yard?

MOTHER HUBBARD: Yes, it did have those flowers growing in the front yard.

RUDOLPH: Did it have Victorian curtains, you know, those lace curtains in the window?

MOTHER HUBBARD: Right!

RUDOLPH: You left me on that porch thirty-two years ago. Mom!
 (*They embrace. All applaud.*)

MOTHER HUBBARD: What a wonderful son you turned out to be, Rudolph. We have so much to catch up on, so much history to go over.

RUDOLPH: I'm proud of you, Mom. You're a tough old broad.
 (MOTHER HUBBARD *turns to* MARGO.)

MOTHER HUBBARD: Margo, what are you going to do now? We've been through so much together.

MARGO: I'm returning to school to get a degree in film studies. But right now I'm going downtown to the movies. They're doing a John Wayne retrospective.

MOTHER HUBBARD: And you, Yvonne?

YVONNE: I'm going to go out and get me a good man.

> (*Footsteps.* DETECTIVE *enters. Handcuffs and leads* MOTHER HUBBARD *away. All exit with them.*)
> (*Sound Up: "Where Have All the Cowboys Gone?" segue to News Signature.*)

ACT II

SCENE 5 (EPILOGUE)

(*Street scene, ten years later. Everybody older, wiser. Sound Up: News Signature.*)

NEWSCASTER #2 (*With* CAMERAPERSON): Ladies and Gentlemen, live from Hollywood we bring you the unveiling of a statue to Mother Hubbard's dog, Rex. As you know, the last request of the late leader of the Hubbardites was that a memorial be created by sculptor Natalie Detroit to honor the dog whose death marked the beginning of the movement. Many dignitaries are arriving to celebrate the unveiling of the statue and by doing so honor Mother Hubbard, bound to be one of the most controversial women of the twenty-first century. The event takes place on the tenth anniversary of Mother Hubbard's death. She was a martyr and liberator to some, a terrorist and demagogue to others. She spent a few years in prison before being given executive clemency by Margo Madison, former follower of Mother Hubbard and current Governor of California. And I think that I see Yvonne Hawkins, Margo Madison's old comrade-in-arms, whom the Governor appointed to head the California Arts Commission. Ms. Hawkins was also a devoted follower of Mother Hubbard.

(YVONNE *enters. She's all dressed up.*)

NEWSCASTER #2: Ms. Hawkins. May we have a word with you?

(YVONNE *approaches* NEWSCASTER #2.)
Could you tell us your emotions on this day of celebration for Mother Hubbard?

YVONNE: I feel proud to have known this great woman. She changed our lives. She made me proud to be a woman. She's responsible for our being what we are.
(RUDOLPH *and* OLYMPIA *enter, arm in arm.*)

NEWSCASTER #2: Also attending the unveiling are Rudolph Greene and former lightweight champion of the world, Olympia Greene. They have become Nike's chief competitors with their line of sporting goods. Ms. Greene, any chance of a comeback?

OLYMPIA: Not a chance. My husband and I have found that challenging corporate greed and paying workers a fair salary and improving their conditions is where the real battle should be waged. Not the ring. Isn't that right, dear?

RUDOLPH: Right, dear. We've established scholarships for the children of our workers and have inspected every detail of their working environment so that it's healthy and free of sexual harassment. That's what my mother would have wanted.

NEWSCASTER #2: Some are still calling your mother a "gynarchist."

RUDOLPH: Mom, a gynarchist? Look at it this way. The women tried to reason. They tried to negotiate. They tried to debate, and it got them nowhere. Sexual harassment continued, ogling continued, job discrimination continued. Their fathers, their brothers, their husbands, and their dates wouldn't let up. Wouldn't raise up off of them. Wouldn't loosen the parameters that the male society placed upon them. Their bosses would send them out for cigars, coffee, and chocolates, and dinner had to be ready when their husbands and children arrived home. What would you do? What would any of us do if they found themselves in a predicament of near slavery? And so my mother came along. Now I admit that I didn't agree with some of her tactics. Kidnapping the Oakland Raiders, now that wasn't too cool. And the camps in the mountains. They weren't exactly the health resorts that the Hubbardites advertised them to be. But sometimes you have to go a little crazy to make an important point. As Thomas Jefferson said, the tree of liberty must be watered with blood from time to time.

(BOBBIE RAT *enters. Wears Churchill mask.*)

NEWSCASTER #2: Bobbie Rat. Strange seeing you here. I thought that you and Mother Hubbard were enemies.

BOBBIE RAT: Mother Hubbard and I had our differences, but before she died we had a meeting. It was a wonderful meeting. We both got a lot off of our chests. But we agreed about one thing. A deal is a deal. Though many dismissed me as a fink for ratting on Ms. Hubbard, so to speak, I brought peace to California. I showed that you can't go shooting your way into power. One should use the ballot. Not the bullet.

(MARGO *enters.*)

NEWSCASTER #2: And now we have Margo Madison, Governor of California.

BOBBIE RAT: Wait a minute. I'm not finished. I have more to say . . .
(NEWSCASTER #2 *and* BOBBIE RAT *begin to wrestle for the microphone.*)

NEWSCASTER #2: But I have to interview the Governor.
>   (MARGO *stands along side* NEWSCASTER #2.)

MARGO: Bobbie Rat. Still his old feisty self. Congratulations on your new face.
>   (BOBBIE RAT *stops arguing. Appears stunned.*)

BOBBIE RAT: Why . . . why thank you, Governor. You really like it?

MARGO: It's very dignified.

NEWSCASTER #2: Governor. As someone who was loyal to Mother Hubbard, this must be a proud moment for you.

MARGO: Yes. She was a woman who suffered for all women. For years after granting her executive clemency, I visited her in her cottage in Santa Rosa. It was a lovely place with peach and lemon trees growing in the front yard. Thousands of sightseeing buses would roll by on any given day as tourists from all over the world strained to get a glimpse of this hero. She was happy with her life and with her new dog, though this dog would never replace her beloved Rex. And that was her last request: that we build a monument to her dog, Rex. If it were not for Rex, and Mother Hubbard's disassociative episodes following his death, we would not have had the Hubbardites. Were her tactics excessive? Maybe. But that's for history to judge. And now, I deem it an honor to unveil the memorial to the creature who brought us this far.
>   (*Unveiling of statue of fire hydrant with dog's head. All applaud.* WILSON *enters, all cleaned up and wearing a Santa Claus cap and apron.*)

WILSON: Merry Christmas, everybody.

MARGO: Who's he?

NEWSCASTER #2: I believe that it's the former Governor, Pete Wilson.

MARGO: Oh, hi Governor Wilson.

OTHERS: (*Anyone in the crowd responds*) "Hello Pete," "What's happening, Pete?" and "What you been up to Pete?"

WILSON: Been up all night waiting for a busload of our Mexican brothers and sisters. They arrived at about 6:00 this morning. It was their homecoming, you could say. California could technically be considered part of Mexico, since we Americans did violate the Treaty of Guadalupe Hidalgo. Hell, we Okies just arrived here in the 1930s, which was just a few seconds ago, historically speaking, while the Spanish have been around these parts since 1539. Have you ever heard of Miguel Algarín? Wonderful poet. I'm studying Spanish. Every time I think of those days when I was an old meanie, and opposed bilingual education, I could just kick myself. Why, this Spanish language is so rhythmic that you can dance to it.
(*Does a quick cha-cha-cha*)
Anyway, after I got the families settled, I washed each member's feet and served them chow.

BOBBIE RAT: What in the hell has come over you, Wilson? You used to be lower than roadkill. They called you Pedro Scissorshands after you cut money for meals on wheels and home care for the aged.

WILSON: I know. I know. But you know, all of us can change.
(*The rest of the cast turn to each other and make expressions of agreement.*)
(*Sound Up, with Latin beat: "You Can Change."*)

WILSON: (*Dances throughout song*) You can be the lowest son of a
bitch
   A guy whose soul's a festering ditch
   A two-timing scoundrel
   A scheming conniving rascal
   But you can change

CAST: Yes, You Can Change

RUDOLPH: You can walk over your own grandmother
   Wage your campaigns in the gutter
   But one day help a fledgling brother
   And help us love one another
   Yes, you can change

CAST: You Can Change

BOBBIE RAT: (*To* WILSON) You can be the lowest vermin
   Indeed a horrible specimen
   A snake in the grass
   A certifiable ass
   But you can change
   Yes you can change

CAST: You Can Change

MARGO: You can vent your seething Rage
   Hating men for the rest of your
   Days
   Or you can change
   Yes you can change

OLYMPIA: You can box women into a corner
  But when they strike back you're a goner
  Just like Aretha Franklin says
  Women wanted respect
  Equal pay
  More than an easy lay
  You can change
  You'd better change

YVONNE: You may be at the bottom of the pile
        (*Stares at* WILSON.)
  A person so detestable and vile
  But you can change
  You can be a skylark
  A spark in the dark
  A walk in the park
        (*The rest of the cast, including* MOTHER HUBBARD, *and any
        others who may not already be onstage, join those already
        onstage.*)

CAST: We came from under the slime
  And over time we climbed
  From the depths of the ocean
  To the far reaches of space
  But we still have a long way to go
  Before we improve our race
  A world of peace and harmony
  Of sister, brothers, creatures
  All friends
  And try to do better
  Until the end
  Both men and women

Tragedians and Clowns
The black, white, red,
Yellow, and brown
Our fates are inexorably bound
On this tiny planet we're
On
So the only question becomes
Why can't we get along?
Why can't we get along?
Why can't we get along?

WILSON: I'm here to tell you that there's plenty of dinner left. I hope that you guys are hungry. Just follow me.

(*Smiling and talking cheerfully, all exit with* WILSON.)
(*Sound Up: Music continues through the bows.*)

CURTAIN

SAVAGE WILDS

Savage Wilds, Part I premiered at the Julia Morgan Theatre, 2640 College Avenue, Berkeley, California, on January 8, 1988, directed by award-winning playwright, Ed Bullins. Another production directed by Ed Bullins in May 1988 was produced at the Black Repertory Theatre, 3201 Adeline Street in Berkeley, California. *Savage Wilds, Part II* premiered at Ed Bullins's own BMT Theatre at 3629 San Pablo Avenue in Emeryville, California, on August 24, 1990, produced by Ed Bullins; Konch Productions presented a second West Coast production at the Zephyr Theatre #2, 25 Van Ness Avenue, San Francisco, that same year. Both productions were directed by Vern Henderson. Rome Neal directed the premiere of *Savage Wilds* as a two-act play on February 7, 1991 at the Nuyorican Poets Café in New York City. Miguel Algarín was producer, with sets designed by Marva Duarte, lighting design by Tommy Barker, costume design by Leslie Dickerson, and sound design by Willie Correa.

CAST OF CHARACTERS, ACT ONE

Dr. Marlin, Host, wild-game show, *Savage Wilds*
Sheena Queene, Co-Producer
Vanessa Bare, Co-Producer
Jackson, Prop Man
Mr. Greenbelt, Owner, Greenbelt TV Network
Uncle Sanford, Comedian, Star of *The Uncle Sanford Show*
Announcer

CAST OF CHARACTERS, ACT TWO

Matron
Vanessa Bare
Sheena Queene
U.S. Attorney Richard Head
Ralph Kincaid, White Agent
Juan Paige, Black Agent
Mayor B. V. Dongson
Mrs. Dongson
Cookie Boggs, Reporter, National Feminist Radio

ACT I

SCENE 1

(*Office. Desk and chairs. Blowup of* TV Guide *cover with* VANESSA *and* SHEENA *in safari outfits: khaki shorts, shirts, and helmets. They are posing, holding guns.* SHEENA *is on the phone pacing up and down.* VANESSA *is listening with anticipation.* VANESSA *is black. A wide-eyed bimbo type. Very attractive. About thirty.* SHEENA *is white. About the same age. Also attractive. But hard and bitter. A feminist. Nouveau white trash.*)

SHEENA: . . . But how could that be? We pulled out all of the stops. All of the publicity and adverti— . . . You're sorry? You can imagine how we feel. We might lose our jobs.

(*Hangs up phone.*)

VANESSA: Sheena, how did we do?

SHEENA: (*Dejectedly*) You can't do any worse. We came in twenty-fifth, behind reruns of the *Mr. Peepers Show.*

VANESSA: (*Tearfully*) We're going to be fired. Oh, I knew it wasn't going to work! You and your bright ideas. Having Dr. Marlin bitten by a Gabon viper. He could have been killed. The ambulance attendants said that in five more minutes he would have been dead. The Gabon viper is one of the deadliest snakes in the world.

SHEENA: I was trying to save our jobs. You know that Mr. Greenbelt is upset that the show hasn't taken off. It's hard to compete with wars, genocide, disasters, massacres, serial murders, riots, and all of the other stuff people are watching while eating dinner. I don't know about you, but I'm heavily into debt. You have to be a millionaire to live in New York these days. I still haven't recovered from the crash of '87.

VANESSA: (*Pouting*) You think that you have problems. I just bought a 1955 fully restored red hard- and soft-top Ford Thunderbird with an eight-cylinder engine and telephone. It cost thirty-five thousand dollars. I'm living in this exclusive East Side condominium that's taking fifty percent of what I earn.

SHEENA: You can kiss that goodbye if this show doesn't start to move. You'll have to get rid of your wardrobe, too. You have more clothes than Jackie Kennedy.

VANESSA: (*Huffy*) There's nothing wrong with looking neat. Presentable. I have a reputation to uphold. I was voted Ms. Virginia, in 1983.
> (SHEENA *eyes her contemptuously.*) (*Pause*)

I just called the hospital. Dr. Marlin has been taken off the critical list. The swelling in his arm has gone down. You have to admit that he is a real company man. Allowing himself to be bitten like that to improve the ratings.

SHEENA: There you go sympathizing with some guy.
> (*Door opens,* JACKSON, *the black prop man, enters. White shirt, tie, pants, and shined shoes. A clean-cut type. He carries a yellow legal pad clamped to a clipboard.*)

SHEENA: (*Rudely*) What do you want?

> (VANESSA *glares at* JACKSON, *folds her arms, and sighs impatiently.*)

JACKSON: I have the prop list.

> (SHEENA *snatches it from him and examines it, while glaring at him, hostilely.*)

SHEENA: Cut out the bookshelves. They look too PBS. And get rid of that pipe rack. It looks too . . . too oral. I hate it when he's waving that pipe about. Have him sit in a red lounge chair. You'll also need some colorful bandages. Something that will look good on TV. The hospital bandages won't look right in color.

> (SHEENA *hands the clipboard back to* JACKSON; *he examines it.*)

JACKSON: You forgot to initial it, sweetheart.

> (SHEENA *and* VANESSA *glare at him, intensely.*)

VANESSA: (*Mean*) Who you callin' sweetheart?

SHEENA: Yeah. What do we look like, a couple of whores to you?

VANESSA: You're always making some flirtatious remark when you come in here.

SHEENA: Next time you do it we're going to kick your ass.

> (JACKSON *smiles sheepishly.*)

VANESSA: So apologize.

JACKSON: (*Swallowing his pride*) I didn't mean to offend you, Vanessa, Sheena.

VANESSA: (*Mimics*) "I didn't mean to offend you, Vanessa, Sheena."
Ms. Bare and Ms. Queene to you.

>   (VANESSA *and* SHEENA *glare at him.*)

Sheena, do we have to continue using him? I know a sister who can
do his job.

JACKSON: (*Humiliated*) Ms. Bare. Ms. Queene.

SHEENA: Now get lost.

>   (JACKSON *exits.*)

VANESSA: The soul brothers are never going to change. I'm thinkin'
about buying me a pistol.

>   (*Phone rings.* SHEENA *picks it up.*)

SHEENA: (*Excitedly*) It's Mr. Greenbelt. He's coming downstairs.

>   (SHEENA *and* VANESSA *hurriedly exit.*)

ACT I

SCENE 2

(GREENBELT *enters. Yuppie type. In power suit. Looks at his watch.* VANESSA *and* SHEENA *enter. They've discarded their safari outfits and wear the San Francisco night-on-the-town outfits that will also be seen in* Savage Wilds, Part II. *They're heavily made-up. They approach* GREENBELT *and begin to cling to him.*)

SHEENA: (*Exaggeratedly*) Ooooooooh, Mr. Greenbelt.

VANESSA: Daddy, oh, Daddy.

GREENBELT: Cut it out, you whores. I don't want no ass. Oh, I shouldnta hired you broads. I shoulda hired a man. One man could do the job of twenty of you cunts. What was the meaning of the stupid stunt that you pulled on *Savage Wilds*? It was boring. Not only did you come in behind that *Mr. Peepers Show*, but you got these animal rights people callin' up here protestin' about the way you treated that snake. The sponsor, Polyester Potato Chips, is threatnin' to drop the show. Oh, Jesus. I got to sit down.

    (VANESSA *and* SHEENA *almost collide with each other, trying to provide* GREENBELT *with a chair. He sits down, gulps down some pills. They unbutton his shirt and begin to massage his chest, panting as they do so.* VANESSA *begins to remove his shoes. He slaps her hand.*)

GREENBELT: Will you two cut it out?

SHEENA: But Mr. Greenbelt. It was a critical success. The newspapers said that it set a new high for live television.

VANESSA: The way we kept our cool as Dr. Martin was writhing in pain.

SHEENA: We might get a Grammy and Emmy.
(VANESSA *nods.*)

GREENBELT: Who cares about statues? I can't put no fuckin' statue in the bank. I need people glued to the set when my shit is on. And that Dr. Marlin. Where'd you get that asshole? Fire his ass.

VANESSA: But Dr. Marlin has been here twenty years. He's an institution.

GREENBELT: The only institution that I know about is Greenbelt Television Network and how I can make a buck or two for the shareholders. They're puttin' pressure on me so I have to put pressure on you. Now I'm going to give you one more shot. If next week's show doesn't come in within the top ten, you broads are out on your fannies.

VANESSA, SHEENA: (*On their knees*) Please, Mr. Greenbelt. Don't fire us.
(VANESSA *tugs at his pant leg; he shakes his foot away.*)

SHEENA: (*Suggestively*) Daddy, can't we talk about this in private? I'll make it worth your while.

VANESSA: I'll pose for those art pictures you wanted, Mr. Greenbelt, honey.

GREENBELT: You women and minorities are always making lewd proposals to me. It's final. If you don't make this show climb by next week . . .

> (GREENBELT *makes a throat cutting gesture with his finger.*)

Anyway, you're the creative people, so create.

> (GREENBELT *starts for the exit, laughing at his last remark.* SANFORD *enters. He is an elderly, gray-haired black man who walks bowlegged, à la Redd Foxx, and wears a plaid sport jacket, rust brown pants, white shoes and a checkered cap. He wears dark glasses with loud pink or green frames.*)

GREENBELT: (*Angrily*) You still here? I told you to pack your stuff and get out in an hour. If you don't get out I'm going to call security and have them throw you out.

SANFORD: (*Pitiful*) Mr. Greenbelt, have a heart. Please.

> (*Begs with hands clasped.*)

I just came by to say goodbye to the girls. You'll let me do that, won't you?

GREENBELT: Make it quick.

> (*Turns to girls.*)

So create.

> (*Laughing,* GREENBELT *exits.*)

VANESSA: (*To* SANFORD) Goodbye? Goodbye for what?

SANFORD: I got fired.

SHEENA: Fired? But you came in #1 last week. You've been #1 for ten years.

SANFORD: But I came in #2 last night.
  (*Sobbing*)
What did they expect? The World Series was on another channel. That Greenbelt has no mercy. He has the heart of the Internal Revenue Service. Look girls. You wouldn't be able to lend me a subway token so that I can get down to the blood bank before it closes? I don't have nothin' to eat.

VANESSA: But what happened to the three homes in Bel Air, Miami, and Lake Tahoe?

SHEENA: The pied–à–terre on Central Park West?

VANESSA: The cash, securities, and diamonds?

SHEENA: (*Sarcastically*) Whaddya do? Toot it up your nose?

SANFORD: (*Squeezing his nose*) What nose?
  (*Squeezing his nose*)
This thing is plastic. I had a Beverly Hills physician fix it. As for my wealth, I lost it because of the different races.

VANESSA: Discrimination?

SANFORD: No. Churchill Downs. Belmont. Golden Gate Fields. I don't have nowhere to go. I called about my last job, you remember the one I had where the customers would drink whiskey and get into fights and where I had to do my make-up in the toilet and when it was time to get paid, the club owner would skip town. They said that they don't want me either.

VANESSA: You poor dear. Here, I'll lend you a subway token.
(*Goes into her purse.*)

SHEENA: (*To* VANESSA) What's the matter with you? Helping some guy.

VANESSA: He reminds me of my father . . . a . . . I can't even remember his name.
(VANESSA *hands* SANFORD *the subway token.*)

SANFORD: Oh, thank you Ms. Vanessa. You know, Ms. Vanessa, this is the first time I've seen you with some clothes on.
(VANESSA *glares at* SANFORD. *He realizes that he has blundered.*)

SANFORD: (*Nervously starting to exit, with a shit-faced grin*) Well, I'd better get going. Look, if you two hear of anything, let me know. I'll do anything. Sweep. Buff.
(SANFORD *exits.*)

VANESSA: (*Reflectively, nostalgically*) He'll make a comeback. His jokes are old, but he's been down and out before and managed to make a comeback. All of those years he spent in obscurity, working one-night stands. He had to work around so much cigarette smoke that one of his lungs had to be removed. Probably gave a lot of his money to his friends. He was always a soft touch. The kind of gentle sweet man who would give you the shirt off of his back. A man like that is hard to find these days. Most of them want to fuck and doze off.

SHEENA: How can you say that about a pig—hey, wait. What did you say?

VANESSA: Most of them just want to fuck and doze off.

SHEENA: No before that.

VANESSA: (*Puzzled*) A man like that is hard to find these days?

SHEENA: Sister, you've given me a great idea. We can make the ratings shoot right through the roof.

VANESSA: Sheena, I knew that you'd come up with something. I hope it won't get anybody hurt.

SHEENA: Don't worry. It'll be as safe as a Girl Scout cookie.
>(JACKSON *enters. He has a bouquet of roses. Begins to read the card.* SHEENA *is puzzled.* VANESSA *seems embarrassed.*)

JACKSON: (*Reads from card accompanying the roses. Teasing.*) "None of these roses is as beautiful as you . . .
>(*Makes melodramatic gestures*)

my sweet. My heart aches for you. Every particle of my being shakes for you. My every pore yearns for your divine love. My heart takes flight like an eagle when I think of you. You are the honey that oozes into my passion. I'd climb the highest mountain for you, swim the deepest ocean, feel pain in the warm September rain over you. My heart is burning and churning for you."
>(VANESSA *snatches the flowers and the note from* JACKSON. *He is cracking up.*)

VANESSA: You fresh thing. How dare you read my mail.

SHEENA: (*Laughing*) Who on earth is that from?

VANESSA: (*Embarrassed*) Just a fan.

JACKSON: The guy really has it for Vanessa. He's been sending flowers from Washington all week. You got these guys falling head over heels in love with you, huh babes.
(VANESSA *and* SHEENA *both turn on* JACKSON.)

SHEENA: Who you calling "babes?"

VANESSA: You may call your Mama "babes," but you don't be callin' we feminists no "babes." Ain't that right, Sheena?

SHEENA: We warned you.
(SHEENA *and* VANESSA *rush* JACKSON *and begin to pummel him. We hear his screams as the lights go down.*)

ACT I

SCENE 3

Prop room.

(SANFORD *is sitting in the red lounge chair. He is snorting from a coke spoon. He drops his spoon. He gets on his hands and knees and starts to sniff the spilled coke from the floor.* JACKSON *enters, halts before* SANFORD, *surprised.* SANFORD *looks up at* JACKSON *with doglike, pitiful eyes.*)

JACKSON: Uncle Sanford. What are you doing here?

SANFORD: (*Slowly gets to his feet*) I thought that I could live down here in the prop room for a while until my luck changes. I mean, Jackson, be a brother. You won't tell, will you?

JACKSON: Yeah, I heard that they fired you from your show. Too bad. Didn't you save anything?

SANFORD: I never thought about it. I mean, the show was number one for ten years. I thought that it would always be number one. I don't have no insurance, and I owe the government five million dollars in back taxes. My creditors are auctioning off all of my things tomorrow. This Las Vegas chorus girl that I married—you know, the one who's thirty years younger than me—she sold a story about me to *The National Enquirer*. You know, about my habits and problems, and those nasty parties we used to throw. I'm the laughing-stock of the nation. I'm afraid to show my face in public after what she wrote. Last night I thought about committing suicide.

JACKSON: (*Disgusted*) There's nothing like always being on top of this business. Look at you. Just think. Last week you still had your own parking space and dressing room. This week you're down here in the prop room asking me if it's okay if you can sleep here. With the little money I have, I've invested in bonds: my wife and I are saving money for college so that our son will have it better than we had it. That's the way you build an aristocracy. Each generation looking out for the succeeding generation. Who knows? Maybe my kid will end up being head of the Federal Reserve, or running some Wall Street brokerage house. Play polo. Join the Republican Party. You had your chance, and you squandered it. Guys like you only live for these days. I don't plan to work in the prop room all of my life. As for you, you're better off dead.

SANFORD: (*Pulls wine from coat and takes a swig*) Look, youngblood. Have a little respect. I was the first black man to fly coast to coast first class. I owned fourteen cashmere sport coats and had thirty Chinese servants. I had a bigger dressing room than Clark Gable. I played golf with General Eisenhower. But then I had a joke crisis. No matter how hard I'd try, the jokes wouldn't come.
   (*Takes another swig.*)
These hip comedians came on the scene, like Dick Gregory, and comics like me were discarded like old phonograph records. But now, my kind of humor is in again. People got tired of Gregory, Mort Sahl, and people like that who worried them and made them think. They wanted somebody like me. Somebody who would just entertain them. Somebody like me. Somebody who wouldn't hassle them with a lot of social issues. I worked hard to get where I am. For twenty years, when I couldn't get into the top clubs, I worked in

these buckets of blood where I had to do my make-up in the toilet and the people would get into fights—

JACKSON: Jesus. Don't you get sick of that story? I know I do.
(SANFORD *offers* JACKSON *a taste from a bottle of Wild Irish Rose.*)

SANFORD: Have a swig. I bought it with the money I got from the blood bank.

JACKSON: Don't bother me with that. I have to get this lounge chair ready for the next show. I have to keep my head clear. The future doesn't belong to cloudy heads.

SANFORD: You don't drink no wine. You don't snort no coke. Man, what kind of blood are you?

JACKSON: (*Pauses. Then proudly*) A twenty-first century blood. Your generation had your chance and you blew it. Now it's our turn. We're going to build dynasties like the Kennedys and the Rockefellers.

SANFORD: Well, if it weren't for the sacrifices we made . . .
(*Takes a swig and makes an ugly face.*)
you wouldn't have had your chance. Malcolm X . . .

JACKSON: Malcolm X. Who's that?

SANFORD: That's what's wrong with you, youngblood. You don't read no history. I'll bet that you don't even read books.

JACKSON: I have a book right here . . .

(*Holds up book.*)
How to Survive the Crash of Ninety-Nine.

SANFORD: All you think about is money, youngblood. Don't you ever think about soul?

JACKSON: Soul. You can't buy no groceries or put a down payment on a house with soul. That's what's wrong with the black people of today. Too much soul. Too much love. Trying to be the nation's conscience. Fuck being the nation's conscience. It's time for us to start acting like . . . like Americans. Making money for ourselves and to hell with the next fellow.
　　　(SANFORD *shakes his head.*)
　　　(*Phone rings.*)

JACKSON: Yeah, Ms. Sheena . . .
　　　(*Sarcastically*)
he's right here. It's for you.
　　　(*Hands the phone to* SANFORD.)

SANFORD: What? . . . That is good news. You can use me? Oh, Sheena that's so kind of you to help out an old man like me. How will I ever make it up to you? Glory be.
　　　(JACKSON *looks at* SANFORD *with disgust.*)
Yes. This will be the first step in my comeback. Before long, I'll be number one again. Hotdog! One thing, Ms. Sheena. How did you know I was in the prop room? Security told you? But how did they know? A camera?
　　　(*Looks around.*)
But I don't see no camera. Okay. Ms. Sheena, I'll be right up. Oh, thank you Ms. Sheena.

JACKSON: What are you so happy about?

SANFORD: Ms. Sheena says that they have a job for me. A walk-on. The *Savage Wilds* show. I'm on the comeback trail. I just keep coming back. Here, she wants to talk to you.

(JACKSON *snatches the phone from* SANFORD. SANFORD *exits, hopping and skipping.* JACKSON *looks at* SANFORD *disgustedly.*)

JACKSON: (*Sarcastically*) Yes, Ms. Sheena. What do you want? I'm preparing the lounge chair that you said you wanted.
(*Pause*)
Dummy bullets. How am I going to find dummy bullets this time of night?

(SHEENA *hangs up so hard* JACKSON *holds the phone from his ear. Hangs up. Mimics* SHEENA.)
"That's my problem." Where the hell am I going to get dummy bullets?

(*Thinks for a few seconds. Then indicates to the audience that he's gotten a bright idea. Snaps his finger. Smiles.*)

ACT I

SCENE 4

Studio taping of the Savage Wilds *TV show. Monitor shows taping of the interior of a subway car.*
(MARLIN *is seated in a subway. He is a distinguished white man, fifty or sixty years old. His arm is in a sling. He is reading the* New York Post, *which carries the headline: "Vigilante Hero Says More Blacks Will Die. Says He'll Run For Gov.")*

MARLIN: Welcome to another edition of *Savage Wilds*, a show on which your host, yours truly, traps some of the wildest animals known to man. First, I want to thank you for all of the get-well cards that you sent during my stay in the hospital. It was your prayers that got me through. I'm well now and eager to bring on this week's exciting show. A lot of you have written in, saying that you're bored with out trapping the same old four-footed animals. Some even complain that we've been cruel to these children of nature. This week's show promises to be different. Exciting. You will see us capture one of the most intelligent animals in North America. Brought to this continent over four hundred years ago in chains, this creature was freed and through cunning and wile has learned to adapt to an alien environment. Though its numbers have declined in recent years, it may still be found in one of its favorite habitats. For this show, we've had to travel to beneath the earth through long tunnels to a place where no sun shines. One usually doesn't have to wait long for one of these creatures to appear. Especially about feeding time. The caves are full of them. They move about constantly.

(MARLIN *whispers to audience.*)

Here comes one now.

(SANFORD *is dressed like a bum. He pushes a shopping cart containing all of his belongings. He enters the car slowly. He reels. He removes a wine bottle from his pocket and takes a swig.* MARLIN *continues to read.* SANFORD *sits down next to* MARLIN. *He looks over* MARLIN's *shoulder at his newspaper.* MARLIN *stares at* SANFORD *with annoyance and rattles his newspaper.* SANFORD *mimes his annoyance.* MARLIN *moves to another seat.* SANFORD *follows him. They begin to quarrel.* MARLIN *shoots* SANFORD. SANFORD *collapses to the floor of the subway car.* MARLIN *smiles. He bends over* SANFORD. *His expression changes. He rises and begins to wave his arm for help. A shocked expression on* MARLIN's *face. Video screen goes blank. A man in the studio, the* ANNOUNCER, *appears with earphones on. He is listening intently. He then realizes that he's on the air.*)

ANNOUNCER: Ladies and Gentlemen we've lost our remote to the *Savage Wilds* show, but I can tell you that something terrible has happened. Uncle Sanford has been shot dead. It's the most terrible thing to happen in my twenty-five years as a news broadcaster.

(*Almost sobbing*)

I'm sorry ladies and gentlemen. This is such bad news. We all loved Uncle Sanford, who has graced our TV screens for so many seasons. They were only supposed to be dummy bullets.

(*Screen goes blank. Stills appear of front-page newspaper stories of* VANESSA *and* SHEENA *in jail. "Protest Innocence." "Wild Game Pair Nearly Lynched." "Thousands Attend Sanford Funeral."*)

ACT I

SCENE 5

GREENBELT: Those coloreds really know how to put on a funeral. They had Sanford laying out there. He looked real peaceful. The undertaker did a good job. He looked as though he had a new face.

MARLIN: (*Pretentious*) Yes, but that . . . that noise they call singing. It becomes obnoxious after awhile. Why do they have to become so emotional? The woman next to me became so excited that she slapped me in the face with her pocketbook. And the preacher. I didn't understand what he was saying half of the time . . .
   (*Pause*)

GREENBELT: We made the papers all over the world. The show will be number one for months to come. I'm thinking of adding a clone. A sort of *Son of Savage Wilds* . . .
   (*Pause*)

MARLIN: Vanessa and Sheena are going to be incarcerated for a long time. The Judge might give them thirty years.

GREENBELT: (*Slight remorse*) I kinda feel a little responsibility. I guess I put a lot of pressure on the girls, trying to get them to boost the ratings and all. But they went too far. I guess they can't handle pressure the way we men can.

MARLIN: Well, you know how women are. They're hysterical. They're born with it.

GREENBELT: I can count on you not to pull a stunt like that . . .
 (*Pause*)
now that you're producer.

MARLIN: (*Pleased and surprised*) I won't let you down, Mr. Greenbelt.

GREENBELT: I know you won't.
 (*Pause*)

MARLIN: Did you see how they broke down and cried when the police came and arrested them? A man would never have conducted himself in such a manner.

GREENBELT: And the way they protest their innocence. I mean, if they didn't replace the dummy bullets with real ones just to boost the ratings, who did? They're the only ones who had a motive.
 (JACKSON *enters.*)

MARLIN: My sentiments exactly.
 (*Notices* JACKSON.)
Hello, Jackson.
 (GREENBELT *ignores* JACKSON.)

JACKSON: Hello Dr. Marlin and Mr. Greenbelt.

MARLIN: What brings you up here, Jackson?

JACKSON: The prop list. I always went over the prop list with Vanessa and Sheena before the show.
 (MARLIN *looks at it.*)

MARLIN: It looks fine, except I'd like to have the bookcase and pipe rack back. The show will have a little more dignity.

    (MARLIN *returns the clipboard to* JACKSON.)

JACKSON: You forgot to initial it, Dr. Marlin.

    (MARLIN *initials it.*)

GREENBELT: How's that youngster of yours, Jackson? He must be ten years old now.

JACKSON: (*Flattered and surprised*) He just turned ten, Mister Greenbelt. What a great memory you have.

    (GREENBELT *presses two tickets into* JACKSON's *hand.*)

JACKSON: (*Examines tickets*) Two tickets to the World Series. Gee, thanks, Mr. Greenbelt.

GREENBELT: Don't mention it. You and your boy go out and have a good time on me, and you know, Jackson, I like your moves. You keep going and you might and end up with your own show.

JACKSON: Thanks, Mr. Greenbelt. Wow. My own show. You know, Mr. Greenbelt, Dr. Marlin?

MARLIN, GREENBELT: What is it, Jackson?

JACKSON: I'm glad that you men are back in charge.

    (JACKSON *puts his arm around* MARLIN *and* GREENBELT's *shoulders. They all smile.*)

ACT II

SCENE 1

Women's Prison.
(*The* MATRON, *a stout, black woman, sits at her desk in the prison, talking on the phone. She wears a housedress, slippers, and a policeman's hat.* VANESSA *is lying on a cot sobbing softly.* SHEENA *is comforting her. They're wearing prison outfits or dresses of the same drab colors.*)

MATRON: They put up a little commotion when we brought them in here, Warden, but they've cooled down. We had to segregate them from the rest of the prison population. Uncle Sanford was popular around here. The white girl—she gave me some lip. I had to bust her one.

(SHEENA *pauses. Glares at* MATRON, *who catches her eyes and glares back.* SHEENA *averts her eyes from* MATRON's *and continues to comfort* VANESSA. MATRON *continues to glare.*)

They complainin' about the prison food. Think that this is the Hilton. This ain't no damn hotel . . . The newspapers? They callin' up. But I told them what you said, Warden. They not allowed to give out no interviews. They trial ain't gonna be nuthin' but a damned circus. Killing that po' man because the people who watched the show was tired of them hunting animals.

(*Glares at the two angrily.*)

Had him shot dead right on that wild game show, *Savage Wilds,* just so's the ratings would go up and they could keep they producin' jobs. I don't know what's wrong with these wimmin of today. Cold blooded if you ask me, Warden. Thank you, Warden. Okay, Warden.

(*Hangs up. Addresses audience.*)

Always want some excitement. Too much excitement in the world if you ask me. The way they tricked that po Uncle Sanford. The man was already down on his luck after he lost his show, *The Uncle Sanford Show*, because he came in second on the ratings for one week. How was that man supposed to compete wit the World Series that was on another channel? Now these two hos told him that they could get a little work on the show. The people they work for said that show needed some excitement. They wanted human meat. Now these two lyin' heifers told Uncle Sanford that he would be the game, and that they were going to use dummy bullets and that he should just play dead when he was captured. They put real bullets in there. They were so hard up for ratings and trying to keep their jobs. Everybody in Harlem was at Uncle Sanford's funeral. There was so many flowers there, the people couldn't get into church. There was all these black limousines from downtown. The rich white people were paying their respects. Well, these two . . .

(*Pointing her head in the direction of* VANESSA *and* SHEENA.)

swore up and down that they didn't put real bullets in the guns, but don't nobody believe them.

(VANESSA *begins to sob loudly.*)

SHEENA: Will you cut that out? I'm trying to think.

(MATRON *rises, stares at them contemptuously and exits.*)

VANESSA: (*To* SHEENA, *delicately*) You should have seen the look on my mother's face at the arraignment. She was so ashamed. I wanted to make her so proud. Be somebody. Now I'm in jail for murder, and it's all your fault. Poor Uncle Sanford. You and your big ideas. We might get life imprisonment.

SHEENA: We'll get out of this. They'll find out who did it.
> (MATRON *comes in and sets down a tray. Beans on paper plates.* SHEENA *and* VANESSA *glare at her.*)

VANESSA: (*Pretentious*) Beans, again? I refuse to eat them.
> (*Haughtily*)
They give me flatulence.

MATRON: (MATRON *puts her hands on her hips and momentarily stares at* VANESSA) Flatulence. Well, whatever this flatulence is it's better than a bad case of the farts.
> (MATRON *laughs loudly.* SHEENA *and* VANESSA *look at her, disgustedly.*)

SHEENA: Why can't we eat with the rest of the prisoners?

MATRON: It's for your own good. Uncle Sanford was real popular around here. Real popular. Every week when his show came on, all the girls would watch it. Why would you go and have him killed? Just to get at the top of the ratings? Did it for money, if you ask me. You some greedy nickel whores, if you ask me.

VANESSA: (*Pleading*) We're innocent. We didn't do it. We just wanted him to be shot with dummy bullets. Somebody put real ones in. Why doesn't anybody believe us? We were just trying to keep our jobs.

SHEENA: Who cares about Uncle Sanford? He used to come on the set with cocaine all over his face, and . . . and you remember all of those paternity suits by those young women. Women who could have been his daughters. Just another dead pig. A womanizer and a drunk.

MATRON: You not going to last long around her talkin' that way, dearie.

SHEENA: (*Angry*) I'm not your dearie.
> (*The* MATRON *grabs* SHEENA *by the wrist and brings it behind her back.* VANESSA *jumps up, comes to* SHEENA'S *defense; the* MATRON *knocks her down.*)

MATRON: (*Releases her grip*) We all have to respect each other around here. That way there will be no confusion.
> (SHEENA *has a pained look; wrings her hand.*)
> (*U.S. Attorney* HEAD *enters. He and* SHEENA *make eye contact. She looks at him, annoyed. He is a round, white man about forty. He is wearing a suit and striped tie. Cordovan shoes. Natty hat.* MATRON *stares at him angrily.*)

MATRON: Who let you in?

HEAD: (*To* MATRON) You can go. I want to be alone with the girls.

MATRON: I'm not goin' nowhere until you show me some I.D.
> (HEAD *flashes his badge.*)

HEAD: United States Attorney for the District of Columbia, Richard Head at your service.
> (MATRON *glares at* HEAD *for a moment.* MATRON *exits, mumbling.*)

SHEENA: (*Rubs her shoulder*) She's got a grip like Mike Tyson.

VANESSA: What do you want?

HEAD: The black prop man confessed. He said that you humiliated him daily and that if it weren't for you he would have been the director of *Savage Wilds*. He blamed all of his problems on the Women's Movement.

VANESSA: What a paranoid.

SHEENA: These black guys are always imagining that people are ganging up on them. Blaming everything on the system or the Women's Movement. What a bunch of crybabies. Always pretending to be the victim.

VANESSA: Does it mean that we're free to go?

HEAD: Yes.

VANESSA: We're free. I can't believe it.
(*Jumps up and embraces* SHEENA.)
Oh, Sheena we're free. Let's go and order the biggest steak we can find. I hated this prison food. Let's go to the Plaza. Let's see . . .
(*Dreamy eyed. Recites slowly with relish.*)
I'll start off with a cocktail, then I want steak, potatoes, green peas, salad with a Thousand Island dressing, custard, and then Cuban coffee—

SHEENA: Not a chance of our getting back on TV, though. I'll have to declare Chapter Eleven.

VANESSA: (*Weakly*) Me, too.

HEAD: I'm in a position to get back you on the air. You can do something for your country, as well.
(VANESSA *looks puzzled.*)

SHEENA: What do you mean?

HEAD: You've heard of the Mayor's problem. Mayor B. V. Dongson of Washington, D.C.
(VANESSA *looks shocked.*)

SHEENA: Who hasn't? There's a guy who can't seem to keep his pecker in his pants. Boy, do I feel sorry for his poor wife. Smokes crack, too.

HEAD: We don't have any evidence. We've been trying to get the guy for ten years, with no success. That's where you come in.

VANESSA: What do you mean?

HEAD: We got the idea from your show. We're going to bag the son of a bitch. Stop the swagger.

SHEENA: Not me. I'm not gettin' mixed up in no murder.

VANESSA: Me, neither.

HEAD: Who said anything about murder?
(*Pause*)

SHEENA: What do you want us to do?

HEAD: We need you two to be lovebait.

VANESSA: Lovebait?

HEAD: You know, a honey trap. We want you to lure the guy into a compromising situation. We'll do the rest.

VANESSA: I'm not going to be your whore.
(SHEENA *nudges her.*)

SHEENA: (*To* HEAD) Do you mind if we have a little confab?

HEAD: Go ahead.

SHEENA: (VANESSA *and* SHEENA *caucus*) Let's hear what he has to say first.

VANESSA: I don't think it's right.

SHEENA: Since when have you gotten so high and mighty? I know all about how you used to entertain Mr. Greenbelt and his television executive friends at those broadcast conventions.
(VANESSA *looks down, embarrassed.*)

SHEENA: (*To* HEAD) What do we get for it?

HEAD: We're looking for someone to produce our new show, *The Founding Fathers*, which is all about how the Contras were freedom fighters who tried to bring democracy to Nicaragua.

SHEENA: I'm not participating in a show that glorifies male violence.

VANESSA: You tell him, Sheena.

HEAD: We're going to have the script written so that the leader of the Contras is a woman. If you like, we can change the title to *The Founding Mothers*.

SHEENA: A woman, I don't believe it.

HEAD: She'll be the commander. A white woman. Vanessa, you may be interested that her assistant will be a black woman, and she'll have a love interest, even.

VANESSA: Oh, Sheena. This is a real opportunity.

SHEENA: How much?

HEAD: Double what you made on the last show.

SHEENA: (*Looks to* VANESSA *who nods her head wide-eyed*) You got a deal, pal.
      (*They shake hands.*)

HEAD: I'm glad that you guys decided to come aboard. Especially you, Vanessa.

SHEENA: What does he mean?
      (VANESSA *looks upset.*)

HEAD: Tell her, Vanessa. Vanessa has been the Mayor's mistress for three years.

SHEENA: What?

VANESSA: It's not true, Sheena. Don't believe him.

> (HEAD *provides photos.* SHEENA *inspects them. Recoils.*)

He victimized me, Sheena. He made me do it. He asserted his male dominance over me. I didn't want to. I was unwilling, Sheena. I was duped. He ... he ... seduced me. He victimized me. You've heard of Stockholm Syndrome. He treated me like a slave on the plantation.

SHEENA: But in this picture you're on top.

VANESSA: (*Suddenly angry*) Let me see those pictures!

> (*Snatches the pictures from* HEAD's *hands. Shuffles the pictures getting angrier with each one. Pauses on one.*)

Why that son of a bitch. He said that he only did that with his wife and me. Before I met him, I thought Crisco was something that you cooked with.

SHEENA: You sure are a sucker for men. You'll never be a feminist. They mold you in their hands like putty. Don't you have any self-control?

VANESSA: (*To* HEAD) What do you want me to do? I'll do anything to get him. He can't treat me as if I was some kind of streetwalker.

SHEENA: That's the spirit, sister.

HEAD: Right on, Vanessa. Get your things together. We have to catch the shuttle to Washington, but not before I buy you two a dinner at the Plaza.

> (VANESSA *and* SHEENA *beam. They exit.* HEAD *has his arms around their shoulders.*)

ACT II

SCENE 2

HEAD's *makeshift secret office.*
(*A desk and a couple of chairs. Photo of President George
H. W. Bush on the wall. A* BLACK *and a* WHITE AGENT *are
in charge of this office. Both are clean-cut American types.*
WHITE AGENT, *in shirtsleeves and loosened tie, is present,
reading a skin magazine. Radio is on.*)

RADIO (Voiceover): This is Cookie Boggs, National Feminist Radio.
People have just about had it with the black mayor of this town
swaggering around Washington as though he owned the place. Giving his black buddies a high five, and saying "hey bro," "hey man,"
and things like that. Slapping women on their behinds, squeezing
their breasts, and generally behaving like a coon with his genitals
wrapped around his neck. Rumors of his cocaine smoking persist,
though U.S. Attorney Richard Head hasn't been able to uncover
any evidence or get a grand jury to indict him. Everybody knows
that Mr. Head is bucking for Attorney General of the United States,
but he won't even be considered if he can't stop this big black buck
from waving his fanny in his face. Head must find some way to
gain the respect of Washington's white people, who are tired of
the daily minstrel show that passes for government here in the nation's capitol—a black jungle. This is Cookie Boggs, from National
Feminist Radio.

(BLACK AGENT *enters.*)

BLACK AGENT: Sure wish I could be transferred. What's wrong with this joker, Head? You've worked under him for three years.

WHITE AGENT: I don't know. The guy's into a fantasy number about the Mayor. It's obvious. He's been unable to get a grand jury indictment. He's losing face.

BLACK AGENT: He's losing ass, too. Why doesn't he get these generals and senators who be attending these freak parties?

WHITE AGENT: If you got everybody who was doing drugs and partying with drag queens, there'd be nobody to run the government. You heard about the president and that young girl who freaked out on acid.

BLACK AGENT: Then why are they doing the Mayor? I think they're racist. What about these guys in the Secret Service and the National Security Council who are doing coke? And what about the Coast Guard? They're supposed to be fighting drug smuggling and it turns out that they're not only doing coke, but taking bribes and telling the smugglers the best times to bring in their cargo.

WHITE AGENT: There you go with that racist shit, again. Seeing conspiracies that aren't there.

BLACK AGENT: Well, why do you think that Head is so antsy about this guy? Look at all these prescription drugs he's gulping down all day.

WHITE AGENT: Maybe he just wants to make the Mayor an example to the rest of them. The Mayor just happens to be the black. Look what they did to Gary Hart and Senator Towers. They were white.

BLACK AGENT: Yeah, but that was the press who caught them. The government didn't have those guys under surveillance twenty-four hours per day. Cameras, bugs, and everything else. They even put a microphone on Mrs. Dongson's cat. The Mayor does something to this guy Head's innards and it's because he's black, that's why.

(*Pause*)

Any luck on the honey trap bait?

WHITE AGENT: Nothing. I even tried one of those high-class girl agencies.

BLACK AGENT: Maybe we'll hire one of those sexual surrogates.

WHITE AGENT: What?

BLACK AGENT: Well, they're not exactly whores, Ralph. They help guys who can't, well, you know, perform.

WHITE AGENT: Are you sure that is legal?

BLACK AGENT: Since when have we been concerned about legalities? Besides, if we get caught we can probably make more money than we make now.

WHITE AGENT: Explain.

WHITE AGENT: Well, look at North, Haldeman, Ehrlichman, Nixon, and Reagan. They made more money at breaking the law than by abiding by it. Lecture fees, books, TV appearances.

(BLACK *and* WHITE AGENTS *laugh. Pause*)

WHITE AGENT: Hey, I got the new Digital Underground rap.

BLACK AGENT: Oh, yeah? Where did you get it?

WHITE AGENT: Over at the FBI.

BLACK AGENT: What was it doing over there?

WHITE AGENT: I guess they're keeping an eye on those rappers. They say that this song encourages anarchy . . .

> (WHITE AGENT *puts a cassette in the tape recorder.* HEAD *enters.* AGENTS *don't see* HEAD. *He stands there glaring at them.* WHITE AGENT *sees* HEAD *and starts trying to warn* BLACK AGENT, *who is dancing, by pointing at* HEAD *standing in the doorway. Finally,* BLACK AGENT *turns around and sees* HEAD. *He is embarrassed. He stands frozen.* WHITE AGENT *turns off the recorder.*)

HEAD: I warned you guys about playing those rap records. I hate that shit. It brings on my migraines.

> (*Gulps down a pill.*)

WHITE AGENT: Yessir.

HEAD: Barbaric ape-people's music.

BLACK AGENT: (*Angry, but controlled*) What the fuck do you mean by that, sir?

HEAD: This stuff is eroding the moral fiber of our society. It's leading to illegitimate babies, and crack smoking.

> (*Pause*)

Where are those photos I asked you to get?

> (BLACK AGENT *removes photos from envelope.* HEAD *examines the photos, while talking to himself.*)

HEAD: Yellow toilet paper. Wonder what that means?

BLACK AGENT: (*Indignant, angry*) Sir. Do I have to photograph the guy in the toilet? Suppose he discovers our stakeout. Shouldn't we permit him to have some privacy? You got pictures of him and his wife in intimate positions.

HEAD: YOU DO WHAT I TELL YOU TO DO. THIS BUCK IS NOT GOING TO MAKE A FOOL OUT OF ME.
> (*Both the* WHITE *and* BLACK AGENTS *stare at* HEAD. HEAD *notices.*)

HEAD: What are you two staring at? And you . . .
> (*To* BLACK AGENT)
You sound like you're on his side. You know, I was against the department hiring your kind. You lack control. Objectivity.

BLACK AGENT: I don't like the guy, sir. But the Washington establishment is full of freaks. Why him?

HEAD: (*Weakly*) He's a poor role model.
> (*B*oth AGENTS *crack up.* HEAD *gives them a stern look. They stop.*)

BLACK AGENT: A lot of people are saying that you're on the guy because he's black. Forty million dollars just to get him a misdemeanor charge. You could have built four neighborhood treatment centers for that kind of money.

HEAD: You're just like all of the other blacks. Seeing conspiracies and plots that don't exist. You're paranoid.
> (*Continues to study photos.*)

WHITE AGENT: Sir. I wasn't able to find anybody cheap enough for the honey trap.

HEAD: I took care of it.

BLACK AGENT: Who are they, sir?

HEAD: Sheena and Vanessa from the *Savage Wilds* show.

WHITE AGENT: But I thought they were in jail for the murder of Uncle Sanford. Man, that was my favorite show. *The Uncle Sanford Show.* Every Thursday night we'd send out for pizza, and the whole family would sit around the tube and watch Uncle Sanford.

BLACK AGENT: Mine, too. Those broads killed the man in order to boost the ratings for their wild-ass game show. How low can you get?

HEAD: They're innocent, you idiots. The prop man did it. He replaced the dummy bullets with real ones. He had it in for the girls. Accused them of hindering his career.
(*Shouts into the next room.*)
Girls! Come in here. I want to introduce you to the fellows.
(VANESSA *and* SHEENA *enter. Introduced all around.*)

HEAD: What do you say we get over to the hotel? The mobile unit has just informed me that the Mayor has left his favorite topless place for home.
(THEY *exit.*)

ACT II

SCENE 3

(*The living room at the* MAYOR's *house. Mrs. Dongson, the* MAYOR's WIFE, *is seated at a table with plates laid out and a candle burning. A bottle of moderately expensive wine is on the table. She is walking up and down, looking at her watch. She is a very attractive woman of about thirty-five. She is dressed as if she's going out on the town.*)

WIFE: Where is that fool? Two hours late. I've called all over town and to his limousine. No answer. What could be taking him so long? I'll bet he's drunk again. He comes home drunk and immediately wants to have sex. He makes love with that beeper on the night table. Gets up and rushes out of the house when it goes off. Hasn't eaten dinner here in four months. My father told me not to marry this fool. A graduate of Spelman like me. I could have done much better. Much better. All of the men who used to ask me out. One of them is now a member of the President's cabinet. Lawyers, Educators. No, I was in love. Fell for his sweet-talking jive. He used to be so tender. So loving. Those days when we were organizing for SNCC. Defying the Klan. Registering voters in Mississippi. He was right there with Martin and Stokley. There was something pure and clean about being on the outside. Now we're on the inside. Big house. A long way from sleeping in tents and freedom marches. Children in private school. Mayor of the most powerful city in the west. The FBI and that nutty U.S. Attorney Richard Head are after him. All of these people saying that they've smoked crack with him. I hope that's not true. And even if it was, he wouldn't be the only politician in town who does coke. Why won't this Richard Head leave us alone? What is he after? That's all B.V. talks about. Richard Head. How he's outfoxing this fool. I know they're tapping the phone. God knows what else they're doing. I feel eyes watching me when I'm out on errands. Vultures' eyes waiting for me to drop. Vultures' eyes crawling up and down my spine.

(*Shivers and holds her arms as though she has goose bumps.*)

Waiting for me to show any sign of weakness. Even when we're making love I feel as though I'm spied upon. Still he won't be cool. I know he has these women. He comes in with their musk all over him. Strands of hair all over his shirt. I can tell. Any woman can tell another woman's smell. They flirt with him in public. Right in front of me. He thinks that they're enjoying him, but they're screwing what he stands for. Power. There are people all over this town trying to get in bed with power. They even have these hideaways in the capitol where these politicians go and meet women or men, whatever their predilection. I know. I wasn't born yesterday. He says it's because of the pressures of the office. I'm tired of these black men who blame their failures on the system. On racism. I'm tired of politics. He told me to stick with him until after the next election and he'd enter the Betty Ford Clinic. I'm not sure I can wait that long. Trying to put up a good front. Well I'm tired of playing the loyal, devoted wife and smiling before the camera when there ain't nothing funny. I don't know why I've stayed with him so long. I try to tell myself it's for the children. But when he looks at me with those dark, snake eyes, and tells me those loving lies, I forget about my anger. And that walk of his. It's more than a walk. The man's walk could have been choreographed by Katherine Dunham. It's like enchantment what he does to me. Something comes over me. He turns me on and off as though I was a spigot.

(*Pause*)

It's our anniversary and he's late. Probably forgot. He should go to a clinic. Maybe a counselor. The children. They have to go to school. Take the ridicule of their classmates who call their father a crackhead. They get into fights with the other children. And the newspapers. And the talk shows. We had to chase away a TV crew the other night. They were using telephoto lenses to spy into the kitchen.

(MAYOR *enters. Has a bobbing street walk.*)

MAYOR: Hi, babe.

(*Goes over and kisses his* WIFE, *who recoils from his affectionate gesture and folds her arms. Glares at him.*)

MAYOR: What's the matter, hon?

WIFE: This is our anniversary and you come stepping in here at two in the morning.

MAYOR: (*Slaps hand against forehead*) Aw, damn. I knew that there was something I forgot. Look, baby, I'll make it up to you. We'll go down to Bermuda after I announce for reelection. I was busy downtown, making the rounds. You know how I like to get out with people. Go to the bars. Talk to my constituency. That way I keep on top of the pulse of the community.

WIFE: Keeping on top of your whores.

MAYOR: There you go getting paranoid, again.

WIFE: (*Shows* MAYOR *a tiny cellophane bag*) B.V. I found this in the bathroom. B.V. This isn't one of those crack bags is it?

MAYOR: (*Reaches for bag, innocently*) Let me see.
(MAYOR *examines bag, continuing to feign innocence.*)

WIFE: Look, if you don't respect me and respect yourself you could at least respect your children.

MAYOR: (*Innocent*) I don't know how it got there.

WIFE: (*Rising, angrily*) You don't know how it got there? You need some help. Everybody knows about it and even though they can't get a grand jury to indict you, they'll get you sooner or later.
(*Sympathetic*)
Why don't you go to a clinic? Get help?

MAYOR: Clinics are for sick people. I don't need any help. Can't nobody beat me. I'm invincible. I'm announcing for reelection next week. There's nobody in the polls who can touch me. You read too many newspapers. You know that the media and the white boys in the U.S. Attorney's office are against me. They hate a black man who . . . dresses well, talks good, and who's a great lover. I don't hear no complaints from you in the bedroom department. You were screaming so loud the other night that one of my bodyguards had to bust down the door. He thought that somebody was robbing us.
(*Starts to mimic:*)
Let me have it. Oooooooh, let me have it. Yes. Yeessss!
(MAYOR *laughs nastily.* WIFE *slaps him and hurries, crying, from the room.*)

MAYOR: (*Puts his hand upside his cheek. Pauses for a moment. Sits down and pours himself a glass of wine.*)

Just like a black woman. Try to get in the way of my career. If it weren't for them we would be ruling the world. We'd be African Kings, striding the world like Atlas. Heroes and champions. Golden, bronze, and ebony Gods. Hot damn.

(*Laughs, then serious*)

They're in cahoots with the white power structure to keep the brothers down. Always accusing me of drinking too much. Smoking crack. Hell, I can quit anytime I want. They can't catch me. They can't prove that I smoke crack. Richard Head. Ha, ha. A simple, corny white boy. Can't get nothing on me. The newspapers. A white racist cabal. Trying to catch me because I'm so great. Hell, as long as I keep the fat cats downtown happy, they can't touch me. The members are crazy about me. Naming they babies after me. Everywhere I go they almost create a mob scene trying to shake my hand. To get a glimpse of me. And the women. Every woman in town is trying to get in bed with me, and the only regret I have is that I can't satisfy them all. How did that singer Maurice put it?

(*Sings: "I got ladies by the dozen, I got money by the ton."*)

(*Phone rings. Picks it up. Grins.*)

Hey, baby what it is? Look, I meant to visit you in jail, but I figured you'd get out. I know you're ambitious, but I figured you weren't so ambitious you'd have a man murdered on television . . . A party to celebrate? Well, allrrriggghhhttt. Just you and me and . . . Oh yeah, the one who was on the show with you. I always did know that she was a freak. She got a nice behind.

(*Puts on coat. Starts out. Yells off stage.*)

Hey, baby. I got to run downtown to take care of a little business. I'll be back in about an hour.

ACT II
SCENE 4

Hotel Room. A crummy dive.
(VANESSA, SHEENA *are present.* HEAD *is on the phone. Off-stage we hear the beginning of the* WIFE's *monologue from Scene 3, being replayed.* HEAD *hangs up phone.*)

HEAD: Okay. The mobile unit says that the Mayor has left the house. Now let's have one more run-through before he gets here. I'll play the Mayor.
(*Referring to the tape of* WIFE's, *which is still running:*)
Turn that thing off!

VANESSA: (*Tired*) Again?

SHEENA: I'm exhausted.

HEAD: You guys ready back there?

AGENTS: (*From offstage*) Ready.
(SHEENA *goes into the other room.* VANESSA *sits on the couch.* HEAD *goes off stage. Bell rings.* VANESSA *answers.* HEAD *enters, taking the role of* MAYOR.)

VANESSA: Oh, Mister Mayor.

(HEAD *enters the room with her. Walks the way he thinks black men walk.*)

HEAD: Come here pretty Mama.
> (HEAD *turns her around and kisses* VANESSA *for a long time. Puts his hand on her behind. She knocks it away.*)

VANESSA: Baby, we have plenty of time for that. Come. Let's sit down for a minute.
> (HEAD *and* VANESSA *sit down on a shabby, dirty couch.*)

HEAD: Where's your friend?

VANESSA: She's in the bedroom getting comfortable.

HEAD: I'm sorry I didn't visit you in jail. I missed you. Whenever I made love to my wife, I'd imagine that it was you.

VANESSA: (*Playing along*) That's so sweet of you, baby.

HEAD: You're more important to me than the stars, the moon, the sun, and the mountains. You my love nourishment.

VANESSA: You talk so nice.

HEAD: You know that these white boys are trying to bust me. They can't stand a black man being all fine, and . . . and invincible. I'm invincible. They can't stand a black man talkin' that talk. And walkin' that walk. A noble and bold brother man. A super cool dude.

VANESSA: I got the new Digital Underground record. Would you like to hear?

HEAD: Oh, yes. Digital Underground are my main brother men. I love them dudes.

> (VANESSA *puts on the rap record.* HEAD *starts to dance. Awkward. Silly. Snapping his fingers.*)

HEAD: Funky down! Funky down!

> (SHEENA *enters.*)

SHEENA: Vanessa. So this is the foxy dude you been tellin' me about. Hey, baby. What's happenins?

HEAD: I can dig it. Yes, indeed. I can dig it.

VANESSA: Mr. Mayor, this is Sheena. She's my partner.

HEAD: Yawl got some blow?

SHEENA: Do we have some blow? Come on into the bedroom. We got that, and we got some other things that you might want to indulge in.

> (*Does a mock bump and grind. Winks.*)

HEAD: Well alllllrrrigghhhhttt. Okay.

> (*Changes to natural voice.*)

Now at this point you all disappear into the bedroom and we make the snatch. Do anything you have to do to get him to smoke the crack pipe.

> (*Bell rings.*)

HEAD: (*Excited*) There he is now.

> (HEAD *disappears into the other room where agents have set up video equipment.* VANESSA, *smoothing her clothes, goes to the door.* MAYOR *enters.*)

VANESSA: Oh, Your Honor. How nice of you to come.

MAYOR: (*Walks in. Looks around. Grins.*) It's been a long time, baby. We have a lot of catching up to do.
> (MAYOR *tries to kiss* VANESSA. *She resists.*)

VANESSA: We have plenty of time for that. Let me take your coat. Why don't you make yourself comfortable?
> (VANESSA *takes the coat off stage.* MAYOR *rubs his hands together and looks about the apartment.*)

MAYOR: How was your trip down from New York?

VANESSA: It seemed to take forever. I was eager to see you.

MAYOR: I knew that you'd get off. The idea of you killing Uncle Sanford was absurd. I knew that they'd made some kind of mistake.
> (VANESSA *returns to the room. The* MAYOR *tries to pull her towards him.*)

VANESSA: Why don't I put on some music? How about some rap music?

MAYOR: I hate that shit. Put on something grown-up . . . Some Barry White.
> (VANESSA *puts on Barry White's "Ecstasy."*)

VANESSA: Would you like something to drink?

MAYOR: Yes. Get me a Scotch.
> (VANESSA *goes over to the bar, and prepares a glass of Scotch. She brings the bottle and the glass to the* MAYOR. *She puts*

them on broken-down coffee table situated in front of the couch. MAYOR *drinks some.* VANESSA *sits in his lap. They kiss briefly.*)

MAYOR: You know I missed you, baby. Plenty of nights I'd be lonesome by the moon longing for your warm embrace. Dying for a plunge between your gentle thighs. These other women—they mean nothing to me. My wife, she doesn't satisfy me the way you do.

(*Pause*)

She's an Episcopalian, you know. Come here. I want to caress your voluptuous breasts and lay my head in your nurturing lap.

(SHEENA *enters.*)

VANESSA: This is my friend, Sheena.

MAYOR: (*Looks her up and down, enthusiastic*) We are going to have some funnnnnnn tonight.

(*Away from his vision,* VANESSA *glares at him, evilly.*)

MAYOR: How are you, Miss Queene? I'm a fan of yours. I used to watch that show of yours and Vanessa's every week. It was great. The way you had the host Dr. Marlin bitten by a Gabon viper to improve the ratings, and then the most daring hunt of all. The way you bagged Uncle Sanford. Of course, the way I look at it, he was volunteering for a stunt like that in the first place. You could say that he staged his own entrapment and was responsible for the tragic consequences.

(SHEENA *and* VANESSA *stare at each other.* MAYOR *doesn't see this.*)

It almost worked except for that prop man having to go and put real bullets in the gun. You know, some of the brothers are really reactionary when it comes to women. Anyway, Vanessa here tells me that you like to party.

SHEENA: I love to party, Mr. Mayor. But not with something as lame as Scotch.

MAYOR: What do you have in mind?

SHEENA: I have some glory nose. You know about that?

MAYOR: I'm willing to try anything.

VANESSA: Why don't we go into the bedroom and make ourselves comfortable?
>   (ALL *rise and go into the (offstage) bedroom. Momentarily, we hear voices.*)

VANESSA: Mr. Mayor, slip into this. Relax. Lay back.
>   (*Pause*)

SHEENA: What am I going to do with all that?
>   (*Giggles. Laughter. Pause. Moans and little cries.*)

VANESSA: (*Husky, passionate voice*) I love it. Godddd, do I love it. Mayor, let me put some more Crisco on.

MAYOR: Do me. Awwww, do me. Right there. Easy now. Right there. Go on, girl.
>   (*Moans and then sighs.*)
Damn, girl. What are you doing? Where did you learn that? Vanessa, your friend is a pure-d-freak.

VANESSA: I told you she was.

SHEENA: Save some for me. Don't hog it all. Andrew Dice Clay was right. It's as huge as an oak tree.

(*Pause*)

MAYOR: Don't be selfish, Vanessa. There's enough to go around.
  (*Giggles. Nasty laughter.*)
  (*Pause*)

SHEENA: This is so gooooooodddd. Yummy. Are you going to drive me out of my mind? No. Oh, God, no. Stop. I mean, I mean keep going.
  (*Moans and cries rise. Get louder. Then cease altogether.*)
  (*Pause*)

VANESSA: (*Weak, tired*) Let me have some more.
  (*Pause*)

SHEENA: Naw. Let's light up first. You want some, Mr. Mayor?

MAYOR: Don't be so formal. Call me B.V. That's what my intimates call me. Listen. I haven't done this before. You have to show me.

VANESSA: You're a liar. You've done it plenty of times. Do you hear that? Plenty.

SHEENA: (*Laughter*) You've got the thing upside down, Mister Mayor. Let me show you how.
  (*Pause*)
There. Now you've got it.
  (*A commotion begins. Screams.*)

HEAD: Okay, Mr. Mayor. Admit that you have a problem. This is the end of your playing the cool dude. Read him his rights, guys. Get your pants on.
  (*Two AGENTS begin to read, and continue to read Miranda rights throughout commotion.*)

Nice work, girls.

> (*Commotion tumbles out into the living room. The* MAYOR *is struggling with the* AGENTS. *He is naked from the waist up. No shoes.* HEAD *follows, rubbing his hand gleefully with a triumphant look. The men sit the* MAYOR *on the sofa.* WHITE AGENT *still reading him his rights. The* MAYOR *puts up a fight. Surrenders.*)

HEAD: Strip him. I'll frisk him personally. He may be hiding something up his cavity.

> (*Both of the* AGENTS *are shocked.* VANESSA *and* SHEENA *nod and smile.*)

WHITE AGENT: (*Shocked*) But—what? Are you out of you mind, sir?

BLACK AGENT: You're not going to strip nobody, Head. This is not some kind of street criminal. This is the Mayor of Washington.

> (HEAD *and* BLACK AGENT *glare at each other intensely for a moment.*)

HEAD: (*Glaring at the* BLACK AGENT, *who has deprived him of an attempt to probe the* MAYOR *rectally*) Okay, pad him down.

BLACK AGENT: (*Sadly*) Put your hands up against the wall, Mr. Mayor.

> (MAYOR *rises. The* BLACK AGENT *frisks him.* VANESSA *and* SHEENA *look to each other, smiling, obviously enjoying themselves.*)

BLACK AGENT: Okay, Mr. Mayor. You can sit back down.

MAYOR: (*To* VANESSA) You set me up. You tricked me. You goddamn bitch. You. You dirty . . . lowdown . . . Why . . .

(MAYOR *tries to get at* VANESSA *and has to be restrained. He shakes himself loose. Sits down on the couch. The* AGENTS *go after him, but* HEAD *nods.* MAYOR *finally begins to laugh. A long sinister laugh.* MAYOR *laughs until he cries. The two* AGENTS *laugh nervously.* HEAD *manages a weak smile. To* VANESSA:)

How much they pay you? Or did you do it on the cheap, as usual?

VANESSA: (*Screams*) You were screwing all of my girlfriends. I hope they give you the electric chair.

MAYOR: And you, Richard. One of your traps finally worked. Congratulations. I had you all wrong. I underestimated you. All of those winters your people spent in Europe taught you patience. Persistence.

HEAD: Why, thank you, Mr. Mayor. And look, it may not turn out so bad. You can resign and seek treatment.

MAYOR: (*Angrily*) I ain't resignin' from a motherfucking thing. And yeah, I'll probably get treatment, but who's going to treat you?
(*Pause.* MAYOR *and* HEAD *glare at each other like bucks pawing the ground before battle.*)
Who's going to treat the people that you work for?
(BLACK AGENT *helps the* MAYOR *off the couch. He drapes his coat over the* MAYOR. MAYOR *glares at the* BLACK AGENT. *Throws the coat to the floor.*)

HEAD: What do you mean by that? I don't need any treatment.

MAYOR: I can clean myself up, but how is a government that lies and sets people up with crack and whores going to clean itself?

SHEENA: Now wait a minute, buster.

VANESSA: What whores? I don't see no whores.

MAYOR: I can get rid of my stains, but how is your government going to get rid of its own? One of the most powerful governments in the world reduced to pandering?
(*Laughter*)
Reminds me of the old African proverb. "No matter how high the vulture flies it can't get rid of its stink."
(*Gives* BLACK AGENT *a look of disgust.*)
What kind of homey are you? Sucker!

BLACK AGENT: (*Pauses before answering*) You made your bed now and you have to lie in it, Mayor. I'm sorry.
(*The* MAYOR *looks to* VANESSA, *who stares back, defiantly, to the* AGENTS, *who lower their heads, and to* HEAD, *who manages a smirk.* MAYOR *straightens his back. Holds his head high. Musters considerable dignity.*)

MAYOR: Yeah, well, may be I have been a bad husband. A substance abuser. A liar. And maybe even a dickhead. But who expects anything more from a politician? There are politicians all over town who've done worse than I've done. Why do you think I'm the one they used these tricks on? Besides. All I did was smoke from a crack pipe. At least I'm not flying it in or bringing it in by ship, like your people are. I get set up while they go to college campuses on speaking tours.
(MAYOR *laughs. The others in the room don't know what to make of this recital.*)

HEAD: That's enough of your paranoid speeches, Mayor.
(*To* AGENTS)

Take him downtown.

MAYOR: Okay. Let's go.

> (*The two* AGENTS *grab the* MAYOR's *elbows. He shakes them off. They look to* HEAD. *He nods. They permit the* MAYOR *to exit without holding his elbows.* MAYOR *exits, head high, walking his arrogant street walk.* VANESSA *and* SHEENA *follow the two* AGENTS *and the* MAYOR.)

HEAD: (HEAD *sits down. A look of satisfaction and peace. He sits there for a moment.*) I wonder whether I should supervise the urine test. Look over the Mayor's shoulder. See to it that the Mayor wee-wees into the paper cup. Guess the boys will take care over it. But then the black agent may substitute the Mayor's sample. Switch cups so that the Mayor won't be trapped. Imagine him, standing in the way of my strip search.

> (HEAD's *eyes light up. Snaps his fingers as if to say, "I got it."*)

The hair samples. I'd love that. Maybe I can be the one who clips off strands of hair for the lab.

> (*Pause*)

Naw. I'll be okay. Finally caught the son of a bitch. Tried to make a fool of me.

> (*Stretches and yawns.*)

Haven't been able to sleep for ten years. Gonna go home. Kick off my shoes. Watch some tapes of *My Little Margie*. That show always relaxed my nerves. Going to stay in bed for two weeks.

> (*Gulps down some pills. Rises.*)

How does he walk like that?

> (*Imitates Mayor's walk.*)
> (*Phone rings.*)

Hello?

> (*Perks up immediately. Stands up at attention.*)

Why, President Skippy. I . . . it's an honor. You canceled your trip to the summit so you could hear the outcome of the sting? . . . Why, Mr. President . . . I didn't know it was so important. The highest priority, huh? . . . The honey trap worked like clockwork, Mr. President . . . He was really mad, tried to harm that black gal, but she was cool . . . No, sir. You have complete plausible deniability. Nobody can trace it to you. Mr. President, may I make a suggestion? . . . I think sir that we ought to put the net on some of these black agents. The one we have told the Mayor that he was sorry . . . These homeys stick together . . . Yessir . . . Yessir . . . The Attorney General is resigning and you want me? . . . Mr. President you can count on me . . . What's the matter Mr. President? You want the bedsheets . . . Deliver them to the White House through the back entrance . . . But Mr. President, I'm sure that the hotel has plenty of clean sheets if the White House wants to borrow them . . . You want the ones in this suite? But they were all lying on . . . Whatever you say, Mr. President. And the videotapes? But we can edit them for you Mr. President. The raw footage. Okay. What else, Mr. President? The Martin Luther King Jr. sex tapes? No inconvenience, sir. We'll get them from the boys at the FBI. You're having a private party, tonight? Coming right over, Mr. President . . . No, I won't tell anybody. Yessir . . . Yessir . . . Goodbye sir . . . Strange request. I guess the deficit must be pretty high. They can't afford to buy sheets for the White House . . . cities are going to look like *Planet of the Apes*. Degenerate apes. Not if I can help it. Those Martin Luther King sex tapes are in real demand around town. Say that the old preacher had the stamina of a bull. Insiders say that LBJ listened to them so much he couldn't concentrate on anything else. That's why we lost the war in Vietnam.

(SHEENA *enters.* HEAD *rises. He tries to kiss her. She resists.*)

HEAD: What the hell's wrong with you?

SHEENA: Why did it take you so long to spring us?

HEAD: We had to persuade the prop man to confess. It took three days. He'll be in the prison hospital for a long time. He was pretty busted up when we finished with him.

SHEENA: And the Contra show. Why didn't you let me know? You took me by surprise. I'll bet you discuss things with your wife.
> (*Pouting*)

HEAD: I haven't been home more than three weeks in the last ten years. This case has taken all of my time. You know that. Look, I don't feel like arguing. You know, I don't know what I see in you. You can be a difficult bitch sometimes. Maybe there's something to that thing about opposites attracting. I mean here I am with you, a raving feminist. I hate feminists. Maybe people are right when they say that I should have my head examined.
> (*Pause*)

Do you think Vanessa knows about us?
> (HEAD *sits down, pours himself a drink from the bottle of Scotch that's been left behind.*)

SHEENA: Not a thing. I put her in a cab and sent her home. She asked me why I wasn't coming. I told her that it was a nice night and I wanted to walk. She had second thoughts about bagging the Mayor. I think that she's still in love with him. She's always falling in love with these pigs.

HEAD: You're attached to her.

SHEENA: (*Pause. Longing look of desire.*) She reminds me of a black woman I once knew. I had a nurturing experience with this woman.

HEAD: (*Pause. Stares at her puzzled.*) You mean that you had a maid?

> (*She nods.*)

My folks had one too. She took care of us more than she took care of her own family. Good nigger.

SHEENA: I wish you wouldn't use that word. I'm telling you, Head, you're such a pig. I must be crazy to be with you.

HEAD: Look, I don't want to get into some political argument tonight. Besides, Eddie Murphy and Richard Pryor say it. Why can't I? Everybody's saying it nowadays.

> (*Pause*)

You really got carried away there in the bedroom.

> (*She looks at him angrily.*)

You went way beyond my instructions. Putting that nasty thing in your mouth like that. You didn't know where that thing had been last. Then you let him penetrate you. He was only supposed to do that with Vanessa.

SHEENA: I was just trying to do a convincing job. You know I'm a professional. I was giving it my all.

> (HEAD *stares at her nastily.*)

HEAD: Did you enjoy it?

SHEENA: Enjoy it? I don't know about you, Dick.

> (SHEENA *thinks for a moment, then with nasty sarcastic laughter:*)

I have an idea. Why don't you get Dongson to get a divorce from his wife so you can marry him? You're just like your old boss J. Edgar Hoover. You know what they say about him.

HEAD: (*Draws a gun and points it at* SHEENA.) What do you mean by that? TAKE THAT BACK. TAKE WHAT YOU SAID BACK, GOD-DAMITT.

(*Begins to cry.*)

Don't you ever say that about Mr. Hoover. Do you understand? Mr. J. Edgar Hoover. What did you mean by that?

SHEENA: (*Frightened*) Nothing, Dick. Just a joke. Dick.

(HEAD *keeps the gun pointed at* SHEENA. *Then slowly lowers it. Puts a hand to his forehead in a gesture of fatigue.*)

HEAD: I'm sorry, Sheena. I got carried away. I been working ten years to put that guy away. I thought that I would be at peace once I trapped him. But his arrest merely raises more questions. Doubt. I hate doubts. These doubts are giving me insomnia.

(HEAD *puts his head in* SHEENA'S *lap and begins to sob. She comforts him and strokes his hair.*)

Did you see the way he walked, Sheena? Were you watching? Doesn't he have a cool walk?

SHEENA: (*Puzzled look*) Yeah. Sure, Dick. I saw the way he walked. Dick, speaking of divorce, you've been promising that you were going to divorce your wife for years, now.

HEAD: (*Lifts his head from her lap and sits upright. Pours two large glasses of Scotch from the bottle in front of the shabby hotel-room couch.* SHEENA *glares at the glass and then at* HEAD.) Let's make a toast.

(HEAD'S *speech is slurred. He offers the glass to* SHEENA.)

SHEENA: (SHEENA *refuses*) I wish you wouldn't.

HEAD: (*Gulps down the glass and starts on the one he's poured for her*) Don't worry. I can handle it.

SHEENA: That's what you always say. You know that this stuff makes you crazy. I'm not gettin' in no car with you. You know how you drive when you're drinking.

HEAD: This stuff makes me relax.

RADIO: (*Hostile, sarcastic*) This is Cookie Boggs of National Feminist Radio. Well, the women of Washington, D.C. can rest tonight, safe in the knowledge that Mayor B. V. Dongson has been put into a federal cage where he belongs.

> (HEAD *pours another glass.* SHEENA *gets up and exits angrily.* HEAD *looks at the door for a moment.*)

Just a few minutes ago, we received a bulletin that the Mayor was caught in the act of smoking a crack pipe . . .

> (HEAD *lifts the entire bottle to his lips and slowly begins to drink the remaining Scotch.*)

in an elaborate sting that was set up by U.S. Attorney Richard Head. Apparently, the Mayor was lured into the trap by Vanessa Bare and Sheena Queene, the former hosts of the wild-game show, *Savage Wilds*. Just a few days ago, our sisters were cleared of all charges in connection with the murder of comedian Uncle Sanford, another one of the brothers who had trouble keeping his britches up and his zipper zipped. Congratulations, my sisters. A prop man who worked on the show has been charged with the murder. Reached at the White House, a spokesperson said that the President had no comment on the arrest, which followed years of rumors in Washington that the Mayor had smoked crack on many occasions. Predictably, a spokesperson for the NAACP blamed the arrest on, what? You guessed right if you said, "a conspiracy against black elected officials." So what else is new? This has been a special report from Cookie Boggs, National Feminist Radio.

> (HEAD *turns off the radio. Picks up the bottle of Scotch. Starts to exit, imitating the* MAYOR'*s walk. Stops. Snaps his fingers.*)

HEAD: (*Mumbling*) Forgot the sheets.

> (*Exits Stage Left. Momentarily returns with the sheets. Places them into bag. Exits carrying the sheets, imitating the* MAYOR'*s walk.*)

CURTAIN

HUBBA CITY

A PLAY IN TWO ACTS

Hubba City is based upon the North Oakland, California, crack wars of the 1980s, but the situation is the same in cities, large, medium-sized, and small, throughout the United States. ("Hubba" is the street name for crack cocaine.) It was written as a tribute to the brave members of the Oakland Crime Watch, who risked their lives to combat the invasion of their neighborhoods by criminal elements. All of those who profited from this nefarious enterprise are exposed, including the local police, federal agencies, representatives in the local government, and the bankers, real estate brokers, and other businesses built upon or profiting through money laundering. Many of these institutions are given credit for the falling crime rates reported across the country in the late '90s and early 2000s, but the role of the citizens and neighborhoods in bringing about this decline has seldom been discussed. *Hubba City* addresses their selfless actions.

Hubba City premiered in 1989 at the Black Repertory Theater at 3201 Adeline Street in Berkeley, California, where it was directed by Vern Henderson. In 1996, Rome Neal directed a revised version of the play, starring Vinnie Burrows as Mildred Warhaus, at the Nuyorican Poets Café. This production received enthusiastic reviews in the *New York Post*, *New York Times*, and *Amsterdam News*. Henderson directed his second staging of *Hubba City* at Potrero Hill

Neighborhood House, 953 De Haro Street, San Francisco in 1998, which was produced by the author through the use of his MacArthur Foundation Award, received in 1998, "because of [his] concern about the demise of American ethnic theater."

CAST OF CHARACTERS

Mildred Warhaus
Sam Warhaus
Jake Nelson
Mabel Nelson
Jack Krud
Bobbie Krud
Joe Handsome
Bump
Crackpot Jenkins
Cop
Martin
Martha Wingate
Banker Krock
Robert Hamamoto
Cameraman
Lady In Red (dancer in Crackpot's dream)
Mrs. Jenkins
Radio Announcer

ACT I

SCENE 1

(Oakland, California. About fall, 1989. Home of the War-hauses, a black couple living in the North Oakland section of Oakland, California. On the wall are pictures of a black Jesus Christ, Martin Luther King, Jr., J.F.K., and a younger Sam Warhaus in cowboy clothes. Also a young black man in an Air Force outfit, with binoculars, etc. SAM *is sitting in a wheelchair with a blanket over his knees. Coughs a lot. He is listening to the baseball game. Enter* MILDRED, MABEL, *and* JAKE. *They're wearing yellow jumpsuits and caps, and carrying flashlights. They wear badges that read "Crime Watch." All of the characters are in their middle sixties.* SAM *is clearly annoyed by this interruption.)*

MILDRED: (*Wearily*) Am I tired. Some of the people in the Crime Watch are in their seventies. I don't know how they do it. Walking up and down these streets. Looking out for suspicious behavior.

JAKE: (*Sits down, removes his shoes and begins to massage his feet*) My feet hurt so bad that when I go home, I'm going to soak them in a pan of hot water.

MABEL: Do you think that this take-back-our-streets program is really worth it?

MILDRED: I don't know. We go to these Crime Watch meetings and hear the people from downtown and nothing changes.

MABEL: Soon as the hoodlums move out of one neighborhood, they show up in another.

JAKE: It's all coming from that apartment building on Forty-Fifth and Market Street. That's the headquarters of Crackpot. You see those runners out there all day with their bicycles. They use that bus bench, pretending to be waitin' for the bus so's the police won't notice them.

MILDRED: I knew that his lawyers would get Crackpot out. He was supposed to do ten years for running down Mr. Johnson, our block captain.

JAKE: He only did two.

MILDRED: You want some tea or coffee?

JAKE: Coffee.

MABEL: Not me. My doctor told me to cut back on caffeine. It's making me a nervous wreck. And with these gunshots going off half the night . . . I'm sorry I left Texas.
> (*She disappears into the kitchen.* MABEL *and* JAKE *glare at* SAM.)

JAKE: It's all over, woman. You know what your sister said in her letter from Houston. It's down there, too.
> (*Turns to* SAM.)
Sam, we could use your help at the Crime Watch meetings.

SAM: I'm trying to listen to the ball game.

MABEL: If this drug war don't stop, you won't have a ballgame. We'll all be dead.

JAKE: Crackpot and his gang are shooting up the neighborhoods and all you want to do is listen to the durn ballgame.

SAM: That's my right ain't it? Since when has it become against the law to listen to the ballgame.
> (RADIO ANNOUNCER *says, "Home run." * SAM *leaves the conversation and returns to his radio. Enter* MILDRED *with two coffees and one tea.*)

MILDRED: You can forget about him. He ain't no help.
> (MILDRED *and* SAM *frown at each other.* SAM *waves her away contemptuously.*)

MABEL: A lot of people are scared to come to the meetings since Ms. Brown's house was burned down by them crack addicts. And that man down on Fortieth Street. They slashed his tires and killed his dog. They using these little boys to peddle their dope because they won't be prosecuted like the older boys.

MILDRED: Well maybe the people are right not coming to the meetings. The police come out to talk to us. The district attorney comes and says that he's doing the best he can. But it don't change nothin'.

MABEL: Did you hear what that old crazy white woman said?

MILDRED: Which one?

MABEL: The one who tries to run the meetings every month and gets mad when she can't get her way. She said that we should go down to the city council meetings and complain.

JAKE: The council meetings are televised. Every gang member in Oakland would know our faces. She must have been a fool to suggest such a thing.

MILDRED: White people live in a different world from us. They're free. They don't have to worry about these crack dealers. Yet they always complaining. Angry about the government. Angry about taxes. Angry about black people. Angry about who knows what else.

MABEL: I'll say, and that other white woman who represents us. The one who s'pose to be our councilwoman. We only get to see her once a year. She has a black man come in her place.

MILDRED: He's her liaison.

MABEL: Is that what he is? I was wondering what he was.

JAKE: Then what is she spending all of her time doing?

MILDRED: She's up at Rockridge where all of those young white professionals live. They worried about the ice-cream factory expanding.
> (*They all laugh, except* SAM *who tries to silence them so that he might concentrate on the game.*)

MABEL: The ice-cream factory. We down here about to be driven out of Oakland by these thugs and she worried about ice cream. We have to drive ten miles to get ice cream. There ain't no stores or nothing. We can't buy fresh vegetables.

JAKE: We have to go to Arab stores.

MILDRED: You can go. I can't. Mabel can't. There are always these young people hanging out in front of those stores. Drinking whiskey.

JAKE: I thought that Arabs didn't drink liquor.

MABEL: They sellin' it all to us.

MILDRED: Next time Jesse Jackson goes to the Middle East and be hugging and kissing—what's the name of that man who be wearing that old nasty head-rag and look like he ain't shaved or took a bath in thirty years.

JAKE: Arafat. Yasser Arafat.

MILDRED: Well maybe he ought to ask that Arafat to close down some of these Arab liquor stores.
        (*Pause*)
We got more liquor stores in Oakland than churches and that's the problem.
        (*Pause*)

JAKE: Sam sure has changed since Port Arthur. Remember?

MABEL: Everybody respected him—

JAKE: Because they know they'd get a mouth full of bullets, that's why—

MILDRED: Texas white folks used to push black people off the sidewalk—

MABEL: But not Sam.

JAKE: Even the white folks respected Sam.
(*Chuckling*)
I remember when we were kids. The Depression. Times was hard and Sam's family got back on their rent. His mother use to take in the wash of these rich folks, but some of them was broke too. Well the landlord came to collect the rent and when Sam's mother said she didn't have it, the landlord slapped her. Then he started calling her all out of her name. Sam took a brick and hit the landlord in the head with it. Nobody did nothin' because everybody thought Sam was crazy.

MABEL: What happened to him?

MILDRED: He hasn't been acting right since his retirement. He says he's sick but the doctor can't find anything.
(*Shots are heard. Everybody scrambles for the floor except* SAM. *Spotlight on* SAM *who's still listening to the ball game. After the shots stop they slowly rise to their feet.*)

JAKE: This is gettin' bad on my high blood pressure.

MABEL: A whole lot of our friends are moving out of North Oakland.

JAKE: Or turning their homes over to their kids. Some of their kids are setting up crack houses. We can put some pressure on some of the landlords, but what do we do when they the landlords?

MILDRED: It's gettin' bad. But I'm not going to move. Nothin' will make me move. We been living in this house for almost thirty years. My child grew up in this house until he went to war. We plan to stay here.

MABEL: Yes, but sometimes I get discouraged.

JAKE: So do I.

MILDRED: I know that it gets bleak sometimes. Looks like we have been abandoned. Looks like nobody cares anything about whether we live or die. But you know what Martin King said.

JAKE: What's that Mildred?

MILDRED: He said, "Walk together children, don't you get weary." Whenever I get discouraged, I think of Martin.
(*She glances up at his picture.*)

MABEL: (*Spontaneously, begins to sing*) "We shall not, we shall not be moved."
(JAKE *and* MILDRED *join in,* SAM *becomes really annoyed.*)
"We shall not, we shall not be moved. Just like a tree standing by the water, we shall not be moved. We shall not, we shall not be moved . . ."

SAM: (*They sing over his lines*) Will you shut up and let me listen to my game?

ACT I

SCENE 2

(*The Warhaus home.* MILDRED *and a* COP *are arguing.*)

COP: What do you want me to do about it lady? I'm telling you that the department is undermanned. Go to the city council and ask them for some more money. We've tried our best to drive these bastards from the streets and into rock houses.

MILDRED: You ain't trying hard enough. We go to these meetings every month and you hand out the same jive. About how you don't have no money and you're working double shifts, yet that situation on Market Street has been going on for years and now with Crackpot out of jail it's getting worse. And tell me this. Another thing I want to know is why do the police seem so cozy with these thugs? Carrying on conversations and acting all chummy.

COP: (*Nervously*) You people don't understand how the system works, Ma'am. It's not just a matter of arresting these people. We have to have evidence—we have to be mindful of the law. The Constitution.

MILDRED: (*Angry*) You mean to tell me that the Constitution was some kind of suicide pact? That the men who wrote it went out and drank poisoned Kool-Aid, afterwards? Crackpot sends these young people into our neighborhoods from that apartment building over on Forty-Fifth Street. They talk nasty and look mean. They make filthy remarks to the women who walk by. They rob us. They mug us and break into our homes. The lady around the corner was raped and murdered, and you talking about some durn system. Are you out of your mind?

SAM: (*Meekly*) No need to raise your voice at the man, dear. He's just doing his job.

MILDRED: (*To* SAM) You keep out of it. All you do is sit around, listening to the ball game all day.
(*To* COP)
If they spent the fifteen million dollars on this drug mess instead of puttin' all the money on that football team, there would be more money for the police.

SAM: Woman what you got against the Oakland Raiders?

MILDRED: You shush. If you and the other men on the block would get together, you could get rid of these hooligans. Every time we have a Crime Watch meeting, a few men show up, but it's mostly women and children. I wish that Mr. Johnson was still alive. He would do something. He would have chased these hooligans out of the neighborhood. They respected him. If James hadn't been shot down in Vietnam, he would have done something. He would have been right here with me. Standing up to these bums. Our son wasn't afraid of anything. Not like his father who is just a shell of his former self. You won't even get up from that chair so's we could take a trip to Washington to see the child's name on the Vietnam Veterans' Wall.

SAM: Aw Mildred, leave me alone. You know that I'm an invalid.

MILDRED: (*Ignores* SAM, *to* COP) It's been three months since I called you. You told me to organize a Crime Watch. So I went around and knocked on people's doors and got them to put those signs in the window saying that they would report any suspicious activities to the police. Next, we got everybody to make a phone tree. We called the police and called the police. We called that special number you gave us and a voice came on saying that the phone had been disconnected. We call all day and all night and they don't come. Sometimes we get a recorded voice and sometimes we don't even get that. It rings and rings. What will it take? One of us getting shot dead? Hell, I thought things would change after we formed our Crime Watch, but now that these boys see they can do anything and the police won't show up, they've gotten bolder. It's even worse now then it was before we organized.

COP: It takes time, lady.

MILDRED: Time? Time my foot. It's been a year. What are you going to do about Crackpot?

COP: (*Clearly uncomfortable with this question*) We haven't completed our investigation. Now if you'll just continue to write down license plates numbers and get the neighbors to call the police, it will be a big help and
    (*Exasperated, looks at watch.*)
I gotta go.
    (*Heads towards the door.*)
You have my card. If there's any more trouble, let me know.
    (MILDRED *looks at* COP *with disgust. He exits.*)

SAM: You sure were hard on him. He's a nice young man. And I told you, you'd better leave those young people alone. You hear those automatic weapons going off half the night. They'll shoot you.

MILDRED: I wasn't raised to be no slave, and I didn't work thirty years of my life to spend my retirement in prison.
(*Pause, then tenderly*)
Why don't we get away for awhile? You know they called up here last week and said I'd won that trip for two to Las Vegas.

SAM: But you know that I can't travel, the doctor said—

MILDRED: The doctor didn't say nothin'. You've been to twenty doctors and they can't find nothin' wrong with you, man.

SAM: It still hurts when I stand up.
(*Shots are heard outside.* SAM *cowers.* MILDRED *falls to the floor. Gets up, slowly.*)

MILDRED: That does it.
(*She reaches for an overcoat and picks up a purse.*)

SAM: Mildred. Where are you going? You have to fix me my lunch.

MILDRED: The lunch can wait.
(*Puts on coat.*)
I'm going downtown to see the council lady who represents our district.

SAM: For what?

MILDRED: This neighborhood, that's for what. These people come into this neighborhood every first and fifteenth of the month to buy drugs. Soon as they get their checks from the county. Everybody on the block knows about it, but nobody wants to do anything.

SAM: That's dangerous. Those young people don't respect nothin'. Why, one of these crack girls got into a fight with her own mother. You remember reading that? The child was selling drugs, and her mother wanted credit, and she told her mother that she, her own mother, was just another customer.

MILDRED: We have to find some way to close down that apartment building. Get it condemned. The landlord don't care. He don't have to live around here. Probably live up there in the Oakland hills.

SAM: You just asking for trouble. You always was like that. Why can't you leave well enough alone? These are our retirement years.

MILDRED: And you want to spend it in that chair, listening to the baseball games, while I bring you lunch, dinner, and breakfast, and rub your back. Wash your clothes. Everything for you, you, you, and nothing for me. This is a time that we should be enjoying ourselves.

SAM: (*Puts hand on back as though he experienced a sharp pain*) Ohhhhhhh.

MILDRED: (*Concerned*) What's the matter?

SAM: My back. Please, Mildred. Rub it for me.

MILDRED: I can't right now. I have to catch the bus.
(MILDRED *exits.* SAM *returns to the baseball game.*)

ACT I

SCENE 3

(*Interior of the private club, The Vassals of the Celestial Ocean. Three club chairs, two facing the audience. A table with a pot of flowers on top. A framed portrait of Theodore Roosevelt in a safari outfit with bagged animal if possible.* KRUD *is a realtor who owns properties in Oakland, including the apartment building used by* CRACKPOT. *He's in his late sixties. Dressed in an expensive suit, shirt, cufflinks, has blow-dried white hair.*)

KRUD: (*To audience*) Sure am glad to be somewhere I don't have to run into a lot of blacks. My club, The Vassals of the Celestial Ocean, allows me to be around my own kind. Men who think the way I do.

> (KRUD *tinkles a little bell.* MARTIN, *a black waiter, appears, in white jacket, black bow tie, black trousers and shoes. Gray sideburns, mustache. He wears a black patch over one eye. Very dignified. About 66. He carries glasses on tray.*)

MARTIN: Yessir, Mr. Krud?

KRUD: Fix me a Manhattan, Martin.

MARTIN: Yessir.

> (KRUD *hands him five dollars.* MARTIN *looks at the five dollars disdainfully. Smiles. Puts it in his pocket.*)

MARTIN: Why thank you, Mr. Krud.

KRUD: Don't mention it Martin. Sure wish we had more black people like you. They're down there in the inner city ruining the good name of the United States. Screwing like rabbits, and spending all of their welfare checks on crack and wine. You know, you can't blame the system or whitey anymore, Martin. You can't blame slavery or history either. Why, the Japanese are over here and you don't see them asking for any handouts. Why, I'm trying to get Congressman Rapp to introduce a bill that would declare them honorary whites.

MARTIN: I lost an eye fighting the Japanese at Okinawa, Mr. Krud. We engaged the enemy in hand-to-hand combat.

KRUD: See there you go. A prisoner of history. You and the other blacks ought to try to come into the twentieth century.

MARTIN: Yessir, Mr. Krud.

> (*With quiet anger,* MARTIN *looks back contemptuously at* KRUD. KROCK *enters. Walks over to* KRUD *and gives him the secret handshake. Sits down in his chair, and begins to read* Barron's.)

KRUD: What's the latest?

KROCK: I feel great today. Deposits are up in the last two months, thanks to these black kids and their crack money. For a while there I thought we were going to have to get the Feds to rescue the company, I okayed so many bad loans to the club members and their friends. The Feds were about to audit our books.

KRUD: Those kids are getting all of us rich. I've rented out houses that I thought I'd never rent out. But I'm glad that we don't have to socialize with them as we do with the rest of our prime customers. It's a good thing that we have this club where we can get away from black people and our wives.

KROCK: You said it. I could make a helluva lot more money if I didn't have women in the way. I have to support my wife, and my mistress in that condo over near the lake. Only my daughter is making money.

KRUD: How is your daughter?

KROCK: Went to a stag the other night and they showed a dirty film. Guess who was the star?

KRUD: Who?

KROCK: (*Proud*) My twenty-year-old.

KRUD: What are you going to do?

KROCK: Buy half interest in the movie company. They've already drawn up the papers. You want in?

KRUD: No wonder you were able to build that chateau in the wine country. All of your investments. Your bank is holding the mortgage on half the property downtown.

KROCK: These young ghetto kids are putting hundreds of thousands in the bank. Kid came in the other day and deposited ten thousand dollars in cash. The next day he deposited thirty thousand. They're making all of us rich. If anything happened to this cocaine traffic, the bottom of the economy would fall out. It's bigger than nuclear power and superconductivity. And the biotech industry everybody thought would be big in the late eighties. This crack stuff is bigger than that. And Jack Marsh, the gun dealer, says he's making so much money he's talking about early retirement. Says these kids have bought so many weapons from him that they could supply three armies.

KRUD: We're getting ours, too. Crackpot, remember him?

KROCK: Do I remember him? He's one of the bank's best customers.

KRUD: He's renting that apartment building of mine over on Market and Forty-Fifth Street. Now he wants me to buy him a home in the country. Those bastards down there could all die if it were up to me. This crack stuff is merely hastening the day, but while the cash is coming in I'm going to get all that I can lay my hands on.
(KROCK *looks at his watch.*)

KROCK: I'll be right back, I have to call the bank.
(KROCK *exits.*)

KRUD: (*Rings the bell*) Where's that Martin?
(MILDRED *enters in her Crime Watch jumpsuit.* MARTIN *walks sheepishly behind her. Sets down* KRUD'*s drink.*)

KRUD: What do you—

MARTIN: We tried to stop her, Mr. Krud—
> (*Out of* KRUD's *view,* MARTIN *grins.*)

MILDRED: You the man who owns that apartment building on Forty-Fifth Street?
> (*She hands* KRUD *the address.*)
That's what they told me at the City Assessor's office.

KRUD: What's it to you?

MILDRED: You ought to be ashamed of yourself. We poor colored people work all of our lives to live in a quiet neighborhood and you come in with this apartment building. They got a rock operation going on. Some of our neighbors haven't had sleep in eight months. They leave these little packages all over the street . . .
> (MILDRED *flings a cellophane package at him.* KRUD *recoils.*)
and that ain't the worst—

KRUD: (KRUD *rises from his chair.* MILDRED *begins to back him up.*)
So what do you want me to do about it?

MILDRED: I want you to evict them.

KRUD: Evict them? Look, I have to rent to whoever can come up with first and last month's security. Hell, you people have been fighting for fair housing all of these years and you're asking me to evict some coloreds—
> (*Laughs*)

MILDRED: You can evict them if you wanted to. You know you can. Besides, I'll bet you wouldn't tolerate any rock houses in your neighborhood. Where do you live?

KRUD: (*Weakly*) Hillsborough.

MILDRED: That's where Bing Crosby used to live ain't it? I knew it. If some of these kids come to your neighborhood selling rock, they'd call in the army.

KRUD: I'm sorry lady. My hands are tied. Why don't you go see your councilperson. Don't bother me with your problems.

MILDRED: I called the police, and the police don't answer. They asked me to start a Crime Watch program and they still don't answer. I go to the councilperson and her assistant tells me to go to the Vice Mayor, and then I go to the Vice Mayor and he tells me to go to the Mayor. The Mayor is never in town. So I decided that since you own that place, I should come and see you about it. I don't blame some of these people saying that they want to take the law into their own hands.

KRUD: I'm sorry I can't help you. I know that you'd like to blame it all on the landlord, blame it on the system, blame it on anything but what deserves the blame—your own self-destructive behavior. These are the eighties. We don't cater to special interests anymore.

MILDRED: Some landlord. That building is the worst one in the neighborhood. It should be condemned. You could at least cut the lawn from time to time. They use our sidewalks for a bathroom.

KRUD: Look. Here's my card. If you can think of something that I can do legally, within the law, I'll do what I can. You people ought to band together like the Asians. You don't see them whining and complaining all of the time. You don't see them asking for affirmative action and welfare or begging to be compensated for past acts of discrimination.

MILDRED: (*Glares at* KRUD *and approaches him. Puts her finger in his chest. He recoils.*) Now you look here. I never asked for no welfare or anything else from you. Me and my husband worked all of our lives. I worked ten years on the night shift at Highland Hospital. Working with sick people. Praying with them, emptying their bed pans, and changing their sheets. Bathing them and entertaining them. I was the one who cleaned them when they were dead and got them ready for the morgue.

KRUD: Now don't get violent.

MILDRED: My husband worked in the aluminum plant ever since we came up from Texas in 1943. We pay our taxes, and our only son was killed in Vietnam. So don't you ever accuse us of taking things from this country. We're the ones who are being bled. We do all of your dirty work and get treated like dogs.

> (MARTIN *enters and takes her elbow. She yanks it from his grip and gives him a contemptuous look.*)

And all we're asking for is that we have a little peace and quiet in our last years. Well, you're not going to help us, but I tell you one thing. That rock house will be closed if it's the last thing I do on earth, and as far as I'm concerned you're worse than those damned kids. You got them packed in schools like sardines and they don't learn nothin', you cut the money you was giving them for college, and you call them all kinds of dirty names—the TV the politicians and the newspapers—so what do you expect?

> (MILDRED *exits.* KRUD's *son,* BOBBIE, *enters. He is dressed casually. He is accompanied by* HANDSOME, *a man with an aviator's cap, knickerbockers, boots, white scarf, dark glasses, and black gloves.*)

KRUD: Bobbie, my boy.

BOBBIE: What was that all about, Dad?

KRUD: One of these black malcontents. Blaming everything on the white male power structure. Demanding things. Some kids I rented an apartment to are operating a rock house. She wants me to evict them.
(BOBBIE *looks to his companion,* HANDSOME, *with anxiety.*)
Anyway, what brings you boys to the club?

BOBBIE: Thought I'd come over and take a swim. Meet my guest, Joe Handsome.
(KRUD *shakes his hand.*)

HANDSOME: Ciao.

BOBBIE: Joe's a pilot.

KRUD: Pilot? How exciting. You know, I always wanted to fly. Took a few lessons even.

HANDSOME: It's an exhilarating experience. I'd rather fly than eat, or be with a woman. Being up there with all of that mystery. What Swinburne calls, "The flowerless fields of heaven." A man is really alone with his thoughts. Sometimes when I'm flying late at night I turn on my tape deck and play Richard Strauss's *Also sprach Zarathustra.*
(*Sound Up in the background.* KRUD *looks to his son, quizzically; his son shrugs his shoulders.*)
And contemplate the moon. I think of the new man. The new god. I think of how we can transcend this puny shell in which we find our souls, or sometimes I put the ship on automatic pilot and read poetry. "When the hounds of spring are on winter's traces, The mother

of months in meadow or plain, Fills the shadows and windy places, With lisp of leaves and ripple of rain."
>   (KRUD *gives* BOBBIE *a puzzled look.*)

BOBBIE: (*Nervous, trying to change the subject*) Joe's just made a trip up from Mexico. He's staying with me for a couple of days.

KRUD: That's nice. You must be really tired, Mr. Handsome. How do you like Oakland Airport?

HANDSOME: I didn't land at the airport, I—
>   (BOBBIE *takes* HANDSOME'S *arm, eager to get him out of the room.*)

BOBBIE: Dad, Joe and I should take our swim now.

KRUD: You boys come over for dinner tomorrow night. We'll barbecue in the backyard and have a round of Old Fashions.
>   (*They exit, and* KROCK *enters.*)

KROCK: Remember Richard Cummings, used to play golf up here with the boys?

KRUD: Yeah. What about him?

KROCK: Just called to ask for another loan. He's defaulted on three and he's two years behind in his mortgage payments.

KRUD: So what are you going to do?

KROCK: What the hell, I decided to go him another million. Anything to help a brother of The Vassals of the Celestial Ocean. Besides, at the peak of the Vietnam War he got my kid a soft cushy job in the National Guard. Cummings was a commander. He had influence.

KRUD: Can't let a lodge brother down. Say you just missed my son. He's here to do the pool with a friend of his, a pilot.

KROCK: That son of yours is a comer. He's going to carry on the tradition. I wish—

KRUD: Look Krock. It wasn't your fault. Your oldest was just depressed. A lot of people suffer from depression.

KROCK: But when he jumped out of that window he took a part of me with him. I was such a hero to him, but when the grand jury indicted me for embezzlement, he took it real hard. Good thing the DA was a brother. He got the whole thing quashed, and fired the young zealot in his office who brought me up on charges. I don't know what I'd do if I didn't have the club, and my friends. Oh, did you hear, they're lettin' in a minority.

KRUD: They what?
  (*Shaken*)

KROCK: Aw, you know the NAACP was raising such a fuss about our being on city land and being an all-white club. The board of directors decided to let one in.

KRUD: Are they out of their minds? Besides, it costs twelve thousand dollars per year to belong to this club. What minority can afford that? They must be crazy.

KROCK: That's what I thought, but they said that if we didn't do it, the city might scrutinize the operation and we don't want to have them up here. Suppose they find out that we're using up all of the water keeping our golf club lawns green, while the people in the flats have to go without because of the drought, or that we're bringing prostitutes to our parties. The board decided that if we let one in, they'd call off the dogs.

KRUD: I don't like it at all. Have you met him?

KROCK: No, but I hear that he's an auto dealer.
> (HAMAMOTO *enters. Snappily dressed, well-groomed.*)

HAMAMOTO: (*Bows*) Gentlemen. My name is Robert Hamamoto of Hamamoto Motors. I'm the new club member.
> (KRUD's *jaw drops.* KROCK *rises and gives him the secret handshake. They both look at* KRUD. KRUD *glares at both of them. Angrily, returns to his newspaper, rattling it in anger.*)

CURTAIN

ACT II

SCENE 1

(*The Warhaus home.* SAM *is sitting in the wheelchair. He's frightened. Cowering. We hear gunshots off stage.* MILDRED *is on the telephone.*)

MILDRED: You can't send nobody right now, but they're out there shooting up the neighborhood . . . What do you mean maybe an officer will be available in an hour? Somebody might be dead in an hour . . . Some neighborhoods are worse?

(*To* SAM)

It sounds like Vietnam outside and she talking about some neighborhoods are worse.

(MILDRED *slams down the phone. She starts out of the door.*)

SAM: Dear, where are you going?

(MILDRED *doesn't answer, but exits. Momentarily, the gun-fire stops. She comes back in. She throws an Uzi to the floor.*)

SAM: (*Petrified*) Where did you get that thing?

MILDRED: I took it from one of those snotty-nosed punks. The rest of them ran away. He gave me some lip, but I aimed this thing right at his privates. He ran too.

SAM: Are you out of your mind? You took that gun out of that boy's hand? You could have been shot.

MILDRED: The way we livin', we better off dead.

SAM: But . . . But they might come back. I'm scared. You know that I'm disabled. They might blame me for snitching on them or something.

MILDRED: (*Sarcastically*) Don't worry, I'll save you.

SAM: Mildred. You done gone too far with this. You becoming one of those vigilantes. Take the law into your own hands. Why, it's unchristian.

MILDRED: I'm like Charles Bronson in *Death Wish*.

SAM: Like what?

MILDRED: Charles Bronson. You know that movie we saw on TV last week where the man's wife and daughter are killed and he goes out and shoots him up a bunch of punks.

SAM: This ain't no movie. This is life. These punks will come back, and blow us away.

MILDRED: We have to take a stand. I organized the Crime Watch in our neighborhood as they told us and that didn't work. I called 911 and nobody showed up. I went to the councilwoman's office and she made me wait. I think that she must have sneaked out the back after she heard the fuss I made in the reception area. I went to the Vice Mayor's office and they said that he was in Chicago. It was impossible to reach the Mayor. I went to the landlord and he laughed at me. What are we suppose to do? Nobody will help us. We have to do it ourselves.

(*Knock on the door*)

SAM: (*Frightened, hiding under a blanket*) There they are now!
(MILDRED *goes to the door. A black middle-class woman, well-groomed,* WINGATE, *and a* CAMERAMAN *enter.*)

WINGATE: Mildred Warhaus?

MILDRED: Yes.

WINGATE: We were in a neighborhood a few blocks from here, filming a crack bust, when the call came on the radio about the shoot-out over here, and when we arrived, the people in the crowd told us that you'd disarmed one of the lookouts and chased him and his gang out of the neighborhood. The phones all over the city are ringing. We'd love to interview you for a few minutes. May we come in?

MILDRED: Word travels fast. Come on in.
(CAMERAMAN *and* WINGATE *set up for the interview.* MILDRED *sits next to* WINGATE *on the couch.*)

MILDRED: (*Smoothes her dress and touches her hair.*) Won't you give me a chance to change into some decent clothes?

WINGATE: You look fine. Don't worry.

CAMERAMAN: (*Counting*) 10, 9, 8, 7, 6, 5, 4, 3, 2—
(*Points to* WINGATE.)

WINGATE: This is Martha Wingate, *Channel 8 News*, in the home of Mildred Warhaus. Mrs. Warhaus has become a celebrity within a half-hour, and crowds are gathered in front of her house. This woman dared to disarm one of the members of the notorious Runners, an Oakland gang that's said to be responsible for the high homicide rate which has made Oakland the Miami of California. Many have begun calling it "Hubba City," "hubba" being a nickname for crack. Mrs. Warhaus, why would you risk your life by taking a gun from a dangerous drug runner?

MILDRED: It's about time somebody did something about these kids. This used to be a good neighborhood, but since Crackpot took over that apartment building on Forty-Fifth and Market Street, life in our district has become a living hell. We have these hoodlums milling about on the street, and the children are scared to come out to play. Our elders are trapped in their homes. I just had enough of it. Just like that lady down in Montgomery whose feet was tired and she didn't give her seat to the white man because she had enough—

WINGATE: Rosa Parks.

MILDRED: Yes, I believe that's the lady's name. Just like Jesus when he chased the money changers out of the temple. He too had had enough.

WINGATE: Why didn't you call the police?

WINGATE: We been callin' and callin' the police. They told us to organize a Crime Watch. We did that. I called the city councilwoman. I went to the Vice Mayor. I tried to reach the Mayor, the City Manager. I even went to the landlord. He laughed at me. We patrolled the streets. We had a block party. Nothin' worked.

WINGATE: You certainly are a brave woman.
(*Turning to* SAM)
Mr. Warhaus, you must be proud of your wife.

SAM: (*Throws a blanket over his head*) Get those cameras away from me. Get them away. Those hoodlums might see me. Might blame me. You see what they do to snitches. You saw them burn up that woman's house. Besides, what she did was unchristian. You're suppose to forgive. There's no sin that can't be forgiven. It's in the Bible.

MILDRED: The Bible also says, "Wherefore lookest thou upon them that deal treacherously, and holdest thy tongue when the wicked devoureth the man that is more righteous than he?" Habakkuk, first chapter, thirteenth verse.

SAM: (*Waves her off*) Aw woman. Nobody can win an argument with you.

WINGATE: This is terrific footage. You getting it all?

CAMERAMAN: Got it.

WINGATE: Thank you very much, Mrs. Warhaus.

MILDRED: Thank you.
(*They exit.* JAKE *and* MABEL *enter.*)

MABEL: Mildred. We just heard the news! You took that boy's weapon.

JAKE: Weren't you scared?

MILDRED: Something just came over me.

SAM: She puttin' all of our lives in danger.

JAKE: (*Ignores him*) It's all over town. People are calling up asking about Crime Watch. They asking Mabel and me where to sign up.

MABEL: All because of you, Mildred.
(*They embrace.*)

SAM: I don't like it. Strange people comin' in my house all day. The TV people will be parked out in the street all day. People will be calling up here. That ain't right. I can't concentrate on my baseball and, and . . . Mildred this rock-house mess is coming between us. I'll bet you going to be going out on these speaking engagements. Talking to clubwomen. Doing interviews.

JAKE: Sam, she's done in an hour what the police and City Hall haven't been able to accomplish in years. Put heat on Crackpot.

MABEL: Seem to me you would be proud, Sam. What's come over you? You use to break all of the horses and kiss all of the women when we were young.

JAKE: You could zydeco better than anyone.

MILDRED: Remember his barbecue ribs? His standing up for people who couldn't take care of themselves? Back in Texas you wouldn't let nobody step on you. That was the man that I loved, and that was the man that I married. Then when we moved here we had our child and you had a good job, working at the aluminum plant. Got your head busted when you led that strike back in fifty-three and then they gave you that foreman's job—

SAM: I was the first black foreman—

MILDRED: It all began to change, you got quiet—

SAM: It was different from the inside. You can't go through your life yelling and screaming—

MILDRED: Then they brought you down to the front office.

SAM: I earned it.

MILDRED: And as soon as you retired you got sick. I think that you're okay. You just sat at that desk for so many years you can't get up. They used you to keep out the other blacks, anyway.

SAM: I was qualified.

MILDRED: There were plenty others who were qualified. Every time the others asked for a promotion the front office said they had you.

SAM: (*Sadly*) Why do you stay with me? A poor broken down patient.

MILDRED: I stay with you because I love you and because one day you will stand up. One day you will be the man I married again.

MABEL: Come on Mildred, we have to go on patrol.

JAKE: It used to only be a few people walking out on crime patrol. But now, thanks to Mildred, we will have to turn people away.
(*They exit.* SAM *returns to the baseball game.*)

ACT II

SCENE 2

(CRACKPOT's *apartment. The room is filthy. Littered with empty fast-food boxes, empty bottles of High Life beer, pairs of running shoes, and clothes strewn around the room. Big sound system.* CRACKPOT, *about 30 years old. Wears jeans and sweater. Gold chains. Sneakers. Do-rag on his head. Lying on a dirty mattress on the floor . . . Veiled* LADY IN RED *appears, dancing to the song, "Lady in Red."* CRACK-POT *is asleep on the sofa with a smile on his face. Toward the conclusion of the dance she kneels down and uses a tape to take* CRACKPOT's *measurements from head to foot.* SAM *comes on. He is smoking a cigar. He is dressed in white shirt, pants, and shoes. He glares at her.* LADY IN RED *sees* SAM *and recoils from* CRACKPOT. *She is frightened. She flees.* CRACKPOT *frowns, and begins to toss and turn in his sleep.*)

SAM: Whatever you're doing son, you'd better quit. She's a bad one and she's got her eye on you. She wants to add you to her harem of lovers. The only catch is that you have to die to get the honor. She was taking measurements for your coffin is what she was doing.

(CRACKPOT *begins to thrash around and moan.*)
You'd better straighten up and get yourself together or you're going to find yourself somewhere where you don't want to be.

(CRACKPOT *wakes up screaming. Sits up. The two figures vanish. His bodyguard,* BUMP, *rushes in.*)

BUMP: Crackpot, what's the matter?

CRACKPOT: That dream. I had that dream again. This woman. There was this beautiful woman dressed all in red. And she was doing this dance. And when she finished she started to take my measurements. Then, a man dressed in white came on. He warned me that this woman wanted to take me as a lover, but I would have to die to get the honor. It was horrible. Must have been the Mama Rosa's pizza I ate last night. I ate two large sizes. Everything on them.
(*Clutches his stomach.*)

BUMP: Damn, Crackpot. I'm sorry.
(MOTHER *enters. She has a frantic look. She's ragged. Her hair is uncombed. She's a mess. No shoes. Hasn't had any sleep for days.* BUMP *and* CRACKPOT *are startled at first.*)

BUMP: Ms. Jenkins.
(*Shocked*)

CRACKPOT: (*Contemptuously*) What do you want?

MOTHER: (*Drowsily. Weakly.*) Crackpot, I haven't had any sleep in five days, please Crackpot.
(*She moves toward them.*)

CRACKPOT: I told you to stay away from here. Besides, I'm busy.
(*She approaches him, arms outstretched.*)

MOTHER: Just a bag, Crackpot. I'll pay you back. Honest I will. I won't bother you no more.

CRACKPOT: Yeah, that's what you said the last time.

BUMP: (*In sympathy with* MOTHER) Crackpot . . .

CRACKPOT: (*Shouts*) You keep out of this.
(*To* MOTHER, *who is now trembling*)
You owe me already. You'd better be glad that we have a special relationship. If you were anybody else, you'd be dead.

MOTHER: (*Drops to her knees. Clasps her hands. Begs.* CRACKPOT *turns his head, arrogantly folds his arms.*) I need just a little bit to get me through to the first. My check—

CRACKPOT: Your check. That's what you said the last time. And the time before that. Bump. Get her out of here.
(BUMP *moves to where the* MOTHER *is kneeling. He takes her arm gently and she rises.* CRACKPOT *turns his back on them. She continues weeping. When they reach the exit,* BUMP *gives her a bag. She looks at* BUMP *with gratitude. She begins to thank him but he moves her off the stage.*)

BUMP: Damn Crackpot. Your own mother.

CRACKPOT: (*Calmly*) She got to pay like everybody else. Ain't no exceptions. Once you start extending credit, people start taking you for a chump. You get a reputation for being easy. I can't afford to give her any more credit. I'd be out of business if word got around that I was easy.

BUMP: But Crackpot. You're supposed to love your mother.

CRACKPOT: Love. Don't be givin' me that love shit. I'll tell you what I think about love. I agree with O. O. Gabugah.

BUMP: O. O. Ga—what?

CRACKPOT: O. O. Gabugah. He's this militant poet we used to read in that community college I went to for a semester. He said that "love is a white man's snot-rag." That's the way I feel. Love is whitey's trick to keep blacks soft, so that he can mold them, and mess over them. The only one that I love is myself. There's no room in my heart for anyone but me.
(*Pause*)
Look, did they find that kid? The one who let the old biddy take his gun from him.

BUMP: Yeah. He was hiding at his mother's house, under the bed. We had to waste his mother. While we were doing that he jumped out of the window. We had two of the runners outside waiting for him. They left his intestines in the middle of the street. It was a mess. Damn, Crackpot. The kid was only twelve. Couldn't you have given him a break? When that old woman took the gun from him he lost his cool.

CRACKPOT: We have to make an example. These kids don't know nothin' about discipline. Now we got people all over the city messing with our people. All because some punk let an old woman take his gun. They having neighborhood rallies and who knows what else. Block parties. This Mildred Warhaus is on TV all day. She's messin' with our credibility. All we have is fear. We keep those people afraid of us, but now that they've lost their fear we've lost our greatest weapon. Now get back to guarding the front door.
(BUMP *exits.*)
(*During the following monologue,* CRACKPOT *paces up and down the stage, haranguing the audience, smoking a cigarette.*)

I have to do all of the thinkin' for this group. That Bump is gettin' soft. We have to enforce our way or people don't have respect. I don't care if the bitch is my own mother, if I find her snitching she would have to go too. As far as the kid being twelve—you got to go sometime. We all got to go. You might be walking across the street and get hit by a car. I'm ready. I know that if I'm in the wrong neighborhood, somebody from another gang might get to me. But while I'm here I'm going to have all of the money, cars, and clothes I can buy. Homes, too. Never had no home. Lived with my mother in these shelters. In the street. Living room was a shopping cart and sometime I was so hungry I cried myself to sleep. Now I got plenty of food and money. Boss hootchies. Respect. Ain't nothin wrong with me gettin' mine. The way I see it, I'm supplying a need. A dirty need, but what I've found in my business is that, in America, few people are clean. You either pimpin' or you ho'in'.

(*Beeper. Dials the telephone number.*)

Yeah. I told you that I can't give you no credit so don't be callin' up here. There's nothin' you have that I want.

(*Hangs up.*)

You know who that was? Bitch's picture be on the society page every week. Always at some charity ball. She was down here yesterday crawling on that floor right there

(*Points.*)

naked, begging me for credit. Asking me whether I wanted her to do nasty things to me. She scared her husband will find out. Dude is a big stockbroker. She don't know that he's a customer too. She don't want him to know, he don't want her to know. Meantime, I have all their money and their jewelry. She spends her whole day chasing the bag, and trying to get credit. You know these people you see who supposed to be so high and mighty. Be talking about family values and running down welfare mothers on TV. I know a lot of them. Lawyers, priests, accountants, you know that congressman that always be saying "Just Say No." My best customer. Sucker be tweaked out all the time. Police too. So the way I look at it, everybody in America is high on something. I'm performing a service. Some people are high on crack, some people are high on smack, and other people are high on things that you don't put in your mouth or up your nose, or in your arm. They high on religion, or love. Or some other spacey thing. All these politicians who be passing these get tough drug laws? They drunk all the time. They just arrested the head of the vice squad last week for driving under the influence. Besides, what about all of the hubba they pushing? So why is everybody coming down on me? I read where one of these men who was running for president, DuPont I think the fellow's name is, ran a company that's responsible for the warming of the earth. Some chemical that you get out of an aerosol spray can and when it get into the space it makes a huge hole in the sky so that in five hundred years mankind will be dead. At least I ain't responsible for something like that, yet the people are mad at me. But this man who could be responsible for the oceans rising and skin cancer is allowed to run for president. And what about the government? They peddling dope too. They sell cocaine and heroin in order to buy arms for the people down in South America who are killing babies and burning down people's houses, yet they talking about the death penalty for drug kingpins. So I don't see any difference between what I'm doing and what everybody else is doing. The way I look at it, the White House is the biggest crack house there is.

(*Pause*)

I don't be planning to be on the street all that long. I'm working with this partner of mine to go wholesale, so that all of these chumps will have to buy from me. I'll be one of the first brothers to be in on this. I can do what the whiteys do. Operate my business from home, with a fax, two computers, and Xerox machine. Get off the streets.

You don't see whitey in the street. He be operatin' from legitimate business fronts.

(*Muses*)

You never see his name in the paper. You never see him being dragged away in handcuffs, placed in leg chains and strip-searched. That's only for the brothers. When they put me out of school for stabbing the teacher they said that my ass was going to end up dead. Now I'm making more money that all of the teachers in school put together. I'm making more money than the president. I'm a new breed. And one day—I may not do it myself—but somebody is going to take over this whole operation for the brothers who spend all of their money buying the very products that they're selling and getting as strung out as their customers. We'll put it in stocks and bonds and real estate. We'll start businesses in the community and hire people like Al Capone, Legs Diamond, Dutch Shultz, and Arnold Rothstein used to do. That time ain't here yet, but it's comin'.

(KRUD *enters with* BUMP.)

KRUD: Crackpot, my boy, I have good news. Good news.

CRACKPOT: Yeah. What's the good news?

KRUD: That house you wanted to buy near Mount Diablo. It's all yours.

CRACKPOT: How much is it?

KRUD: Three hundred thousand dollars. I'll have to draw up the papers. There's usually a ten-percent down payment, but I can get you in for five.

CRACKPOT: That won't be necessary. Bump, go over and get that bag.

> (BUMP *goes over and fetches a bulky mailbag, which rests in the corner of the room.* CRACKPOT *reaches in and removes some cash. He pays* KRUD. KRUD *is shocked.*)

CRACKPOT: Anything wrong, Mr. Krud?

KRUD: No, I just—do you mind if one of the boys helps me carry it to the bank? I just don't want to walk around the streets with this kind of money.

CRACKPOT: Sure. Bump, get one of the fellas to take the money back with Mr. Krud.

KRUD: Nice doing business with you, Crackpot.

CRACKPOT: Sure. And get the place ready. I want to drive up with my girl this weekend.

KRUD: I'll send the keys and the directions back with the boy.

> (KRUD *exits with one of* CRACKPOT's *gang.* CRACKPOT *puts on a hip-hop cap, backwards.*)

BUMP: Where you going, Crackpot?

CRACKPOT: (*He picks up a pistol and puts it into his waist pocket*) Get the car. We're going to make a visit on this Mildred Warhaus. We have to teach these people to respect us.

BUMP: But . . . but, Crackpot. She's a sixty-eight-year-old woman—she—

CRACKPOT: Did you hear what I said?

> (BUMP *looks at him for a moment. His fear is obvious.*)

BUMP: But she was on television. She's all in the news. Aren't you taking a chance?

CRACKPOT: I know what I'm doing. One thing I learned in prison. You let one person walk over you, soon your body will be a highway. Bump, you actin' like a regular little ho these days.

> (*Mocks him in an effeminate manner.*)

"She's all in the news. Aren't you taking a chance?" Bump, I chose you to be second in command, now if you becomin' some kind of pussy then maybe I should get somebody else. That means we'll have to burn yo' black ass. You know too much.

BUMP: (*Trembling, excitedly*) No Crackpot. I'm . . . I'm the same Bump. I just don't think we should be takin' chances. I'm lookin' out for you, Crackpot.

> (BUMP *glares at* CRACKPOT *with hostility for a moment.*)

CRACKPOT: Okay. Let's go.

> (*They put on ski masks and exit.*)

ACT II

SCENE 3

(*The Warhaus home.*)

SAM: (*Whiny*) You hardly spend any time with me anymore. I have to go the bathroom by myself. I have to shave myself. You always at meetin's or answering mail. Now you talkin' about running for city council.

MILDRED: I haven't made up my mind.

SAM: The phone rings all day. I can't hardly concentrate on the ballgame. And now you want to travel to Washington to make a speech. Who is going to take care of me? Wash my clothes? Turn on the TV?

MILDRED: I'm taking you with me. With the contributions people have sent me, we'll be able to hire an assistant for you. While we're down there we can see our son's name on the Vietnam Veterans' Wall.

SAM: I don't know about flying. Them planes ain't safe.

MILDRED: Sam. I'm worried about you. You haven't been out of the house in two years now. I'm thinking about getting a head doctor to come and look at you. You haven't been acting right ever since you retired.

(*Doorbell. She goes to answer offstage.* SAM *can hear* CRACK-
POT *ask :* "Are you Ms. Warhaus? Mrs. Mildred Warhaus?"
Shots are fired. SAM *is shocked. Wearing an expression of
great agony,* MILDRED *staggers onto the stage, holding her
chest. Her blouse is bloody and she collapses.*)

SAM: (*Screaming*) Mildred! Mildred!!!
    (SAM *slowly rises from the chair. With much effort he walks
over to where* MILDRED *lies. He lifts her head.*)

SAM: (*Looks at his legs. Goes to phone.*) Hello. 911? My wife has been
shot. Please send an ambulance . . . A half hour? What do you mean
a half hour? I . . .
    (SAM *goes to* MILDRED. *Struggling, picks her up and carries
her offstage. Blackout.*)
    (*Spotlight Up on* WINGATE, *reporter.*)

WINGATE: Hundreds of people have gathered outside of Highland
Hospital waiting for news about the condition of Mildred Warhaus,
who was shot earlier today by unknown assassins at her residence
in North Oakland. Mrs. Warhaus received national attention when
she disarmed a crack dealer, one of many who had been terrorizing
her neighborhood for over a year. For her heroism she has been
called the Rosa Parks of the anti-drug movement. Mrs. Warhaus
has been in surgery for five hours, and according to attending phy-
sicians, the prognosis is not good. The police have no suspects in
the shooting but word has it that the shooting may have been a re-
prisal by the notorious Runners led by Crackpot Jenkins, a notorious drug kingpin who served two years as part of a plea bargaining
deal struck with the District Attorney. This gang leader was charged
with the murder of Ezekiel Johnson, a leader in the North Oakland
community.

(*The Warhaus home.* JAKE *and* MABEL *are sitting at a table having coffee. They are glum.* SAM'*s wheelchair is empty. The phone rings.*)

SAM: (*From offstage*) Will you get that?

MABEL: (*On phone, excitedly*) Hello . . . She's out of surgery . . . She's going to make a full recovery. Well thank the Lord for that.
        (MABEL *hangs up the phone.*)

JAKE: That woman is made of lead. I knew that she would recover.
        (SAM *enters. He is dressed in cowboy clothes. Campy, like in the movies. With sequins and other glitter.*)

MABEL: Sam, Mildred's going to be okay—what—
        (*The sight of* SAM *shocks her.*)

JAKE: Sam, what's the matter with you?

SAM: I'm going to take care of that punk who shot my wife.

MABEL: You don't have to be no hero, Sam.
        (JAKE *tries to block his way.*)

SAM: Get out of my way, Jake.

JAKE: The police will take care of Crackpot—
        (SAM *laughs.* JAKE, *realizing what he's said, backs away dejectedly.*)

JAKE: (*To* MABEL) You try to talk some sense into him, Mabel.

MABEL: Sam, what's the use of Mildred coming home to a dead husband? You don't have a chance against those boys. They'll kill you as soon as smash a bug. You know they don't care about life.

SAM: I have to do what I have to do.

JAKE: Sam, you ain't in Texas no more.

SAM: The hell I ain't. Texas is anywhere hell is. Now move out of the way and let me do my business.

(*Blackout.*)

ACT II

SCENE 4

(*Crackpot's apartment.* WINGATE *is on TV. Picture of* MILDRED *flashes on. Then picture of* CRACKPOT.)

BUMP: Damn Crackpot. They trying to trace it to you.

CRACKPOT: Change the channel.
(BUMP *changes the channel to a cowboy movie. They watch it for a few minutes.*)

BUMP: Crackpot, you don't seem worried. The public wants to ice you for what you did to Mildred.

CRACKPOT: Don't worry about it. Just like the other times, they'll pick me up, and my lawyers will have me out the next day.
(*Same* COP *whom we've seen in the scene with* MILDRED *enters.* CRACKPOT *nods his head to* BUMP *and* BUMP *goes to the bag and takes out some bills and hands them to the* COP.)

COP: No, I didn't come for that this time, Crackpot.

CRACKPOT: What are you talking about? You know the arrangement.

COP: (*Nervously*) That Warhaus woman, Crackpot. There's a lot of pressure downtown to take you out, Crackpot. Why the hell did you have to go ahead and do it?

CRACKPOT: How am I going to maintain authority if I let a sixty-eight-year-old woman call my bluff? Everybody would be on my case. I wouldn't be able to go nowhere without risking a drive-by by these people who think I'm weak.

COP: It was a big mistake.

CRACKPOT: What the fuck do you know about it? You livin' out there in the suburbs with your family. I clothed your wife and I sent your children to college. Every additional room you built on your house, I paid for. When your mother was sick I paid for her bills. And now, with the first sign of trouble, you cut and run—why, you little cunt!
(*Grabs him by the collar.*)

COP: I'm sorry, Crackpot. I won't be coming around anymore.
(*Exits hurriedly.*)

CRACKPOT: (*Shouting*) Well run then, and I tell you what. If I go down, a whole lot of these high and mighty people downtown will go down with me. All of these people who drive in here in their Mercedes and BMWs will go down. I will name names and tell everybody where the dogs are buried. Do you hear me—
(HAMAMOTO, *the auto dealer, enters.*)

CRACKPOT: Hey. You get that order?

HAMAMOTO: Came in three days ago. It's in your garage next to the Mercedes and the Porsche. You have quite a collection.

CRACKPOT: Yeah. Well I don't like to drive the same car every day.

HAMAMOTO: I need eighty thousand dollars.
(CRACKPOT *goes and shoves some money into a bag.*)

HAMAMOTO: Nice doing business with you.

CRACKPOT: Hey, didn't I see you in the paper last week?

HAMAMOTO: Yeah. Everybody in town must have seen it.

CRACKPOT: You got into some club.

HAMAMOTO: Yeah. They made me a Vassal. The club's name is The Vassals of the Celestial Ocean. I'm getting a lot of orders up there. Some of the big shots in Oakland belong to the club. We Vassals look out for each other and are always passing each other tips on the stock market and helping some of the brothers who suffer setbacks. We play tennis, golf, get massages, and have Christmas dinner together. It's a real fraternity. There are great opportunities for networking.

CRACKPOT: Maybe you can get me in. I have a lot of money. I have cars and houses.

HAMAMOTO: Takes more than that, Crackpot.

CRACKPOT: What do you mean it takes more?

HAMAMOTO: Look at it this way. You're black. They know that the kind of wealth you have is transitory. Guys like you are a dime a dozen. As soon as somebody takes you off the scene, somebody else will take your place. Mr. Krud will sell him houses. I'll sell him these Suzuki Samurai hubba jeeps. And Banker Krock will keep his money under lock and key. Every time they look at you they see a loser. Every time they look at me they see Japanese power, because even though my family has lived here for a few generations, I'm still an alien to them. But the biggest banks in the world are in Tokyo. That backs me up. When they look at me they see all of that yen. You don't have any banks. You don't have any insurance. Suppose they legalize the stuff or somebody concocts a synthetic version and corners the market? You'd be back in some corner lot playing basketball.

(*He starts to exit, laughing.* BUMP *comes in the room with* BOBBIE *and* HANDSOME *and they see* HAMAMOTO. BOBBIE *and* HAMAMOTO *exchange secret handshakes.*)

CRACKPOT: What was that all about, Bobbie?

BOBBIE: Oh that was one of the brothers from the lodge. Every time we see each other we exchange the secret handshake. Look, I got some good news.

CRACKPOT: What news?

BOBBIE: The guys in Colombia have come up with a new hit. Smokable Heroin. It should be on the market in the fall. And get this. It'll be five k's per kilo.

CRACKPOT: Man can you imagine the profits? Joe, they're going to have you flying in day and night. Think you can handle it?

HANDSOME: Can I handle it? As long as they pay me the money I can handle it.

BOBBIE: All of mine goes into stocks and bonds. When you come back from Rio next year, the operation will be in full swing.

CRACKPOT: (*Pause. Studies* BOBBIE.) Rio. What are you talking about?

BOBBIE: We've decided that it might be a good idea for you to disappear for a while until the heat's off.

CRACKPOT: I don't understand.

BOBBIE: That woman. Look, I understand that you might have been under a little stress, I mean, hypertension is hereditary among black people, but you went too far when you shot that Mildred Warhaus. It's all in the papers and on television. I've decided that Bump should take over for a while.
> (CRACKPOT *looks at* BUMP, *shocked.* BUMP *lowers his head.*
> *Shrugs his shoulders.*)

You're excitable. You need to rest your nerves on the beach for awhile. If that woman dies, it'll be murder one.

CRACKPOT: I'll be out on the street in an hour. You get that lawyer who's always defending me.

BOBBIE: He says you're at the end of your rope. He got you a light sentence for running down that old man, but now they have to give you some hard time. The cops say that they can't cover for you anymore.

CRACKPOT: They're gettin' their cut. Anyway, Bump does what I say. Right, Bump? Bump, home?
> (BUMP *looks at his shoes.*)

Hey wait a minute, man. Bump. What's going on, man? Don't let this white boy come between me and you just because of some bread. Man, you and me, all the ass we used to chase, the way we used to get high together, remember when we took the principal and had him hanging out of a window, man? Remember when we stabbed that teacher?

(BOBBIE *goes for his gun.*)

CRACKPOT: Hey, Bobbie, what are you doing?

BOBBIE: Look, Crackpot, nothing personal, but the Cartel has decided that you're just too flighty to be of any use to us any longer. The days of wild men are over. We need a clean efficient operation. We want this thing to be operated like IBM.

CRACKPOT: (*To* BUMP:) Bump, help me Bump. I'll give you all of my cars. My women, you can have them. Look, Bump there's all the money in that sack, you can have—

(BUMP *draws a gun. But before he can fire,* HANDSOME *shoots him.*)

BOBBIE: (*Shocked*) Joe what—what's going on?

HANDSOME: Drop it, Bobbie.

BOBBIE: Joe, I don't understand.
(*Drops his gun and raises his hands.*)

HANDSOME: I have decided to make it a two-man operation. Crackpot and me.

(CRACKPOT *is relieved.*)

BOBBIE: You, you're siding with this—this spade against me? Why, we were roommates together at Harvard and pledged for the same fraternities, double-dated at the Yale Winter Fest; I was the one who recommended you for the Elite Club. We had that apartment in Greenwich Village.

HANDSOME: We've decided that we don't need you anymore. Cut out the middle man and I can deal directly with Crackpot.
(CRACKPOT *laughs*.)

BOBBIE: But, but . . .
(HANDSOME *shoots him. He falls and begins to squirm in agony until he is dead.*)

CRACKPOT: (*Laughing. Shouts to offstage.*) Hey, somebody come in here and clean up this mess.
(*Two men in ski masks enter, and drag the corpses out.*)

HANDSOME: Two less to share with. From now on when I fly in you meet me and I'll deliver the goods to you directly. Deal?

CRACKPOT: Look. You drop it, I'll distribute it. That Bobbie was slick but he wasn't as slick as you and me, huh, Joe? And Bump. How could he have ever thought that Bump could replace me?

HANDSOME: This is a big operation, Crackpot. Bigger than you ever thought. My orders come directly from the White House basement.

CRACKPOT: The White House basement? It must be big then!

HANDSOME: (*With a glazed look, begins to paint his vision with gestures. First few strains of* Zarathustra *again.*) I'll explain, Crackpot. You see, billions of dollars are going back and forth across the border. Some of it is making a lot of people rich. But some of it is making our country stronger, Crackpot. We're helping freedom fighters all over the world, Crackpot. From the jungles of Angola, to the mountains of Afghanistan. Crackpot, you and I are patriots. Do you follow me, Crackpot?

CRACKPOT: (*Bewildered*) I guess so.

HANDSOME: Crackpot, there are people, bad people, all over the world, who are aligned with the traitors in this country to undermine our traditional values. Some of the profits from this operation are going to men and women who are keeping our liberties alive. Bobbie didn't understand that, Crackpot. He always felt that these sentiments were corny, Crackpot. He used to mock the small band of patriots who were outcasts at Harvard, Crackpot. There's plenty of red in that *Harvard Crimson*, Crackpot. He always had the fast cars, and the women, Crackpot. He didn't understand what was at stake, and so when we got into this business after graduation, all he saw was an opportunity to make quick money. I saw it as a way to achieve a higher and nobler purpose, and I found plenty of brave and selfless men in the government who agreed with me, Crackpot. Crackpot, with the profits we're making from crack we're stockpiling weapons in three western states and as soon as we get the signal that Armageddon is on—the final battle between the forces of good and evil—our patriots will heed Gabriel's call.

CRACKPOT: What call?

HANDSOME: For the day when we take back our government and restore justice to the American people.

> (SAM *has entered. He's dressed up like Gene Autry. Has two guns drawn. He looks comical. Both men laugh.*)

SAM: I got your justice. Stick 'em up.

> (SAM's *hand trembles as the holds the gun.* HANDSOME *and* CRACKPOT *continue to laugh. They're in stitches.* SAM *tries to twirl the gun around his thumb, like in the movies, the gun falls to the floor. They really laugh then.*)

HANDSOME: (*Laughing*) Who's this clown?

CRACKPOT: (*Laughing*) He's the husband of that woman we hit. Thinks we don't know that he's carrying a toy gun.

> (*As* SAM *picks up the gun, it goes off accidentally. This even startles* SAM. CRACKPOT *and* HANDSOME *are shaken up.* SAM *holds the gun again.*)

HANDSOME: (*Panicky*) Look pal, I didn't have anything to do with it. It was this lunatic, Crackpot. He shot your wife. We can do without him. You and me. That's it. We can split the cash. Cut him out. I'll deliver directly to you.

> (SAM *waves* HANDSOME *away, gesturing with the gun toward the exit.* HANDSOME *flees.* CRACKPOT *gets on his hands and knees.*)

CRACKPOT: (*Sobbing*) Hey man. Let's talk this over. It was Bump's idea. I didn't want anything to do with it.

SAM: Bump. Who is Bump?

CRACKPOT: My partner. It was his idea to hit Mrs. Warhaus. He ordered me to run down that Mr. Johnson, too. He drove the car.

SAM: I don't believe a word you say. Now get ready to meet Satan. I'm going to give you the same chance that you gave my wife.

CRACKPOT: Man, you don't have to do it. Please . . .

    (*Sobbing*)

don't kill me. Look, I got some cash. There's over $100,000 in that bag over there. You can have it.

> (SAM *walks over to the bag and removes some cash. Examines it. While he is doing this,* CRACKPOT *reaches for a small pistol that he has in his shoe. He shoots* SAM *in the arm.* SAM *grabs his arm. He prepares to shoot again. Shots are fired from offstage, mortally wounding* CRACKPOT. SAM *turns to the entrance. This dramatic pause should be milked. Momentarily,* JAKE *enters. He too is dressed in corny cowboy clothes.*)

SAM: Thanks, partner.

> (*They embrace.* SAM *then goes over and picks up the bag.*)

JAKE: (*Gazing upon* CRACKPOT'*s corpse*) What a waste. Bright kid like that. No telling what he could have done with his life if somebody had given him a break. What's that?

> (SAM *removes some stacks of bills from the bag. Shows it to* JAKE. SAM *has a broad grin.*)

What are you going to do? Turn that over to the police?

SAM: That's not what I had in mind, exactly, Jake. Seems to me that if we don't take it, these police will take it and spend it in the suburbs. If we take it, it goes back into the community.

JAKE: Put it back.

SAM: Are you crazy?

JAKE: (*Insistent*) I said put it back, Sam.

> (*Growing anger. As* SAM *returns the bag,* JAKE *turns his back*

to SAM *and faces audience. He folds his arms in a manner of moral superiority. He doesn't see* SAM *take a few stacks of bills and put them in his pocket, but the audience does.*)
We have to be better than these people. We're Christian people. The Bible says, "Woe to him that increaseth that which is not his."

SAM: Yeah, uh, thanks Jake. Thanks for reminding me.
(*They exit. Blackout. Spotlight on* WINGATE.)

WINGATE: We interrupt this program to bring you further news on the bizarre murders discovered this morning in an apartment building located in North Oakland. The bodies of three men: Crackpot Jenkins; Bump Disney his sidekick; and Bobbie Krud, son of the well-known realtor and community leader, Jack Krud. Neighbors said that they heard a number of shots and called the police. When the police arrived an hour later they were too late to catch the assassin or assassins who escaped without being noticed by the drug kingpin's neighbors. The police had no explanation for how the three came to be found in the apartment together, but surmised that Bobbie Krud had been kidnapped by Crackpot, and members of his notorious gang, the Runners, in an attempt to collect ransom from Mr. Krud's father. The young Mr. Krud's red Porsche was found parked outside the building, a clear indication, the police say, that he was a victim of a carjacking. Jack Krud, the civic leader and philanthropist, was in tears after identifying his son at the morgue. He said that the young man had been doing well in his investment firm and was presently expanding his business to foreign markets. Mr. Krud offered a fifty thousand dollar reward for anyone who has information leading to the perpetrator or perpetrators of his son's murder.

ACT II

SCENE 5

(SAM *enters carrying some luggage. He is dressed in a suit and wears a Stetson hat. He's smoking a cigar.* JAKE *and* MABEL *enter. They are also dressed well.* MABEL *wears a corsage.*)

JAKE: The car is ready. Where is Mildred?

SAM: Oh, you know that woman. Take her hours to get ready.

JAKE: (*Looks at watch*) Well, we'd better get going. The plane leaves in an hour.

SAM: What's the weather in Washington?

MABEL: Say it's going to be seventy.
>   (MILDRED *enters. Looks great. Hair done. Corsage. Mink. Walks with a cane.* SAM's *eyes widen.*)

MABEL: Mildred. Now don't you look nice.

JAKE: Like a million dollars.

SAM: She do now don't she. I knew what I was doing when I married the most pretty girl in Port Arthur.

MILDRED: (*Flattered*) Sam, you still know how to talk that trash. And it was awfully nice of you to arrange for all of us to fly to Washington. Then to New York. Puttin' us up in the Mayflower Hotel in Washington and this fancy New York hotel called the Plaza. Hiring that limousine driver—we can see our son's name on the Veterans' Wall before we die. Thank the Lord.

MABEL: How are you able to afford all of this, Sam?

SAM: Oh, been saving a little on the side for all of these years.
(JAKE *and* SAM *make eye contact.* JAKE *frowns.*)

MABEL: Well I appreciate it, Sam. Jake and I never go nowhere.

JAKE: That ain't true woman. I took you to Reno on that gamblin' special bus, once.

MILDRED: When we go up to New York, I want to see Radio City Music Hall. The Statue of Liberty. The Empire State Building.

SAM: Maybe me and Jake can check out one of those fights at Madison Square Garden. Or even go to one of them OTB establishments.

JAKE: Harlem, I want to see Harlem.

MILDRED: And Abyssinian Baptist Church where Adam Clayton Powell used to preach. That man was a fighter. He took on the whole Congress and beat them. He's the kind of fighter that I want to be when I run for city council.

SAM: Now Mildred, you get that foolishness right out of your mind.

(*All three of them glare at him. He backs down, sheepishly.*)
But on the other hand, I think that you will make a fine council . . .
person.

(*They exit, carrying bags. Turning out the lights.*)

CURTAIN

THE PREACHER AND THE RAPPER

A TWO-ACT PLAY

The Preacher and the Rapper premiered November 10, 1994 at The Nuyorican Poets Café. Miguel Algarín was executive producer and Rome Neal directed the production. Chris Cumberbatch designed the set, which was nominated for a 1995 Audelco Award. Sound design was by Anthony Rivera, light design by Marshall Williams, costume design by Marcel Christian, and the stage manager was Rodney Gilbert.

CAST OF CHARACTERS

Preacher
Rapper/Attorney General
President
Chairperson/Secretary
Aide/Newscaster/Sister
Pope/Messenger
Guard, Sergeant-at-Arms
TV Cameraman
Soldiers

TIME

The 1990s/20 Years in the Future

SCENES

ACT I

PROLOGUE
SCENE 1, St. John's Baptist Church
SCENE 2, Congressional Hearings
SCENE 3, St. John's Baptist Church
SCENE 4, The Oval Office

ACT II

PROLOGUE

SCENE 1, Jail Cell

SCENE 2, St. John's Baptist Church

EPILOGUE

ACT I

3 STRIKES: Ladies and Gentlemen, we're turning down the lights
    to show you a rap about a cultural fight
    about 3 Strikes, a rapper, and Jack Legge, a preacher
    I'll give you some background
    till I hear from my beeper
    The country's turned right and the politicians have found
    that the sure way to election
    is by dissing black sound
    The preachers and the journalists
    are not far behind
    Using columns and pulpits to hasten rap's decline

Chorus
The preacher and the rapper
One's dreadlocked, and one's dapper
A man of the cloth
and a man of the streets
The issues are old
and the passions run deep
and try as they might
will their minds ever meet?

2
They're blaming hip-hoppers for all that's gone wrong

Say the source of our misery can be found in their songs
That the children tune in and get carried away
and pick up an Uzi the very same day
That the women are bitched and the women are ho'ed
And the mind of a rapper is the mind of a toad

Chorus
The preacher and the rapper
One's dreadlocked, and one's dapper
A man of the cloth
and a man of the streets
The issues are old
and the passions run deep
and try as they might
will their minds ever meet?

3
Now Congress is preparing to put rap on trial
Claiming words on these records are nasty and foul
And the volume they're played at is enormously loud
And that nudity and profanity should be banished from sight
As a surefire way to end this terrible blight

Chorus
The preacher and the rapper
One's dreadlocked, and one's dapper
A man of the cloth
and a man of the streets
A man with a beat
and a sailor in God's fleet
They're on opposite sides
Will their minds ever meet?
> (3 STRIKES's *beeper goes off. He exits.*)

ACT I

SCENE 1

(St. John's Baptist Church, in the 1990s. REVEREND *is about fifty-five years old, prosperously robust, with gold teeth. He wears an expensive black clergyman's outfit. Kente cloth draped over his shoulder. His black shoes are fastidiously shined and he wears rings on three of his fingers.* REVEREND *is praying. He has one follower. The* SISTER *is sitting in a chair, her back to the audience. She is dressed in Olosun cult clothes: white gown, turban, etc. On the wall is a poster of Charlton Heston in* The Ten Commandments. *The* REVEREND *is on his knees, praying.)*

REVEREND: . . . and Lord, we pray to You to end this drought. Replenish our congregation, so that we may fight the evil of this time, Heavenly Father. Save St. John's Baptist Church. Fertilize our garden. Make us a wellspring of Christian hope. We call upon You, Heavenly Father. You know our situation. You know that Your membership has dwindled. That Your children are being persecuted like never before. That Thine enemies now rule this country. That our great and beloved United States of America has been taken over by worshipers of alien gods. Of strange and exotic idols. Serpent cults. Bizarre chants are being uttered in the street of our capital and we are like Paul, a stranger in a strange land when he tried to spread the Gospel, but finding opposition at every turn. They have reduced our once powerful church to a congregation, trembling with fear as our rights are trampled by worshipers of the Mother Goddess. You must help us, oh God. Restore us to the pinnacle as You did for Daniel and Joseph, preparest a table for us in the presence of our enemies and have our cup runneth over. I implore You, oh Lord.

> (REVEREND *rises from his knees. He begins to sing and clap his hands.*)

REVEREND: This little light of mine. I'm gonna let it shine,
This little light of mine. I'm gonna let it shine.
This little light of mine. I'm gonna let it shine.
Let it shine. Let it . . .
> (*Stops singing.*)
Sister. Why ain't you singing along?

SISTER: I didn't come to worship this morning, Reverend. I came to say good-bye.

REVEREND: Good-bye? Good-bye? But you the last faithful follower. At one time St. John's Church had ten thousand members. Look at us now.
> (*Frowns*)
People have abandoned Jesus for sin and fornication, and are living loose in a variety of new familial relationships. Sister, you give me strength. Because I know that if I just have one faithful follower, I can rebuild. Slowly build up a congregation so that we will be ten thousand strong as we were in the beginning. With far-flung missionary posts. Bible sales. And our television ministry theme parks and the Jack Legge Bible College. Why, we built a replica of the Wall of Jericho which was still the major tourist attraction for the state of South Carolina until this woman Barbara Sung and the Wicca party began running things.

SISTER: I'm sorry. I've made up my mind.

> (REVEREND *places his arm around* SISTER'*s shoulder. She removes it.*)

REVEREND: What's the matter?

SISTER: I've joined the Yemaja temple.

REVEREND: The Yemaja what?

SISTER: O dab o, Reverend.

REVEREND: Ya-what? A-what? But, but, you been a member for twenty years. You going to give up the Lord, just like that? You mean, you not going to worship in your home church no more? Sister what's come over you?

SISTER: I'm sorry Reverend Legge. But according to our teachings, Christianity and Islam are invader religions. They are not indigenous to West Africa, the ancestral home of most African-American people.

REVEREND: Sister, who be putting these wicked ideas in your head? You know you'd better be careful. God don't like one to put no strange idols before Him. Jesus said, "He who is not with me is against me." You'd better not mess with the Lord.

SISTER: I'm sorry Reverend, but we've been taught that Jesus is not our problem.

> (REVEREND *expresses shock.*)

Africans didn't kill Jesus, the Romans did. So why would we share the guilt for an offense that we had nothing to do with? Good luck Reverend and may Olodumare be with you.

(*She exits.*)

REVEREND: (*Sits down. Wipes his face with a handkerchief.*) Another one gone over to the forces of Satan. What am I going to do? I'm six months behind in my Cadillac notes. Lost that TV hour. Got evicted from my fifteen-room rectory.

(*Pause*)

That sexual harassment suit caused me a lot of damage. A lot of damage. But I weathered that storm. I had to pay one third of the Church's coffers to settle out of court. That greedy Jezebel. It was worth it though. She had a butt that you could grow tomatoes on and a pussy as tight as a bulldog's grip. Still, things have changed since the 1990s. Boy, I was steppin' high then. The delectable juices of filet mignon dripping from my lips, banquets honoring me. Plenty of parish sisters in case I needed to relieve the tension that's an occupational hazard for public men like me. The finest Scotch from Ireland and three kinds of wine. Hanging out with high-class folks. Statesmen, clergymen, and the most powerful business leaders in America. Invited to do op-eds in the *Wall Street Journal* in which I traced the problems of the black community to their forgetting to honor Jeeeessssusss. I called for the politics of conversion. Congressional committees calling upon me to testify about the moral evil that was vanquishing America.

(*Lights Fade to blackout.*)

ACT I

SCENE 2

(Congressional hearing room. Lights up on a table topped with microphones with the call letters of different stations on them. A TV CAMERAMAN is photographing the scene. Mabel Johnson, with a wide hat, fur collar, and gaudy tasteless dress, wearing high heels and a blonde wig, is CHAIRPERSON of a committee. 3 STRIKES, a rap star, is seated next to the REVEREND. He wears dark glasses, baseball cap, and other hip-hop attire.)

CHAIRPERSON: And Reverend Legge, tell the committee the effect that these nasty rap records have on the minds of the youth of today.

REVEREND: What effect do they have? They do have plenty of effect, sister. Plenty of effect. They have made them into licentious slaves to the passions of the flesh; they have turned them into violent predators. Why when I look over my shoulder on a dark street and see that it's a white person walking behind me and not black, I am relieved. They put evil thoughts in the mind of the young men. Get them to disrespecting they women. Using filthy words to express theyselves. Cussing out and issuing threats against our fine gentleman in blue who provide a thin line between the jungle and we law-abiding citizens. I have a lyric right here that illustrates the viciousness of this nasty music. It's called "Put It in the Butt," by Luther Campbell.

3 STRIKES: That's not the title. It's "Put It in the Buck."

CHAIRPERSON: (*To* 3 STRIKES) Shut up, you.

3 STRIKES: I've been sitting here for an hour listening to this ignorant rant.

CHAIRPERSON: (*Banging the gavel*) 3 STRIKES IF YOU DON'T SHUT YOUR MOUTH I'M GOING TO HAVE THE SERGEANT-AT-ARMS—

3 STRIKES: This insane ignorant attack on rap by this—

REVEREND: Watch what you say, sonny, I'm a man of the Lord—

3 STRIKES: Charlatan—

REVEREND: Charlatan? You call me, a man who walked with Martin Luther King, Jr., who was with the leader in Selma, Montgomery, and Birmingham—
    (*Preaches*)
whose clothes were soiled with the blood of the prophet as his life ebbed away on the ground of the Lorraine Motel—you call me a charlatan. Young man, you owe me an apology.
    (*Catches eye of* CHAIRPERSON, *who nods in agreement.*)

CHAIRPERSON: I'm going to hold you in contempt of Congress, 3 Strikes, if you don't let the Reverend continue. You young people have no breeding. Your parents don't care anything about you. No wonder you're producing this pornographic smut.

REVEREND: As I was saying, Madame Chairperson. I think that it is time for the Congress to step in and stamp out this rot as though it were the evil one underneath one's foot. These records ain't doin' nothing but putting people up to violence and misogyny.

(*Applause*)

They are causing the country to be threatened with a tidal wave of carnality.

(*Applause*)

CHAIRPERSON: Now, do you have something to say, 3 Strikes? Make it brief. The committee has to take a lunch break. By the way, where did you get such a ridiculous name as 3 Strikes?

3 STRIKES: The way I look at it, Madame Chairperson and Reverend Legge, the black man has three strikes against him. He is born black, a man, and poor.

REVEREND: (*Laughing*) Ain't he crazy.

CHAIRPERSON: I sure do get tired of you young punks, wallowing in your misery. You ought to go out and get a real job instead of disrespecting our women with these seedy songs of yours. Now proceed.

3 STRIKES: Madame Chairperson, Reverend Legge, both of you are wrong about rap. What we do is merely reflect the attitudes of the community. We didn't invent the social conditions which led to the breakdown of social values. We're merely the messengers.

REVEREND: That ain't no excuse.

3 STRIKES: You can slay the messenger but you can't slay the message. Besides, if you black leaders were more accessible to the needs of young ghetto people maybe we wouldn't have a generation that's gone buck wild. It seems that you're using rap as a scapegoat for

your inability to reach young people. Every time I see you in the papers Madame Chairperson

(*Sarcastically*)

you're playing golf or at some posh resort or on a vacation in Bermuda paid for by your big business sponsors, who are doing more to pollute the country than all of the music ever written.

CHAIRPERSON: You're out of order, sonny boy.

3 STRIKES: And you Reverend Legge—the only reason that you're in on this is because of your insatiable need for publicity. Why, with all of the money that you raked in from your TV ministry, why haven't you built a recreation center for the youth, or a senior citizens' home?

CHAIRPERSON: How dare you insult Reverend Legge. He is the kind of role model that our community needs instead of you rappers with your half-dressed nasty girls, your swimming pools full of Budweiser, and your gold teeth and chains. Look at some of these awful lyrics.

(CHAIRPERSON *puts on glasses and reads from paper*)

"S my D," from 2 Live Crew, and "Won't you lick my clit bitch." Such foul wicked words, I have to gargle with mouthwash after uttering them.

(*Pulls out a bottle of mouthwash, gargles, and spits in a cup.*)

I've never had an occasion to use such words as "shit," "bitch," "fuck," and "dick"

(*Said lustfully*)

until I began this investigation. It makes me feel . . . dirty all over. Needless to say, the experience has been trying.

3 STRIKES: You artless, tasteless, boo-gee negroes. You tried to stop ragtime and you failed, you tried to stop the blues and you failed, you tried to stop gospel and you failed, you tried to stop rhythm and blues and rock and roll and you failed, you tried to stop the rhumba, the samba, and the salsa and you failed—

CHAIRPERSON: (*Banging gavel, furiously*) Mr. Sergeant-at-Arms!!

3 STRIKES: You tried to stop bebop and Charlie Parker—

CHAIRPERSON: Mr. Sergeant-at-Arms!!

3 STRIKES: lives! (SERGEANT-AT-ARMS *grabs* 3 STRIKES *and begins to escort him from the hearing room.*) When you stop rap here where do you go next? There's Hawaiian rap, Japanese rap, Togoland rap, Italian rap—

REVEREND: The boy don't respect nobody.

3 STRIKES: —people are rapping in Russia, Afghanistan, Madagascar; they're rapping in Beijing and Paris, Amsterdam and Hamburg, Singapore, Lagos and Tokyo, Kinshasa. You'll never stop it. Never, never. Vive la Rap! Rap Libre!
(3 STRIKES *exits with* SERGEANT-AT-ARMS)

CHAIRPERSON: I wouldn't be too sure about that. Reverend Jack Legge, I'm sorry for his outburst. We have the votes. The votes that will outlaw this filthy music once and for all. Let me read the newest song by 3 Strikes:
(*Passionately*)
"Ream my dick, my Buttercup
Lick it till it shrivels up

Make me come all
in you mouth
Suck me, love me
Sex me, south
Let me tickle
your warm wet cunt
stroke your bush
with my hard thick runt
you give me a pull
and I'll give you a push
and then I'll play with
your cute little tush"

(CHAIRPERSON *stops, and gazes into the distance, longingly.*)

REVEREND: You needn't read further, Madame Chairperson.

(*She recovers.*)

Having to listen to these filthy CDs and watching these old MTV videos must have been trying for you. These wicked videos show half-clothed women, gyrating like savages in the darkest Africa. Ah . . . er . . . so I've heard. Every Christian in the country is grateful to you Madame Chairperson for coming down hard on this generation of youth who are a shiftless, evil bunch. And I pledge my support and all of the resources at my disposal to fight to the end. We can win. With the help of the virtuous and moral individuals of this great nation, we will defeat rap, this ugly monster, this fiend from the bottomless pit who has put our Christian values at risk.

(*Blackout*)

(*Spotlight Up on* NEWSCASTER. REVEREND *is being interviewed.*)

NEWSCASTER: Ladies and Gentlemen. Here is a late-breaking story. The Senate has followed an earlier House vote in banning rap music from the airwaves. The President says that he will sign the bill that will make it a federal crime to record, disseminate, purchase, or even hum a rap tune, or even to imagine the lyrics of a rap song. Those convicted of breaking this law can be given a mandatory sentence of life imprisonment. So jubilant was a public weary of this filthy, uncivilized music invading the sanctity of our alabaster land, America, that Monday has been declared a national holiday. Church bells will ring. The horns of ships will blast. Reverend Jack Legge, the sensible black leader who led the drive to ban rap music will receive the Medal of Freedom, during ceremonies that will be held in the White House next week.

(*Light Fades to blackout, followed by Stage Lights Up on Act I, Scene 3.*)

ACT I

SCENE 3

(*St. John's Church. Twenty years into the future.* REVEREND *appears, twenty years older.*)

REVEREND: Boy those were the days. *Meet The Press. Face the Nation. People Magazine.* The *Times, Newsweek, Time.* My face was everywhere.

(*Reveals empty pockets*)

Now my bank account is about the size of a mosquito's peter. All these people are into this old Africa mess. Little do they know that lions and tigers are still walking through town over there. Santeria. Yoruba. And this strange heathen belief that the Chinaman smuggled into the country. Goes by the name of Buddhism. What nonsense. God must be mad. A woman sitting in the White House. A follower of Sophia. S'posed to be some kind of woman earth goddess. Saint John said that at the end of time women would be going with women and men would be lying with men. People don't seem to have the time for Jesus no more. They better get right or something terrible is going to happen to this nation, if the people and their leaders don't shape up. Praying to false idols and . . . and . . . and worshipping a woman. Speaking of women.

(*Pulls out small black book.*)

This stress is getting too much for me. I need a date.

(SOLDIERS *arrive.*)

FIRST SOLDIER: Reverend Jack Legge—

REVEREND: That's me.

FIRST SOLDIER: You're under arrest.

REVEREND: For what?

     (SOLDIERS *carry him off kicking and protesting.*)

I know my rights. What is the meaning of this? Why, I marched with Martin Luther King. He wouldn't make a speech without having me okay it. I kept the shirt which bears the prophet's blood. Hey, not so rough. I'm a man who demands respect. You best not mess with a servant of the Lord. Hey, hold it, stop. Stop it.

ACT I

SCENE 4

(*The Oval Office. The* PRESIDENT *of the United States, an Asian-American woman, is seated on the floor in a lotus position. Her eyes are closed. New Age music can be heard in the background, incense is floating up.* 3 STRIKES *enters, also older and grayer. He is now the* ATTORNEY GENERAL. *He is dressed in white: traditional* sokoto *and a* fila.)

ATTORNEY GENERAL: (*To audience*) She's in the Oval Office all day. "Into her meditations," she says. Not a single piece of legislation has been passed. The government is at a standstill. Mail hasn't been delivered in months. All of the postal employees are meditating. The Wiccan members of Congress haven't returned from their retreat in Arizona. They're attending some spiritual edification conference. Our people can't do business for lack of a quorum. I don't know how long the Santeria Party will be able to maintain an alliance with these people. Before the Chinese entered Tibet, a sizable part of the adult male population was freeloading off of the working people. They justified this on the grounds that they were receiving wisdom and that this was work. With the Wicca people in power, as well as their religion—a mishmash of Orientalism, self-improvement philosophy, California mysticism, and purist ecology—a similar kind of parasitism is happening here.

(PRESIDENT *blinks her eyes until they are fully open. She sees the* ATTORNEY GENERAL *and smiles. He smiles back.*)

PRESIDENT: (*To audience*) Him again. I made him Attorney General as a conciliatory gesture to the Santeria after the last election. Wonder do they really sacrifice people? That's the rumor. All of the animals that they sacrifice to spirits. And then that drumming. There are drums all over Washington, D.C. The whole city sounds like Washington Square Park. They're such a noisy people. When they call their members for a vote, in the House of Representatives, they insist upon using a conch horn instead of the electronic system. I hope that they won't gain more seats in the House. It's a good thing that we Wiccan people run the Senate. They talk a good game about their devotion to women's rights, but women priests, or what they call Babalawo, are very rare. Also, how can they revere such demanding, egotistical, and authoritarian gods? Gods who drink rum. Eat meat. And have sex with people.

ATTORNEY GENERAL: Ms. Prez. I consulted with members of the department. We've decided to arrest the Christian leaders and reprocess them. Close down the remaining churches. Of course, there will be those who will complain about the infringement upon first amendment rights, but it'll blow over. The public has lost its patience with these Christians. The violence. The misogyny.

PRESIDENT: I think this is the best course of action.

ATTORNEY GENERAL: Outside of the mayhem and the grisly murders still taking place in the Christian sections, the country is at peace. The temples are filled with people. Crimes of violence are way down. People are not shouting at each other anymore. Everybody goes around talking like Avery Brooks in *Star Trek: Deep Space*

Nine. But in the Christian corridors, crime, violent crime, child and spousal abuse are still taking place. People in these areas lose their tempers with the slightest provocation. Everybody is armed.

PRESIDENT: They're nothing but trouble. They have these shoot-outs in their places of worship. On the day that they celebrate their so-called "savior," even. Some of the bloodiest battles occur on Christmas and Easter. Crazed disciples enter temples, mosques, and synagogues and engage in shoot-outs. Seems that religions that originated in the Middle East are run by hotheads. Nothing but jihads, crusades. Witch hunts. Maybe it has something to do with their all worshipping a volcano god.

ATTORNEY GENERAL: The public is through with the behavior of these Christians. Nothing but homicide and genocide wherever they go.

PRESIDENT: What do you propose, Mr. Attorney General?

ATTORNEY GENERAL: We're going to ban the Bible, the Koran, and the Torah. These books, as you know, Ms. President, are full of sexist comments and instructions. Hostility toward women is the hallmark of these religions.

PRESIDENT: Do you suppose their unruliness has something to do with their diet? Their breathing methods? Maybe a crackdown is in order.
(*To audience*)
This is an election year. Right? If I can get rid of these people I will win reelection with no problem. The Wicca Party will come in with another landslide.

ATTORNEY GENERAL: (*To audience*) Fat chance. I sense a growing disillusionment with this regime. Everything is so cool and calm. People miss the excitement of former times. The Wiccans have declared a curfew all over the country. From 10:00 P.M. to 8:00 A.M. is the national quiet hour. There's no fun in Wicca, unless you're on the inside. People want to party. To let the good times roll again. Carnivals. Mardi Gras. We'll go through the motions of cracking down on these Christians. Get rid of their leaders. Then their followers will be up for grabs. They will have no choice but to side with us. With their support we will have a new religious majority in the country. After all, we use Christian saints as "ways." Ways to get to our loas. The Christians have nowhere to go. They will have to join us. They hate the Wiccans. Christians use to burn people like her at the stake.

PRESIDENT: (*Starry-eyed*) Just think. Twenty years ago I was a minor poet and then I won a fellowship from the Only Oil Foundation to spend three weeks in residence at a country estate for poets they had established in Marin County, California.

ATTORNEY GENERAL: That was the beginning of a notable career.
    (*To the audience*)
She tells this goofy story at every occasion.

PRESIDENT: And one day while strolling through the meadow a beautiful white horse galloped up from nowhere and spoke to me. Told me that destiny had great plans for me. That I would bring peace to a country nearly destroyed by random mayhem and violence. It was then that I swore off porterhouse steaks forever. Much later Sophia came to me in a dream and revealed to me that yes, indeed, she was that horse. The rest, as they say, is history. I defeated an obese freak who was addicted to country hams. So grossed out on hydrogenated oils he was until he couldn't go two minutes without fatigue. This glutton was a symbol of the Age of Greed. For breakfast he ate steak and eggs. Those awful calorie-laden western omelets. After I was elected, meditation centers were established in every neighborhood. Compulsory low-fat diets were forced upon the public. Fruits, natural grains, cereals, beans. A big market emerged for psyllium hydrophilic mucilloid.

ATTORNEY GENERAL: (*To audience*) There have been riots all over the country protesting this bland diet. We'll promise to restore barbecue. French fries. High-fat ice cream. Steak. There are so many sacred cows wandering around that traffic is tied up from Pittsburgh to Riverside, California. The black market in steaks is making millions in profit. The compulsory diet issue alone should gain us seven states.

PRESIDENT: The first thing I did after the election was to declare war on meat-eaters. I banned the marketing of steaks. But now some person is involved in a hot black market in steaks. Oh, I wish that I could get my hands on that person. I'll put him under the jail. Why haven't you caught him?

ATTORNEY GENERAL: We're doing all that we can.
    (ATTORNEY GENERAL *hands* PRESIDENT *a document.*)

PRESIDENT: What is this?

ATTORNEY GENERAL: It's the Executive Order that will allow our soldiers to raid the mosques, churches, and synagogues. Drastic steps must be taken to end the Judeo-Christian threat to civilization once and for all.

PRESIDENT: You have my unequivocal support. Once again, we'll show the country that the Santerians and the Wiccans, regardless of their differences, are capable of working in harmony for the common good.

(*They eye each other suspiciously for a moment.*)

ATTORNEY GENERAL: Thank you, Ms. Prez.
(*He exits.*)

PRESIDENT: One thing about them. They certainly wear beautiful clothes. I wonder who his designer is?

(*Female* AIDE *enters.*)

AIDE: Your Excellency, we have the final draft of the official prayer in school that all schoolchildren will be required to recite before the beginning of classes.

PRESIDENT: Read it to me.

AIDE: "Our Maker Sophia, we are women in Your image. With the hot blood of our wombs we give form to new life. With nectar between our thighs we invite a lover. We birth a child. With our warm body fluids we remind the world of its pleasures and sensations."

PRESIDENT: Wonderful. Simply marvelous.

AIDE: I have a question though.

PRESIDENT: What?

AIDE: Won't the boys be upset having to recite this prayer?

PRESIDENT: Women have had to recite creeds for thousands of years that addressed a god of the male gender. It's time for payback.

(*Snaps fingers, vogue-like, a gesture made popular in the film* Paris Is Burning.)

AIDE: And the Santerians?

PRESIDENT: Don't worry about them. They're very adaptable. You see how quickly they incorporated Sophia and Gaia into their pantheon. They're just two more spirits to them. I think that they feed Sophia macrobiotic food. Those people have so many spirits to obey that they spend all of their time in ritual. No wonder they were the runners-up in the last election. They didn't have enough time to campaign. If we win the House in the next election, we may have to crack down on the Santerians. I don't trust them. We can run ads accusing them of Satanism and cannibalism. They're meat-eaters like the rest. Only they have an exemption from the Supreme Court. They say it's part of their religion. After the next election, we'll see about that.

CURTAIN

ACT II

PROLOGUE

3 STRIKES: What you visit upon others
   can happen to you
   Now Jack Legge the preacher
   is in a hell of a stew

   In the 1990s
   He was riding a wave
   Now it's twenty years later
   And he's considered a knave
   A different regime
   Is running things now
   And they and the Christians
   Don't see eye to eye

   The prisoners in jail
   include eaters of steak
   and that's not all strange
   in this off-the-wall state
   so sit back and chill out
   and hear this weird tale
   about 3 Strikes and Jack Legge
   and a Pope making bail

Chorus
The preacher and the rapper
One's dreadlocked, and one's dapper
a man of the cloth
and a man of the streets
the issues are old
and the passions run deep
and try as they might
Will their minds ever meet?

ACT II

SCENE 1

(Jail cell. POPE *is being interviewed by the* NEWSCASTER. *He's playing solitaire and isn't looking at her.)*

NEWSCASTER: The world press is focused upon this federal prison today. Inside this jail cell is a man who used to be one of the world's most powerful. But now, as a sign of the declining power of the Christian church, the Pope has been thrown in jail, after being seized on the eve of his American tour. Your Holiness, how are you holding up?

POPE: I have had better days.

NEWSCASTER: The Sung government has said that because of your stand on abortion and women priests, they couldn't guarantee your safety. They have placed you in protective custody. But insiders say that it's because of a complaint made by a young boy.

POPE: A baseless lie. I am not guilty.

NEWSCASTER: It's going to be hard to prove it, Holy Father. After the scandals of the last three decades and the cash the church has paid out to quash suits made in connection with these complaints, people are wondering whether the charges are true.

POPE: Let them believe what they want to believe.

NEWSCASTER: How do you feel when you see your photo on the cover of all the magazines? The lurid copy. The press almost obsessed with every development. Every detail about your private life on display in supermarkets.

POPE: I don't feel a thing, to tell you the truth. I just want to get the whole thing over. Clear my name.

NEWSCASTER: Thank you for giving us this exclusive interview, Your Excellency.

POPE: My pleasure.

NEWSCASTER: This has been an exclusive interview with the Pope, who has been held in an American prison for six months. The government says it's because there have been threats against his life as a result of the church's stand on abortion and women priests, but few believe the official story.
　　(NEWSCASTER *writes a check and hands it to the* POPE.)

POPE: Thank you.

NEWSCASTER: Don't you think it's degrading for a man of your stature to benefit from checkbook journalism?

POPE: Hey. I'm just trying to make bail.

NEWSCASTER: Thanks for the interview anyway.
　　(NEWSCASTER *exits.*)

POPE: A thousand bucks more and I'll have my bail money.

> (POPE *goes over to his tape player and puts in a tape. Some music by Giovanni Gabrielli. Begins to do push-ups.* REVEREND *is roughly shoved into the cell that holds the* POPE. REVEREND *brushes off his clothes.*)

REVEREND: (*To guards, who are leaving*) You'll pay for this. You'll pay. Why I marched with Martin Luther King, Jr. It was I whom he asked for advice when he was composing his famous "March on Washington" speech. I was with him in the Birmingham jail. I wear his blood on my clothes. I have proof.

> (REVEREND *turns around and notices the other jail occupant. Then he starts talking to himself.*)

REVEREND: Well at least they put me in a cell with a white man. I'm afraid of these young brothers. When I walk down the street and someone is following me, I'm relieved when I discover that it's a white person behind me. Aren't you—why yes, Your Excellency . . .

> (*Kneels. Kisses* POPE's *ring.*)

It's an honor, sharing my cell with you . . . I read about your . . . er . . . troubles—they're persecuting us Christians all over the globe, it seems. Look at me. Why, I was one of the top strategists for the Southern Christian Leadership conference—thrown in jail like a common tramp—

POPE: Take it as a learning experience. I've learned a lot in these past few months of incarceration. I've read much of the opposition's work. Marx. The Protestants. Buddhism. Santeria. I've even delved into this Sophia business that's been sweeping the West, posing the greatest threat to the Christian Church since the cult of Isis.

REVEREND: A woman God. Ha! That'll be the day.

POPE: I wouldn't be so sure. As I said, I've had a lot of time to think. This isn't the same as viewing the world from my Vatican apartment of plush red carpets and Pre-Raphaelite paintings. This is real. This is what my fellow inmates would call the nitty-gritty. You know what I'm saying. What are you in for?

REVEREND: They won't say. Came to my church. Hauled me away.

VOICE: Help me! Please somebody help me!

REVEREND: What's that?

POPE: It's a young *Village Voice* reporter. He was always praising prisoners as the true voice of the disenfranchised masses. Said that they were "the vanguard of the revolution." Said he read it in a book. He got himself arrested so that he could write a book from the inside. Poor fellow. They're passing him around and trading him for cigarettes and candy.

REVEREND: That's not going to happen to me. I'll be out of here as soon as my lawyer hears about this.

> (*Television comes on. New Age spacey music. A bald white woman in a* Star Trek *outfit reads the news.* REVEREND *and* POPE *watch the broadcast.*)

NEWSCASTER: This is Violet Ray with the main points of the news. Thousands of people from all over America converged upon Florida today for the annual Odun rites. Master priest, drummer Babatu Olatunji, and his dancers and chorus excited Miami's largest stadium, which was filled to capacity. Many African deities came down and joined in the celebration. Shango, Oshun, Oya, Orungan, Dada, Babalu, Ifa, and many others. Unlike the old Christian days, not a single episode of violence was reported. President Barbara Sung congratulated the worshipers for being so well behaved. Though she disapproves of animal sacrifice and meat-eating, she said that she would continue to respect the religious freedom of Santeria, guaranteed by the Supreme Court. In other news, President Barbara Sung has declared the January holiday of Martin Luther King, Jr., the prophet of nonviolence, to be a day of national celebration. If the celebration is not observed in New Hampshire, President Sung has promised to send in troops. As you know, the celebrations for George Washington, Abraham Lincoln, and Columbus have been eliminated from the calendar, President Sung having declared it inappropriate to celebrate the births of men associated with violence. Troops are beginning to withdraw from occupying the Christian zones where they were sent after the Christmas riots. Each year during Christmas the Christians get drunk and begin to engage in a rampage of violence. The 911 calls increase beyond the capacity of our law enforcement agencies to handle them. On Easter, as you know, many of the more fanatical devotees of the Christian cult drive nails through their hands in imitation of their lord, a character who allegedly rose from the dead. Experts say that one of the reasons that followers of desert religions are so violent is that their core belief is based upon mutilation and blood sacrifice.

(NEWSCASTER *shivers with disgust.*)

Ms. Sung has decided to take stern measures against the Christians who are still engaged in misogyny and are promoting violence and racism, all of which are against the law. Millions of Bibles have been confiscated and burned. As part of the new crackdown, several prominent ministers have been arrested and will be reprocessed

(REVEREND *is stunned.*)

as a way of cleansing society of Christianity and its cousin religions, which have led to the death of millions over the centuries. The charlatan and impostor, Reverend Jack Legge, has been seized and now shares a cell with the criminal Roman Pope, who was arrested on the eve of the Pope's tour of America after a youngster came forth and identified the Pope as the man who molested him in a fantasy.

REVEREND: Reprocessed? What is that! I ain't done nothing wrong. Why, that's crazy.

(*Goes to bars of his cell.*)

Guard! Guard! There has been a mistake! I was with Martin Luther King, Jr. from his early days. Why I used to write his term papers in college. It was me who researched his Ph.D. dissertation.

(ATTORNEY GENERAL *approaches the cell.*)

Who are you?

ATTORNEY GENERAL: I'm the Attorney General—

REVEREND: Well, that's more like it. The government has realized its mistake and sent you to apologize, right?

ATTORNEY GENERAL: (*Ignores* REVEREND) Pope, you're free to go. The child has changed his testimony. He says that it wasn't you who seduced him in his fantasy. It was Elvis. There's an all-states bulletin out on the King of Rock and Roll and he's been sighted in a number of places. We believe an arrest is imminent.

POPE: (*Rising, exiting from the cell, shaking his head.*) You Americans are crazier than anybody would have ever believed. You arrest me as soon as I land in New York on the first leg of my American tour. You throw me in jail and won't allow me to consult a lawyer. All because of some kid's fantasy.

ATTORNEY GENERAL: A fantasy, huh? What would you call the notion of Virgin birth, or the Ascension?

REVEREND: Look, you. Me and the Holy Father ain't going to stand for none of your blasphemy.
>(POPE *and* ATTORNEY GENERAL *ignore* REVEREND.)

POPE: Young man, you have a lot to learn.
>(REVEREND *nods in agreement.*)

REVEREND: You tell him Pope.

ATTORNEY GENERAL: Half the graves in Europe are filled with heretics whom your church put to death for denying those revealed truths, as you call them. Fantasies, as I call them.

POPE: How did a fantasy become the same thing as reality in American law?

REVEREND: Good question, Pope. Answer the man, how did it?

ATTORNEY GENERAL: (*Ignores* REVEREND.) You know as well as I, Pope, that in the West it begins with Plato's cave allegory and continues through Immanuel Kant's *Critique of Pure Reason*. Both argue that objective reality can never be known, right?

POPE: God knows objective reality. Besides, Plato was a pagan and Kant couldn't make up his mind about whether to be a pagan or a Christian.

REVEREND: You right, Pope. God knows everything.
>(*To* ATTORNEY)

I guess he told you, chump!

ATTORNEY GENERAL: You don't know whether God knows objective reality because you cannot know God.

POPE: His being is manifest.

REVEREND: I know him in my heart.

ATTORNEY GENERAL: Max Weber's comment that the objective interpretation of human meaning necessarily involves the subjective viewpoint of the observer is echoed in Heisenberg's Principle of Indeterminacy. The Japanese have a concept known as *Shin-nyo*, which could be translated as "suchness," the true nature of things that eludes all description, for which the word *fu-ka-shi-gi* is used.

REVEREND: There you go with that old heathen Africa mess again. You embarrassing me. You make the Pope think that we still savages. In the jungle. There ain't nothin' in Africa but reptiles and drums.

POPE: He's a real *fregnacciaro*.

ATTORNEY GENERAL: *Fregnacciaro.* That's a bullshitter, right.
> (POPE *nods.*)
We're just amateur bullshitters next to you fellows. You invented the cosmological and teleological and ontological proofs for the existence of God. That's a real con-job, in which the proof for the existence of God was rigged in the premise. Something like God exists because God exists.

POPE: Those proofs lasted for seven hundred years. You should be so lucky.
> (*Pause*)
Besides, what about your God, Olodumare?

REVEREND: He got you now, you infidel—

ATTORNEY GENERAL: Olodumare is rarely mentioned in Santeria. We respect his intermediaries who provide us with services. Unlike your god who allegedly interferes in the affairs of men. Olodumare is sort of like a CEO who presides over a large staff of messengers. Also unlike your god, who has sent armies into the field for centuries, sometimes backing both sides, there is seldom an army that can claim its mandate from Olodumare. Olodumare never punished children who mocked a prophet by sending bears out of the woods to tear them to pieces. Olodumare never turned cities to sand simply because the inhabitants within engaged in unorthodox sexual practices. We even have a hermaphrodite god, Olokun. She/he lives on the ocean floor. Other Santeria gods are also gender-neutral. Christianity condemns gays and lesbians to death. Leviticus says, "They shall surely be put to death." (20:13)

POPE: (*Pause*) You have a strange country here. You can be sure that when my lawyers sue you for false imprisonment, it won't be a fantasy. It will be real. Am I free to go?

> (ATTORNEY GENERAL *nods.* POPE *gathers his Bible and rosary, puts on his skullcap. Begins to lift suitcase.*)

REVEREND: Can I give you a hand, Pope?

> (REVEREND *reaches for suitcase.*)

POPE: No, that won't be necessary.

REVEREND: I insist.

> (*They begin to struggle with the suitcase.*)

POPE: (*Annoyed*) I said I'd handle it.

REVEREND: I know that we have had fallings out, Your Excellency, but maybe now that the church is under attack, we Protestants and Catholics ought to make up. Bury the hatchet.

POPE: Maybe so.
>   (POPE *begins to exit.*)

REVEREND: As for you—
>   (*To* ATTORNEY GENERAL)
You should be ashamed of yourself, humiliating the Pope. Putting a Pope in jail for the first time in history.

POPE: Not true.

REVEREND: What?

POPE: Pius VII was detained by Napoleon. The Church survived Napoleon. In the 1840s Pius IX was imprisoned by the revolutionary Committee of Public Safety. The Church survived that challenge, too.
>   (POPE *and* ATTORNEY GENERAL *are studying each other as*
>   *he delivers these lines.*)
We'll survive you, too.

ATTORNEY GENERAL: Pope?

POPE: Yes?

ATTORNEY GENERAL: Didn't you wonder why there was no outcry against your arrest?

POPE: That did bother me. How do you explain it?

ATTORNEY GENERAL: The church is dead in this country. The mother goddess that your early church supplanted has made a strong comeback. Maybe back there in the nineties, when you had a chance, you should have ordained women priests.

REVEREND: Ha! Ha! That's crazy. Don't listen to him Pope.

POPE: He has a point.

ATTORNEY GENERAL: And your stubbornness at the Cairo Conference, refusing to make even the slightest concession to the pro-choice movement, didn't help.

POPE: You're right, we didn't budge. Maybe we'll change. This time in jail has given me time to think. When do you have time to think? To sort of kick back and mull things over?

ATTORNEY GENERAL: I don't follow.

POPE: You and the New Agers are in charge now, but the same crowds who are applauding you today may be shouting for your crucifixion tomorrow. History always seems to be eager to get on to the next act. Good day, Attorney General. And Reverend Legge, keep carrying the cross. The forces of the Lord are down but not out. Maybe all of what is happening is merely a wake-up call.

    (POPE *exits.*)

REVEREND: Goodbye Pope. Have a good trip back to Italy and I'm sure that the rest of America's dwindling Christian band apologize for the awful treatment you've suffered at the hands of these heathens and idol worshippers . . . A wake-up call from the Lord. Yes indeed.

    (*To* ATTORNEY GENERAL)

You're on top now, but we are united. Catholics and Protestants. Why, even though we may have disagreements, me and the Pope believe in the same thing.

ATTORNEY GENERAL: How about celibacy?

REVEREND: (*Pause*) Well, I . . . a . . .
> (REVEREND *removes a handkerchief and begins to wipe his brow.*)

ATTORNEY GENERAL: Do you recognize me?

REVEREND: (*Stares for a moment.*) Can't say that I do.

ATTORNEY GENERAL: You don't remember the Congressional hearings in the 1990s? The hearings that led to the criminalization of rap music?

REVEREND: Oh, yes. Mabel Johnson and I were successful in our attempt to get rid of that nasty music. Made it a federal crime to create, manufacture, disseminate, and listen to rap music. That hothead 3 Strikes resisted, though. Made a bootleg version of the music, was arrested, and got a long . . .
> (REVEREND *recognizes the* ATTORNEY GENERAL *as* 3 STRIKES)

sentence—hey it's you, 3 Strikes—

ATTORNEY GENERAL: That was my name before my transformation. My new name is Ogun JagunJagun.
> (REVEREND *bursts out laughing.* ATTORNEY GENERAL *ignores it.*)

That long prison sentence gave me a chance to think. I decided that you were right, Reverend. That violence and sexist attitudes toward women should be curbed. The way they're smacked around, humiliated, bruised beaten raped murdered. I read a lot of books and decided that of all of the books that I read, the most influential was the Bible.

REVEREND: I'm glad to hear that son. Glad you see it my way.

ATTORNEY GENERAL: Not exactly. The Bible, as you know, is the paradigm, the frame of reference of the Judeo-Christian religion, and it was after a close line-by-line reading of the scriptures that I decided that it was the Bible that created the basis of our culture's attitudes toward women and violence. From the beginning of the Bible, the book of Genesis, where women are made from the rib of a man and one woman is blamed for the introduction of sin into the world, to the ending, where women are called whores, the Bible is a manual for woman-haters. Not only that, but there are constant instructions to commit violence against women, as in "Thou shalt not suffer a witch to live" (Exodus 22:18), which led to the extermination of women during the Middle Ages—the women's holocaust—to the reference to Babylon the great, the mother of harlots and abominations of the earth (Revelations 17:5). There are constant admonitions in this Bible of yours to fight against the enemies of this psychotic god that your people worship. A god who receives fiendish pleasure from the sufferings of his followers and even his own son. A god who, unlike our Orishas, can't eat and can't dance and won't make love to a woman, a brooding, dangerous, and melancholy god who dwells alone. The greatest taboo in Yoruba is to dwell alone. I regret the songs that I recorded back there in the '90s that disrespected women and that were filled with scatology. I joined the Yoruba temple and became a follower of a female Orisha. I dedicated my life to eliminating violence and misogyny from American life. And Reverend, you gave me the idea by leading the fight to banish rap from the airwaves; you struck a blow for women's rights. I am to blame for making those underground recordings that got me arrested. But it was during that time in jail that I learned the truth.

(*Slowly, deliberately*)

That if criminalizing rap was a good way of getting rid of misogynist culture, then criminalizing Christianity would help to end misogyny and violence once and for all.

REVEREND: Look here buddy, you'd better not fool around with God—God don't like ugly.

ATTORNEY GENERAL: Your god is a racist, sexist homophobe, and a misogynist. Throughout your Bible there are demands that women be subservient to men: "Wives, submit yourselves unto your own husbands, as unto the Lord," says Ephesians 5:22; "The husband is the head of the wife," again Ephesians 5:23; "The head of the woman is the man," says Corinthians 11:3.

Your God doesn't like women talking back, or challenging men; for doing so they got labeled "contentious," as in "A continual dropping in a very rainy day and a contentious woman are alike." Proverbs 27:15.

For your Bible, women are evil: "Keep thee from the evil woman . . ." Proverbs 6:24.

They are seen as causing the downfall of men: "She hath cast down many wounded; yes, many strong men have been slain by her." Proverbs 7:26.

How can we tolerate a religion that condemns nonconformist women and homosexuals to death? Your god? Your god is a cruel god. What does he do to Hagar, concubine of the patriarch Abraham? Sends her and her son into the wilderness without any means of providing for herself. I can't think of anything so cruel.

REVEREND: It's not for us to judge the ways of the Lord. We just suppose to have faith and obey like sheep.

ATTORNEY GENERAL: Think of the wars, the genocide, the hate crimes, the persecution of blacks, women, and homosexuals as a result of these ugly Biblical instructions. The massacres, the show trials, the lynchings. Mass suicides at Jonestown and The Order of the Solar Temple. And you had the nerve back there in the 1990s to accuse rappers of misogyny. No rapper ever stoned a woman because he read it in some crazy patriarchal book.

REVEREND: You ought not be saying these things. God will punish you.

ATTORNEY GENERAL: I'll take my chances. Your god versus mine.

REVEREND: (*Mutters*) Pagan savages. Look, I'm about fed up with this conversation. I demand that I be released. I still have some powerful friends. When Mabel Washington hears about this, you will have some explaining to do. She is one of three Christians who still have a seat in Congress.

> (CHAIRPERSON *is led into the cell. She has aged like all of the other characters who appeared in Act I. She wears a leopard-skin coat.*)

CHAIRPERSON: Get your hands off me. I have Congressional immunity. You can't do this to me.

REVEREND: Mabel. What are you doing here?

CHAIRPERSON: Some of these crazy Wicca police came to my house in the middle of the night. Turned the place upside down. Said they were looking for evidence.

REVEREND: Evidence. Evidence of what?

ATTORNEY GENERAL: She's been making a profit from illegal steak sales. She's raked in millions.

(PRESIDENT *enters with* GUARD.)

PRESIDENT: I just wanted to see for myself the face of a person so vile as to sell steaks when I personally prohibited the marketing of such poison.

CHAIRPERSON: You can't prove a doggone thing.

PRESIDENT: Oh, we can't, can we? All of your cohorts have confessed. They're making deals with the prosecutors. They said that you were the mastermind behind the whole scheme.

CHAIRPERSON: They what? Those dirty lowdown sneaks.
        (*Mutters*)
Those disloyal motherfuckers.

REVEREND: That ain't the reason they're persecuting you, Mabel. Don't you recognize this man? It's 3 Strikes.

CHAIRPERSON: (*Shocked*) 3 Strikes. That filthy-mouthed rap singer.

ATTORNEY GENERAL: We're looking at some serious time here. And to think, you hauled me before a Congressional committee for singing rap songs.

PRESIDENT: As much as I detest rap music, no rap music ever gave anybody a heart attack.

CHAIRPERSON: Selling bad meat was the only way that I could stay in office. It takes a fortune to be a candidate these days.

PRESIDENT: You won't have to worry about running for office anymore.

ATTORNEY GENERAL: You'll get ten years for raising the cholesterol level of the population.

CHAIRPERSON: Ten years. That's ridiculous.

PRESIDENT: Ten years my foot. I'm going to have to reprocess these two. We must rid the nation's gene pool of characters like these.

ATTORNEY GENERAL: Reprocessing? But Ms. Prez. Isn't that extreme?

PRESIDENT: You keep out of this. Oh, now I get it. You're in cahoots with your fellow meat-eaters. I knew it. You barbarian. Guard, take these people to the reprocessing center.

ATTORNEY GENERAL: What? You would . . . me? You're asking for it. The Santeria party will have you impeached.

PRESIDENT: Let them.

REVEREND: Now wait a minute. Reprocessing—isn't that a little extreme? What is it anyway?

ATTORNEY GENERAL: If you are such a loyal follower of your god, then maybe he will save you from the fate that awaits you.

CHAIRPERSON: Reprocessing? It's probably unconstitutional. I know my rights.

REVEREND: Yes, good question.

ATTORNEY GENERAL: They're going to make us an example the way I was made an example by those Congressional hearings that took place in the 1990s.

PRESIDENT: Don't worry, you won't feel a thing. It's painless. We take you into a little room and—The Wiccan way of execution is much more civilized than the crude and barbaric gas chamber, the electric chair. You'll die smiling with enlightenment.

REVEREND: Now hold on a minute. Ain't nobody said nothing about no execution. Let me out of this place. Help! Help!
(GUARD restrains him.)

CHAIRPERSON: You won't get away with it. I knew I should have voted for the Immigration Bill barring these people from coming over here. These chinks have taken over the country. They worse than white people.

PRESIDENT: Now look here dearie. Don't try guilt-tripping me. The Chinese never owned black slaves.

ATTORNEY GENERAL: Only yellow slaves. I suspect that this meat business is just a cover. She wants to use us to gain reelection. She wants to distract attention from her failed policies. The meat prohibition. The national quiet hour. Compulsory aerobics.

PRESIDENT: Nobody cares anything about you. Who would protest? A lowly high-fat peddler, wearer of animal skins and carnivorous steak thief, a has-been broken-down preacher and a follower of
(*Contemptuously*)
VooDoo. The public will thank me. They're tired of your cult and its disgusting practices.

CHAIRPERSON: You're just persecuting us because we're black.

PRESIDENT: Race race race. That's all you people think about. You can't tell us about oppression. We lived under the hated Japanese occupation. Your so-called servitude was a picnic in comparison to that. The slave-master took care of all of your needs. That's why you people developed a welfare mentality. You people are loafers.

CHAIRPERSON: (CHAIRPERSON *lunges for* PRESIDENT. *She is stopped by* GUARDS.) I'll wrap your sorry ass around my fist you mother-fuckin' slope . . .
(REVEREND *is shocked. Sheepishly:*)
excuse my French, Reverend.

PRESIDENT: That's it, that's it, resort to violence. You people are the most violent in the world.

ATTORNEY GENERAL: When the Santeria hear about this, there will be a civil war that will make the one of the 1860s seem like a playground spat. I would advise you against proceeding with this madness.
(GUARDS *begin to remove* ATTORNEY GENERAL, MABEL, *and* REVEREND)

PRESIDENT: Let the Santeria try. I'm way ahead of you, my friend. I ordered raids on Santeria party headquarters on my way over here.

Tonight I will make a speech to the nation. Tell the public what was going on inside those places. After that whatever public support that you had will plummet.

REVEREND: Can't we talk this over? Please.

CHAIRPERSON: (*To* GUARDS) Get away from me. Let me go. Take your hands off me.
>   (CHAIRPERSON *kicks one of the* GUARDS *in the shins.*)

REVEREND: Help me Jesus. Please help me! I don't want to be reprocessed. I want to live. Have mercy. Somebody help me!
>   (*We still hear the* REVEREND's *screams for help from offstage.* PRESIDENT *checks to see if coast is clear. Sits down. Puts on a Yankees baseball cap. Removes a hamburger from a McDonald's bag. Begins to eat. Really enjoys it.*)

ACT II

SCENE 2

(*St. John's Church.* SECRETARY *hears* REVEREND *screaming. Rushes in. She is played by the same actress who plays* CHAIRPERSON. *The* REVEREND *is seated at a desk. The TV is turned on to the* Oprah Winfrey Show, *with the sound off.*)

REVEREND: Help me. Please. Somebody.
(REVEREND *is breathing heavily and sweating profusely.* SECRETARY *wakes him.*)

REVEREND: Mabel. You're alright.

SECRETARY: Mabel? What's wrong with you? My name is Jacqueline. I'm your secretary, Reverend. You been hittin' the Scotch again?

REVEREND: Oh yes. Of course. I . . . I had a bad dream.
(*Calmly, thoughtfully*)
"Thou scarest me with dreams and terrifiest me through visions." Job 7:14.

SECRETARY: What did you say, Reverend?

REVEREND: Forget it. Look, what is my sermon for Sunday?

SECRETARY: "Her Abominations Spilleth Over."

REVEREND: Change that. Make it something like "Mary Magdalene: Holy Witness."

SECRETARY: But Mary Magdalene was a prostitute. Why preach a sermon about her?

REVEREND: There's not a scintilla of proof in the Bible that this divine person was a prostitute. For too long the role of women in the Bible has been denied. It's time to give them their due. After all, had there been no Magdalene, we would have never have had a witness to the resurrection, and without Mary, Christ's mother, there would have been no Christ. While the men betrayed our Lord, these women stood by him to the end and beyond. And daughter . . .

SECRETARY: Yes Reverend?

REVEREND: I want you to put an ad in the *Amsterdam News* and the *City Sun*. We could use a new assistant pastor. A woman. All of the ones under me are men. I want you to get me a qualified woman who can handle pastoral duties. People get tired of looking at the same old hardheads every Sunday. We need some innovative approaches.

SECRETARY: Reverend, what's come over you? You once said that you'd die and go to hell before you'd share a pulpit with a woman.

REVEREND: (*Ignores this remark.*) I want you to sell the two Cadillacs. We could use the money to set up a soup kitchen in the church here. Take . . . take these rings . . .

    (*Removes them*)

and cash them in. We could start a youth program. Keep kids off the streets. And Sister, call my maid. Tell her to give my three hundred suits and ninety shoes to the Goodwill. Don't look right. Our basking in luxuries while our people go hungry. As for my twenty-room mansion in Brooklyn. I want you to see about converting the place into a home for senior citizens. I'll move into an apartment. Hell, Jesus didn't live in no palace. He moved from town to town, living in different people's houses. Another thing. That greedy Jezebel—I mean my daughter, with whom I was supposed to have a private prayer in the home. Cancel that engagement indefinitely. Now what you got for me today?

SECRETARY: Connie Chung's show. You're supposed to debate Ice-T and Dr. Dre and this new rap star, 3 Strikes.

REVEREND: Call it off.

SECRETARY: What?

REVEREND: I said call it off.

SECRETARY: But Reverend—this will give you an opportunity to harangue against this music that encourages violence and degrades our women. You know how you love photo opportunities. You've become the lightning rod for those who want to banish this music from the airwaves.

> (MESSENGER *enters. Dressed in a suit. Same actor who played the* POPE.)

MESSENGER: Reverend Jack Legge . . .

REVEREND: That's me.

(MESSENGER *hands* REVEREND *an envelope.*)
Haven't I seen you somewhere before?
(*Opening the envelope.*)

MESSENGER: I don't think so.
(MESSENGER *exits.*)

SECRETARY: What is it, Reverend?

REVEREND: It's a subpoena from Congress asking me to appear before some committee that's out to do away with rap music.

SECRETARY: That's a wonderful opportunity, Reverend. It'll probably be broadcast on all the networks.
(REVEREND *rips up subpoena.*)

REVEREND: I'm not participating in no drive that would criminalize the free expressions of hip-hoppers, beboppers, hard rockers, or anybody else. I may disagree with the music and the lyrics, but I can't subscribe to any proposition that would smack of censorship. Do you think that Martin Luther King, Jr. and I made all of those sacrifices so that words and music would be censored? That artistic expression would be criminalized? I doubt it. What would have happened had Jesssusss, the greatest rapper of them all, been reluctant to propose such radical ideas in his time? Had he lacked the nerve to speak out, to address taboos? If he'd held his tongue? The world would be quite different. I mean if we began outlawing groups whose expression we object to, where would it end?
(*Pause*)
Who would be next? These kids are sending out a wounded shrill cry from those who are shut up in these festering inner cities. Police brutality, media harassment, unemployment, malnutrition, low

birth weight, landlord exploitation. They didn't create these conditions, they are merely exhibiting them for us.

As for sexism and misogyny, the Church has plenty enough of its own to take care of without worrying about others. And if we can't straighten out the Lord's house, how are we going to straighten out the house of popular music. We would be hypocrites. Jesus Christ hated hypocrisy. Some of his strongest statements are against hypocrisy. "Ye also outwardly appear righteous unto men, but within ye are full of hypocrisy and iniquity." Matthew 23:28. Or, "What is the hope of the hypocrite, though he hath gained, when God taketh away his soul?" We don't want to be hypocrites like the Pharisees whom Jesus condemned to woe. Now daughter, I want you to take a letter. Address it to the Pope at the Vatican.

(SECRETARY *begins to take dictation.*)

Dear Pope,
As a fellow Christian, I was ashamed of the way your organization clowned and carried on at the recent Cairo Conference.

Where do you get off telling a woman when she can and when she can't have a baby. You ain't no woman. Have you ever been pregnant? No you haven't. Have you ever had an accidental pregnancy and didn't know how you were going to feed the child? Or been raped by some man or by your own father, the height of iniquity? The answer is no. Until you have done these things, you should keep your mouth shut. And one more thing. I'd be real careful about trying to rule other people's morality. I read the newspapers.

(*Lights begin to dim.*)
And it seems to me that you have plenty of problems yourself without going around condemning others. The Vatican debt is about fifty-six million dollars, ain't it?

(*Dimmer*)
You remember what Jesus said about the Pharisees in Matthew

23:27. "Woe to you, scribes and Pharisees, hypocrites! For you are like whitewashed tombs, which outwardly appear beautiful, but within they are full of dead men's bones and all uncleanness." Seems to me that

(*Rap music begins to come up*)

this pretty much describes the condition of the church, Pope. We put up a good front, with our swell edifices and rich congregations, but inside . . . inside . . . deep into the soul of the church, there is rot and disease and the bones of dead men. Before we pretend to cleanse others, we should root out the evil in us.

(*Lights Down, Sound Up, spotlight on* 3 STRIKES.)

EPILOGUE

3 STRIKES: And so we conclude
　　The Preacher and the Rapper,
　　our queer story and rhyme
　　about the hazards and drawbacks
　　of making art into a crime
　　You have your tastes and I
　　have mine and that's just fine
　　So give me one good reason
　　why we should fight all the time

　　Some like Bach and others Mozart
　　the Count, the Duke, and the
　　venerable Earl Hines
　　Some like Celia Cruz
　　Willie Bobo and others, my man Dr.
　　Funkenstein
　　There's only good music
　　and bad music
　　Lenny Bernstein
　　was heard to say
　　That's a pretty good point
　　Why don't we keep it that way

　　That's a pretty good point
　　Let's keep it that way

Chorus
The preacher and the rapper
One's dreadlocked, and one's dapper
a man of the cloth
and a man of the streets
The issues are old
and the passions run deep
and try as they might
will their minds ever meet?

CURTAIN

THE C ABOVE C ABOVE HIGH C

A PLAY IN TWO ACTS

The C Above C Above High C was premiered at The Nuyorican Poets Café, New York City, on April 24, 1997. It was produced by Miguel Algarín and directed by Rome Neal.

Louis Armstrong
Gloria Brown
Bebopper
Dwight D. Eisenhower (Ike)
Kay Summersby
Black Woman
Mamie Eisenhower
Lil Armstrong
J. Edgar Hoover
Newscaster
Joe Glaser
Nathaniel (Nat)
Aide to the President
Lucille Armstrong

SETTING

New York City and Washington, D.C. Late 1950s to Early 1960s.

SCENES

ACT I
SCENE 1, Dressing Room of Louis Armstrong, New York City
SCENE 2, Bedroom in the Shoreham Hotel, Washington, D.C.
SCENE 3, News Bulletin

ACT II
SCENE 1, Dressing Room of Louis Armstrong, Washington, D.C.
SCENE 2, Map Room of the White House
SCENE 3, Street Scene
SCENE 4, Lucille's Home/Dressing Room of Louis Armstrong,
New York City

ACT I

SCENE I

(Dressing room of Louis Armstrong. Photos of Armstrong on the mirror. Sound Up: Offstage, we hear the final strains of Louis Armstrong singing, playing "Keyhole Blues," followed by applause. Momentarily ARMSTRONG *enters. He is dressed in a tuxedo and carries his trumpet in one hand and a big white handkerchief in the other. He is sweating and grinning fiercely, but then changes to a serious look. Removes his tuxedo jacket and drapes it over a chair, facing the mirror, loosens tie. Puts on stocking cap. Sits down. Looks into the mirror. He begins to slowly dab cream on his face and doesn't stop until his face is white. On the video monitor, without audio,* Young Man with a Horn *is playing throughout the scene.)*

ARMSTRONG: It's gettin' harder and harder to get control of these grins.

(Makes several types of grins)

One day they're going to leave and take off to the next gig. One day I won't be able to turn them off and on so easily.

(Removes his black tie. Shirt. Wears an undershirt underneath. Studies his face in the mirror. Rubs his jaw, etc. Turns grin on and off.)

My face doesn't belong to me anymore. The public sees one face.

The record companies see another. My Lucille doesn't even get to see me and my agent only sees money.

(GLORIA *appears. She's dressed like a graduate student. Black dress, stockings, shoes. She wears glasses. An intellectual woman's hairstyle. She carries a shopping bag. She wears a trench coat. Removes the coat and sets down the bag.*)

ARMSTRONG: (*To audience*) And here's that little pest Gloria. All she sees in me is a dissertation.
(*To Gloria*)
Gloria you haven't let me have a break all night. What do you want now? I'm tired of answering questions.

GLORIA: Mr. Armstrong. We have some time before your next set. Can we continue the interview? I just have one last question.

ARMSTRONG: (*Sighs.*) Do I have any choice?

GLORIA: (*Removes bottles of mineral water from a bag. Offers to* ARMSTRONG.) I brought you some mineral water, sir.

ARMSTRONG: (*Pleased. Grins.*) Mineral water. How did you know? This is a habit I developed in Paris. They sell water in the bottle over there. Doesn't have the impurities of the water that comes out of the faucet. You know, those French people are high class. Gave me and the cats a royal reception when we were there in 1934. And to think. I couldn't get a reception like that in my own hometown, New Orleans . . .
(*Sad*)
Where did we leave off?

GLORIA: (*Takes out a pad and begins to write.*) You were talking about Sidney Bechet—about the first time—

ARMSTRONG: (*Gazes in the distance. Strokes his chin.*) I never will forget it. There was this bandleader named Henry Allen. He'd come over from Algiers.

GLORIA: Algiers?

ARMSTRONG: Oh, not that place in North Africa. But a place across the river from New Orleans . . . That's supposed to be the place where the heavy VooDoo goes on. Anyway, Allen was playing at the Odd Fellows Hall and needed a cornet player. He hired Bechet.

GLORIA: The way he played stood you on your ear.

ARMSTRONG: You could put it that way. Stood me on my ear.

GLORIA: It's from your autobiography.

ARMSTRONG: Damn, girl. What don't you know about me? You know my fondness for French water. You've read all about me.

GLORIA: That's my job, Mr. Armstrong. That's what writing a dissertation is all about.

ARMSTRONG: I thought that those dissertations were supposed to be about dead people. I still have my chops, and I can still hit those high Cs.

GLORIA: You're the best Mr. Armstrong. Critics all around the world say so.

ARMSTRONG: You know, my second wife went to college. A Fisk woman.

GLORIA: Yes, you were married to her between 19—

ARMSTRONG: (*With teasing indignation*) Gloria you have inspected every aspect of my life. I don't know whether I should go on with this.

GLORIA: Please. Mr. Armstrong. You promised. You said that you would in your letter.
(*Pulls out letter.*)
You said, "Ask as many questions as you wish."

ARMSTRONG: Guess I have to keep my word, huh.

GLORIA: Yes you do.

ARMSTRONG: You come all the way from Los Angeles to interview me? Where are you staying?

GLORIA: I got a room at the YWCA uptown. It's covered by a grant.

ARMSTRONG: A grant?

GLORIA: Yes. The grant pays some of my expenses. You should have seen all of the questions I had to answer. All of the forms I had to fill out. The people in these foundations still don't believe that jazz is music. I lucked up and found a program officer who's one of your big fans.

ARMSTRONG: You're a real fighter, huh? What do you think of those demonstrations down South?

GLORIA: I plan to go down and join the sit-ins next summer.

ARMSTRONG: (*Continues to apply cream to his face.*) These little school children in Little Rock are gettin' bricks thrown at them. Just for trying to go to school. That little girl, Elizabeth, was attacked by that mob of hyenas.

(*Slide projection: Central High mob and black students.*)
These kids are being spat upon. And the only thing on my mind is whether I can hit a higher C on my trumpet than before.

GLORIA: You're doing your part, Mr. Armstrong. You're loved by millions of people. Both the white and the coloreds buy your music.

ARMSTRONG: But the beboppers are calling me an Uncle Tom.
(*They freeze.* BEBOPPER *in spotlight. Has a goatee, wears a beret, dark glasses. Sound Up: Fats Navarro's "Move." The* BEBOPPER *begins to move his feet around in a bop dance. Sound Out.*)

BEBOPPER: (*Arrogant, jive.*) That old Uncle Tom shit that Louis Armstrong plays is embarrassing. The man has no velocity. He doesn't know about chord changes. He can't give you the theory upon which his music is based. All the dude is doing is playing blackface orphan home march music. That's where that hokey tuba sound comes from. And the banjo. An anachronism. A quaint remnant of plantation life and minstrel shows. Only squares listen to Pops now. We're all listening to Prez, Bird, Monk, and Fat Girl. He can't stand it. He can't challenge us so he calls us names like in that whippoorwill song. He greets the world with a watermelon grin.
(BEBOPPER *mocks* ARMSTRONG'*s grin.* BEBOPPER *goes dark.*)

ARMSTRONG: Maybe they're right.

GLORIA: They love you, Louis. But they feel that they have to replace you in order to succeed. The society makes black men do that to each other. They'll never understand your need to entertain the audience. All of your mugging and carrying on. They don't understand that this is a tradition that goes all the way back to Commedia dell'arte. Beyond that to the traditional theater of West Africa. It's called talking with your face. They see themselves as artists. Not performers. That's why Miles Davis turns his back on the audience.

ARMSTRONG: (*Grinning*) I'm not that kind of musician. I see my mission as giving everybody a good time. Bringing people together. The black and white, the yellows and the browns. When I go abroad, warring factions drop their weapons. They come to where I'm playing and party together. This wonderful music that the Lord has given us—I want to spread it around. People break into smiles when they hear my music. It washes out all of that hate from their heart. You know, a lot of my fans are doctors. One of them said that there are killer cells that attack the ones that are viral. He said that the music I play kicks in the killer cells and these killer cells start fightin' them evil ones. Something like that. He said that my music builds up the
　　　　(*Hesitantly*)
immunity. He said that I was a healer. Now take that bebop. Ever go to a bebop club? The first thing you notice is that the people are unhappy. Nobody smiles. The women? Bebop bunnies. They look thin. Emaciated. The musicians look scruffy, bumified. They wear shiny pants and sometimes they don't even wear a tie. We all keep our shoes shined and our creases starched
　　　　(*Slide projection: Jelly Roll Morton*)
A tradition that goes back to old Jelly Roll. Well anyway, the doctor says that the killer cells get confused when they hear that bebop music, they can't go to war against the enemy. That's why the fans and the musicians of bebop look sickly. That's why they die young.

GLORIA: Mr. Armstrong. That's unnecessarily harsh criticism. Look, one day they'll be as famous as you and then a new generation of black men will be calling them names. Besides, if it weren't for you, they wouldn't have their precious bebop. By the way, Mrs. Armstrong called while you were onstage.

ARMSTRONG: I'll call her. She must feel lonely stuck out in that house in Queens. I will have a chance to at least to spend a weekend with her. After that I take off for England. The Royal Family is asking for a command performance.

GLORIA: (*Examines watch.*) Look, Mr. Armstrong, I have to go. The Y closes at 10:30 and the last train is about to leave.

ARMSTRONG: (*Reaches for cash. Hands* GLORIA *some.*) Here, take a cab.

GLORIA: I can't.

ARMSTRONG: You go on. Take it. Pops is not going to let someone who is writing a dissertation about him worry about catching a train. Besides, a young woman like you should be careful about these New York streets.

GLORIA: I can take care of myself.
    (*Pecks* ARMSTRONG *on the cheek and rushes out.*)

ARMSTRONG: There's a kid with spunk. Where's my agent Joe Glaser? He doesn't come down anymore. Rumor has it that he won't come within five feet of me. Says that white people who come near me turn black. That's the most ridiculous thing I've heard.
    (*Pause*)

But then again who knows.

(*Sound Up: "Black and Blue."*)

I often wonder why God made me so black and blue. All of my life. Maybe being that makes me special. Maybe there is a mission for those whose skin is the color of the cosmos. Whose color contains all colors. Who better to unite the world? I read somewhere that most of the universe is composed of dark matter, yet they're always calling us a minority.

(*Removes a huge reefer from a shoebox. Takes a drag.*)

How can that child defend those beboppers? They do that terrible drug, heroin, while my generation does weed. Smoking reefer helps me to get through another day in the United States of America. Reefer is mellow. It was a recreational drug for artists in the '20s and '30s. But then, after the war, they brought in that heroin. The gangsters would give the best of the singers and musicians spots. If it wasn't for them and the New Orleans club owners I sometimes wonder how jazz would have thrived. We could have a gig, jam. But then those heroin people came on the scene. People with no class and no taste took over the clubs. There was heroin before, but then it was the Jews who sold it. Only the rich could afford it then. But then the Italians took over. They're the ones who introduced needles. They brought a cheaper variety into Harlem. It went over big with these young bebop musicians. Guys waking up in the alley with vomit all over their clothes. Robbing their relatives and their best friends. Shitting blood. These bop musicians—if they ain't on the bandstand they're in the emergency room. And that one they call Bird. He's a bad example for these youngsters. People think that just because a person's a genius they should be given license to do whatever they desire. Hell, down in New Orleans everybody was a genius. What about that wicked genius, Hitler. These white critics are calling Bird an alto saxophone great. He should be called The Pied Piper of Death. He is a big mistake. Bebop is a big mistake.

These young players have left the melody. Have left the dance. It's all about tempo. How fast you can play. It has no grace. No nuance. It sounds like a beheaded chicken running around. He's responsible for this and so his name shouldn't be Bird. It should be Chicken. What was the word that that child Gloria used for people who don't believe in anything? Ni-hi-lism. New York jazz is ni-hilis-tic. They call their music cool and refer to what me and the boys play as hot. They think that they're engaged in some kind of revolt. Well, the way I look at it, hot jazz, as they call it, is contributed to the war effort. I understand that even some of the Nazi generals listened to my music. They risked their lives smuggling in the records of the Hot Five and the Hot Seven. Hitler said that my music Negrified Europe. Well maybe Europe could use a little Satchmo to melt the ice that you hear in some of the music over there. Maybe one of the problems with Hitler was that he subjected himself to the torture of sitting through the music of this man Richard Wagner. I once attended one of this man's operas. The thing was nine hours long. It was real ice music with these fat people with pigtails screaming and hollering at the top of their lungs. Whewww!

(*Mops his brow with handkerchief.*)

After sitting through something like that over and over again, who wouldn't want to go out and start a war.

OFFSTAGE VOICE: Five minutes, Mr. Armstrong.

> (ARMSTRONG *straightens tie. Puts on tuxedo jacket. Puts his shoes on chair and wipes them with a cloth, applying some saliva. Struts offstage humming his solo from "Keyhole Blues."*)

ACT I

SCENE 2

(*Bedroom of the Shoreman, a downtown Washington, D.C. hotel. A king-sized bed. There is a portrait of George Washington above the bed.* IKE *wakes up screaming. Sits up. He is wearing long johns. The woman lying in bed is* KAY. *She is a middle-aged redhead and very handsome. She is wearing a fancy slip.*)

KAY: (*Irish brogue*) Ike, what's wrong?

IKE: I had a dream that it was the year 2000. That China had the world's largest economy and that Africa was moving up. That even the smallest countries had A-bombs and were sending up Sputniks. Maybe Douglas McArthur was right. Maybe we should have nuked China.

(KAY *begins to hug* IKE's *back.*)

KAY: Ike. It was just a dream.
(*Pause*)
It will take one hundred years for China to catch up with the West. And Africa is one hundred years behind China. That's why we have to take care of them.
(*Pause*)
Ike last night was so lovely. I was always amazed that a warrior like you could be so gentle in bed.

(IKE *kisses her hands. He gets out of bed and begins to change
into a golf outfit. Golf bag is leaning against the wall.*)

And then toward the climax, the way you . . . you stormed my Normandy Beach, riding the crests of my waves.

IKE: Would you like more champagne?

(KAY *holds out her glass.* IKE *pours. Then pours himself one.
They toast.*)

To our love. May it always be as scintillating as champagne.

(*They drink. They stare into each others eyes longingly, put
down their glasses, and kiss passionately.*)

KAY: Remember the champagne we had after the German surrender. The best champagne in Reims.

IKE: Afterwards we had that buffet supper at the Dorchester Hotel. Then the theater.

KAY: That was the first time you'd eaten in a restaurant in three years. You were mobbed. All of those well-wishers. Congratulating you. Begging for your autograph.

IKE: Yeah. The response of the people. It made all of the hell I had to go through worth it. The quarrels with Montgomery and Patton.

(*Two slide projections: Montgomery and Patton.*)

The setbacks. And all of those youngsters killed.

(IKE *lights up a cigarette.*)

That's what always depressed me. Every time I had an opportunity, I'd visit the cemeteries. Pay my respects. You know. I was known as a general who was not only after victories but the welfare of my soldiers. That was always uppermost in my mind.

(*Sniffles*)

The proudest moment of the war for me was when I showed up as the boys were prepared to land in Normandy. They saw me and they started to chant, "Good old Ike. Good old Ike."

KAY: I know about your suffering, Ike. I was there by your side.
(*They clasp hands.*)
It had to be done, Ike. Just think how the world would be under Hitler, that . . . that racist. The presidency must be boring next to being the Allies' Supreme Commander. You triumphed over that bigot, Hitler. In one of the most spectacular victories of all time. Greater than Napoleon or Caesar.

IKE: I ran because I thought I could do some good. The Democrats were in too long. Harry Truman and the Kansas City mob. It was unhealthy . . . It's not as demanding as leading the Allies. I have a good staff. Things are run smoothly. Except . . .

KAY: Except what, Ike?

IKE: The Negroes. They want to go to school with white kids. The Southerners are good people. They don't want their children going to school with some big overgrown Negroes.
(KAY *recoils. They freeze. Spotlight on* BLACK WOMAN. *Could be the same one who plays Gloria.*)

BLACK WOMAN: (*Walks slowly across the stage.*) When I was a little girl, my mother and I saw a lynch mob dragging the body of a Negro man through the streets of Little Rock, Arkansas. We were told to get off the streets. We ran. And by cutting through side streets and alleys, we managed to make it to the home of a friend. But we were close enough to hear the screams of the mob, close enough to smell the sickening odor of burning flesh. That was 1927. Little Rock.

KAY: Ike, what are you saying? That it's okay for blacks to fight against bigotry in Europe, but it's wrong for them to do it here?

IKE: It just won't work, Kay. It'll not only handicap the black kids but the poor whites as well. Why I talked to this man Arthur Krock, a big man at *The New York Times*. He told me in private that he didn't want to send his kids to school with Negroes either, and he's a big liberal.

KAY: I don't believe you Ike. I thought that we fought to rid the world of racial hatred, and anti-Semitism.

IKE: Oh, Kay. That's your Irish talking. We treat the Negroes well. They're a helluva lot better off here than in Africa. Kay, I even have one of them working for me. Look, I have to go.
(*Silence.*)

KAY: Ike.
(*Hesitant.*)
How's Mamie doing?

IKE: She's in a bad way. There's no peace at home. She hasn't been the same since she saw that picture of you and me in that theater box seat. She takes a drink in the morning and doesn't stop until she's dead drunk. She lies around in bed until noon, watching soap operas. She has to go to these Midwestern spas to dry out. I think that she hates me. We haven't had sex since the . . . since she had that . . . that er, female operation . . . She still thinks that I was responsible for our son, John, becoming a soldier. She thinks that all soldiers are sluts. During the war she wrote me about the loose morals of the American army in Europe. You remember? I read it to you. She acts as though men start wars as an excuse to establish traveling whorehouses. Like . . . like General Hooker.

KAY: We didn't mean to hurt her. It's just this love between us is so mighty, so powerful, we couldn't help ourselves, Ike.
>   (*They kiss for a long time.*)

IKE: You know, Kay . . . the times we spent in our little cottage outside of London were the happiest of my life.

KAY: Mine, too, Ike. We were like a family. You, me, and the dog, Telek. You remember when he peed on General Marshall's bed?
>   (*Laughter.*)
You were furious. You said,
>   (*Mocking him.*)
"Get that dog out of here God damn it!!"

IKE: (*Laughing*) I never will forget the look on the General's face.
>   (*Pause*)

KAY: Remember those long golden afternoons when we'd lie near the fireplace drinking our gin and tonics?

IKE: And the poker games.

KAY: You never had any money. You always had to borrow.
>   (*They laugh. Look into each other's eyes, longingly.*)

IKE: Goodbye, Kay.
>   (*They hold hands.*)

KAY: "In my heart will ever lie, Just the echo of a sigh. Goodbye." Ike.
>   (IKE *approaches* KAY. *Sound Up: Glenn Miller's "Starlight and Music." They begin to dance. Spotlight Up on* MAMIE *while they're dancing.*)

MAMIE: (*Glares at* IKE *and* KAY. *Her arms folded. She's wearing a fox fur cape, and bangs. Speaks to audience.*) She checked in here under an assumed name. The Shoreman Hotel. Hotels are where these men do all of their dirty work. Meeting their whores. He kept me locked up in a hotel for two years while he was away in Europe with this woman. I used to be so attractive.

(*Slide projection: younger, attractive* MAMIE.)

I sacrificed myself for this man. He couldn't afford me. He's always broke. They wanted to pay him some good money to do his biography. The fool turned it down. The president of the Philippines offered him thousands of dollars to stay there and live in luxury. And to think, I could have had any man in Texas. I was so glamorous. My date book was filled. I had my own maid and a generous allowance. I could have lived for the rest of my life on my father's meatpacking money. I gave it up to become an army wife. Went from pheasant under glass to chicken livers and rice. I could have had a career. Instead, Ike became my career. We married in 1916. Moved thirty-nine times. We didn't have a home we could call our own until 1952. He was nothing but a rube when I met him. Farm boy. Didn't even know what a soupspoon was and thought that a bidet was a bird's bath. I had to teach him the social graces

(IKE *and* KAY *are talking but we don't hear them. He puts his golf cap on and kisses* KAY *on the cheek. They kiss.* IKE *exits.*)

Had to polish his English. West Point couldn't take Kansas out of this hayseed.

(KAY *puts on a WAC's uniform and begins to apply make-up in front of the hotel's mirror.*)

LIL: (*Enters. Tall, smartly dressed, intellectual type. Victorian blouse, hip velvet suit, granny shoes.*) I know what you're going through, Mamie.

MAMIE: Who are you, the hotel maid?
> (KAY *embraces herself and begins to whirl about in happiness.* LIL *glares at* MAMIE.)

LIL: Hotel maid. You white women are all alike. Think that all a sister can do for you is your laundry and your floors.

MAMIE: Just asking.

LIL: I was married to Louis Armstrong.

MAMIE: Oh, yes. I have some of his records. Can't play them while Ike is home. Know what his favorite songs are?

LIL: What are they?

MAMIE: "God Bless America" and "You'll Never Walk Alone." He gets all teary-eyed when he hears that one.
> (LIL *laughs.* MAMIE *keeps her glum expression throughout.*)

LIL: Well, Louis has better taste, but he and Ike have one thing in common. Fixated on their mothers. Ida and Mayann. Both of them chose careers that would keep them on the road so's not to get into trouble with their mothers. You know.

MAMIE: Never thought of it that way—Your name again?

LIL: Lil Armstrong. Lil Hardin Armstrong.
> (KAY *puts on a coat and begins to leave the hotel room. Exits.*)
And who may she be?

MAMIE: My husband's whore. Kay Summersby.

LIL: Spindly little thing.

MAMIE: You think so?

LIL: Flat as roadkill.

MAMIE: Well, these men and their wars. They meet women and pour out their souls to these tramps. Yet Ike wouldn't have gotten anywhere without me. All that he wanted out of the army was to be a colonel. Now he's president of the United States.

LIL: You're not telling me anything. I practically created Louis. When he came to Joe Oliver's band, he didn't even know how to wear a hat.
   (*Dressed in drag,* HOOVER *enters the room and begins to take photos of the bed, etc.*)
Wore his hair in that odious New Orleans style. Those ugly bangs.
   (*Sees* MAMIE's *bangs.*)

LIL: I'm sorry, I . . .

MAMIE: (*Relaxes.*) Forget about it. I was thinking of getting a different style.

LIL: Well, I had to teach Louis, the way you had to teach Ike. When he came up from New Orleans he was just a sack of remains with a trumpet.

MAMIE: That bad? What happened?

LIL: Got turned out by one of these green-eyed Creole vampires. Everybody told him not to marry this crazy bitch. When they were courting she'd do evil things like make love to him while knowing full well that her boyfriend would walk in at any moment. There are lots of women like that. Get off by having men draw blood over them. Louis barely escaped one encounter. She was a real wildcat. Liked to fight men. She'd even fight the police. They were together four years, going back and forth between the bedroom and attempted murder. Kind of woman who carried a razor. Her name was Daisy but it should have been Venus. As in Venus flytrap. Louis was the fly who got stuck. Jealous. She was paranoid. Thought people were ridiculing her behind her back. A first class manic depressive.

MAMIE: How did he get rid of her?

LIL: Well Louis hardly knew his father and the only thing his mother taught him was how to hold his liquor. Doesn't it tell you something about his relationship with her that his most vivid memory is of him and his mother carousing the bars and falling down drunk in the streets. So he adopted Joe Oliver as his father, Joe got Louis to leave New Orleans for Chicago. He worshipped Joe. But I found out that Joe was stealing money from Louis and the other band members. I hipped Louis to that but he still wanted to stay with Joe. Louis didn't know how good he was. When he first started hitting those high Cs he didn't know what he was doing. I had to play it on the piano to show him what he was doing. He didn't know anything about the mechanics of music. I told Louis that I wasn't going to be married to somebody who played second trumpet. It was because of me that he left Joe Oliver's band and went to New York to work with Fletcher Henderson. We broke up.

MAMIE: Why?

LIL: I was always independent. I played in bands when I was a teenager. Could write music and I could play piano as well as any man. I was playing in these bands with men who were my inferiors. They'd never let me play solo. All they wanted was to get into my pants. Louis wanted a mother. If he could have married Mayann he would have.

MAMIE: You sound like a woman of good upbringing. Why did you marry him?

LIL: I've asked myself that. Here I was, educated at Fisk. I thought that it may have been a rebellion against my mother. We fought all the time. She hated jazz. If it were only that simple. What about you and Ike?

MAMIE: Our grandmothers and mothers told us that we should be helpmates. I never thought anything different. The biggest compliment Ike made to his mother, Ida, was that she was a wonderful helpmate.

LIL: What's that man doing?
> (HOOVER *is still creeping around the hotel room, emptying drawers, etc.*)

MAMIE: Oh, that's J. Edgar Hoover. He's blackmailed everybody in Washington. He was the first to know that Kay was registering in the hotel under an assumed name.

LIL: I didn't know that he was black.

MAMIE: Oh, everybody knows it. He's never been accepted as a white man by Washington society. He says it's a tan, but we all know better. Nobody talks about it. They're scared. He's ruined people. You'd be surprised the people he's spied on.

LIL: Who, who?

MAMIE: You know that pompous ass, Douglas MacArthur? My husband calls him a big baby.

LIL: Who hasn't heard of General MacArthur?
        (*Mockingly*)
"I Shall Return."

MAMIE: "Old Soldiers Never Die."

LIL: They just live to testify.
        (LIL *and* MAMIE *both laugh.*)

MAMIE: (*Whispers to* LIL) MacArthur was diddling this Chinese teenager into bad health. Edgar knew and so did Drew Pearson.
        (*After primping in front of the mirror,* HOOVER *exits.*)

LIL: Douglas MacArthur?

MAMIE: The same.
        (*She sees champagne that* KAY *and* IKE *have left behind in a bucket next to the bed.* MAMIE *walks over. Lifts the bottle.*)

MAMIE: What you say we finish this off?

LIL: Why not.
        (LIL *walks over to where* MAMIE *is standing.* MAMIE *pours herself a glass of champagne. Pours* LIL *one. They sit on the bed and quietly begin to sip. Sound Up: We hear a recording*

of LIL *on piano in the background playing "Lonesome Blues."*)

MAMIE: Lil, how does that expression go? "Behind every great man is a woman."

LIL: Should be, "Behind every great man there's a chump."

MAMIE: I guess I was one. I think about him and that woman and how I had to live alone in that Washington apartment and those headaches and the insomnia and that double lock on the door between me and the world. I developed symptoms. The doctor said that I had agoraphobia. He came to visit me once. Kept calling me Kay. I was furious.

LIL: You had every right to be, Mamie. No wonder they call that war a crusade.

MAMIE: Come, again.

LIL: They call World War II a crusade because that's what they did in the old days. Lock up their women in towers and go off to these foreign lands where they'd kill the Arab men and sleep with their women.

MAMIE: I can follow that. Well, you remember that TV series they did called *Crusade in Europe*.

LIL: I remember. What about it?

MAMIE: They tried to sneak his girlfriend, Kay Summersby, into the film.

LIL: What did you do?

MAMIE: I had the bitch cut out.

LIL: (*Laughing*) Mamie, you didn't.

MAMIE: I sure did.

LIL: Well, I'll be damned.

MAMIE: And I'll tell you another way I'm gettin' even.

LIL: How's that, Mamie?

MAMIE: I'm on strike. I stay in bed until noon under my rose-colored sheets and watch soap operas. I refuse to do a damned thing around the White House. And his public relations say,
> (*Mockingly*)

"Why don't you at least show up in the kitchen once in a while, and scramble some eggs like Eleanor Roosevelt did?" I told them, why should I scramble eggs when I could be getting in a good game of bridge?
> (*They laugh.*)

Oh, I know they talk about me. Call me a drunk and all. The staff calls me "Sleeping Beauty" behind my back. But you know what, Lil?

LIL: What, Mamie?

MAMIE: As Bessie Smith says, "Ain't nobody's business if I do."

LIL: I'll toast to that.
> (*They toast.*)

ACT I

SCENE 3

(Three people wearing ski masks holding signs that say "Basta Auslander," "Invasione Africaine," "Keep Central High White," and "Nigerians Out of Zimbabwe." Blackout on them. Slide projection: Central High School. A Governor Faubus speech could be heard here.)

NEWSCASTER: The crisis at Little Rock's Central High School continues. Governor Faubus continues to defy a court order

(Slide projection.)

that Negro students be admitted to classes. A mob is building up and sporadic outbreaks of violence are being reported. Famed trumpeter Louis Armstrong has said that President Eisenhower should show some guts, go to Little Rock and escort the children into the school.

(In amazement)

Louis Armstrong?

ACT II

SCENE 1

(GLORIA *is interviewing* ARMSTRONG *in his dressing room. He's removing the cold cream from his face and testing his grins.*)

GLORIA: (*Taking notes.*) What was it like working with Bessie Smith?

ARMSTRONG: (*Laughs, then frowns.*) That woman always wanted top billing wherever we'd play. She usually got her way, too. I was twenty-five years old and nervous, because Bessie was a legend. A big star. And here I was, playing with her. She thought that I was going to try to upstage her, but I stayed in the background, because I respected her. Besides, Bessie was hot tempered, especially when she had that gin in her. She also had a mean right hook. Well, by the end of the '30s Bessie's type of music had played out. You couldn't give away the blues in those days. You must always remember that, Gloria. In this life, you always have to learn how to adapt. Always have something to fall back on. If they ain't buying your blues, be prepared to provide them with show tunes, ragtime, or spirituals. Never depend upon one shtick to get you over.

GLORIA: You recorded nine sides with her.

ARMSTRONG: That's right, I—

> (GLASER, *Armstrong's agent, bursts into the room, but keeps his distance from* ARMSTRONG. *He's a balding, middle-aged man. Neat suit. Shirt and tie. Very ethnic. Carries a newspaper.*)

GLASER: (*Keeping his distance.*) Are you out of your mind, Louie? Since when have you been so political? Insulting the President of the United States.

> (*Points to newspaper, angrily.*)

You're calling President Eisenhower a coward. This is the man who liberated Europe. Are you mad?

ARMSTRONG: It just came out. Before I could do anything, I had said it. It just came out.

> (*Mumbles*)

Well, it accomplished one thing. It got you down here.

GLASER: Look at all of these cancellations.

> (*Waves papers.*)

ARMSTRONG: (*Unperturbed*) There comes a time when all of us have to take a stand.

GLORIA: That's telling him, Mr. Armstrong.

GLASER: And who might I ask are you?

GLORIA: My name is Gloria Brown.

ARMSTRONG: She's writing a dissertation on me.

GLORIA: Mr. Armstrong took a stand. The President should exercise his constitutional prerogatives. Governor Faubus promised the President that he would maintain law and order at Little Rock. He went back on his word. It is he who is insulting the President. Not Mr. Armstrong.

(ARMSTRONG *beams*.)

GLASER: (*To* GLORIA) You keep out of this. What's come over you, Louie, where is the grinning lovable clowning Louis that the world has begun to demand?

(*Seeing that he has hurt* ARMSTRONG.)

Look, I'm sorry, I apologize.

ARMSTRONG: You needn't. That's what people expect. But this is different. When I saw that Orval Faubus prevent those children from entering that school in Little Rock and being threatened by that mob of ignorant crackers, something came over me. I had to say something. And that cat Eisenhower. Let that joker Faubus defy him.

(GLASER *has a concerned look*.)

Is there anything wrong?

GLASER: I didn't want to bring this up, but ever since you blurted out that remark, three goyische men have been following us. They were on the plane down here to Washington and I noticed them in the hotel.

ARMSTRONG: Who could they be?

GLASER: I think it's the Feds. Look, I tried to get you an interview with Eisenhower, so's you could explain, but his staff has nixed the idea. That letter you wrote asking Ike to legalize marijuana didn't help.

(ARMSTRONG *grins*.)

They said you could see Nixon when you're in Washington next week. That's better than nothing. Maybe that will take some of the heat off. People are criticizing you. Sammy Davis, that young colored dancer, criticized you. Said, "Who does he think he is, speaking for black people?" Look I got to go.

ARMSTRONG: One minute.

GLASER: What is it, Louis?

ARMSTRONG: Why are you standing way over there?

GLASER: I . . . I . . .

ARMSTRONG: Afraid that you will turn black?

GLASER: I'm sorry Louis, but I've seen it happen. Take that Teagarden fellow.
(*Slide projection: Jack Teagarden*)
You got him talking and acting like a black man. I'm already a Jew. To be that and a black, too. I'm sorry Louis, but I ain't takin' no chances.
(GLASER *exits. Pause.*)

ARMSTRONG: (*To* GLORIA) Sammy Davis, Jr. criticizing me, huh. Feds on my tail. That son of a bitch Hoover. I'm sorry Gloria. I didn't mean to swear before you child.

GLORIA: I understand, Mr. Armstrong. Don't let them break you, sir. You have to take a stand for all of those people who had to do demeaning things in order to display their talent. Bojangles, your hero, who had to be decontextualized and emasculated, sanitized and mammified by having to perform with Shirley Temple. Bert Williams and George Walker, that brilliant team who were pursued through the streets of New York by mobs. All of the women who had to play maids, and the men who had to play butlers, all of those who had to take the insults of directors and script writers, whose talents were blighted and cheapened. All the ones who had to shuffle, bow, and scrape, all of the black women who could only play prostitutes, and all of the black men with no love interests, who had to play Jim to somebody's Huckleberry Finn. You have to do it for them, sir. Besides, if they put their hands on you, your fans will riot all over the world.

ARMSTRONG: They say they want me to go to the Soviet Union. Put my black face out there to show how liberal we are. Well I ain't going nowhere. They can cancel the trip. They can send that no-playing Benny Goodman in my place.

GLORIA: That's the spirit, Mr. Armstrong.

OFFSTAGE VOICE: One minute Mr. Armstrong.

> (ARMSTRONG *puts on his coat, ties his tie. Looks in the mirror one more time. Pats down his hair. Picks up his trumpet and slowly begins to walk offstage.* GLORIA *stops him. He has left some white cream on his face. She wipes it off with some tissue. He continues to walk offstage until we hear applause.* GLORIA *puts on her trench coat and exits.*)

ACT II
SCENE 2

(*Map room of the White House. A large map of the Pacific with notes scribbled on it indicating World War II zones of combat. A couple of folding chairs.* IKE *is waiting for* HOOVER *to arrive.* IKE *is dressed in his golf outfit and is practicing some puts.* NAT, *a black man, is pouring him a cup of coffee.* NAT *then returns to his position against the wall.* HOOVER *enters. He is a dark skinned, short, rotund black man. Nattily dressed like a gangster.*)

HOOVER: Mr. President I asked you to come to the map room because I didn't want to show you this material in the Oval Office. Who knows; the phone might be tapped.

IKE: Of course, J. Edgar. I understand. What's on your mind?

HOOVER: This Louis Armstrong. He's leading the blacks in some kind of revolt.

IKE: Is that so?
    (IKE *is swinging his golf club.*)

HOOVER: (*Sheepishly*) I've been watching him closely Mr. President, he's a clever one all right. Take that song, "Dinah," for example.

(IKE *stops swinging. Scratches his head. Gives* HOOVER *a curious look.*)

HOOVER: Listen to this, Mr. President.
(*Puts the record on and plays a couple of choruses of Armstrong singing "Dinah."*)

IKE: Not my kind of music, but what's wrong with it?

HOOVER: You don't get it General. He's not singing it the way it goes: "Dinah, is there anyone finer / In the state of Carolina / If there is and you know'er / Show'er to me / Dinah, with her Dixie eyes blazin' / How I love to sit and gaze into the eyes of Dinah Lee"
(*Following lines should be spoken dramatically:*)
"Every night, why do I shake with fright / because my Dinah might change her mind about me"
(*Singing again*)
"Dinah if she wandered to China / I would hop an ocean liner, just to be with Dinah Lee." You see, Mr. President. He's singing it a different way. He's singing in some kind of code. He's sending a message to the Negroes. Telling them to rise up and kill white people. And when they start their rebellion, the Chinese will invade from Mexico. It's all a big conspiracy. But don't worry, Mr. President. My agents are watching all of the borders.

IKE: You don't say.

HOOVER: (*Insistent.*) General, will you put down that golf club and listen.
(IKE *glares at him.*)

HOOVER: A . . . Mr. President, I need your permission to wiretap his phone. We already have a couple of men tailing him.

You heard what he said. Said that you ought to take those black children into the school down there personally. He said that you should take those children by the hand and walk through that crowd of God-fearing white citizens and escort them into Central High School.

IKE: He said that, J. Edgar?

HOOVER: That's not all he said, Mr. Eisenhower. One of our men overheard one of his sidemen call your mother, "a Negro." He said that you were passing for white. A lot of Negroes believe that.

IKE: (*Laughs.*) That's a new one. I've been called a Jew by the Taft people, a Communist by McCarthy's people, and now a Negro.

HOOVER: He said that you lacked guts.

IKE: (*Angry.*) What?

HOOVER: After we finish with him, he won't have such a smart dippermouth.

IKE: Dippermouth?

HOOVER: That's his nickname.

AIDE: (*Enters.*) Mr. President, may I speak to you in private?
(*They go to the side of the stage and begin animated conversation which we don't hear.*)

HOOVER: (*Dials telephone.*) Yeah . . . he stepped out of the room . . . I think that we'll get our tap on Louis. I'm prepared to tell him about the letter. The one he wrote to Marshall asking permission to divorce Mamie and marry Kay Summersby. That'll get him to play ball.

> (HOOVER *and* NAT *begin a staring contest as the conversation between the* AIDE *and* IKE *is heard. With dignity,* NAT *stares through* HOOVER, *who begins to wilt under his gaze.*)

AIDE: But Mr. President, the situation is deteriorating. Every Klansman in Dixie is headed for Little Rock. The Governor has abandoned his duties and become the mob leader.

> (*Slide projection: Governor Faubus*)

We can't assure the safety of those kids. Suppose one of them is killed. How would that look to the Russians and the Chinese?

IKE: (*To* AIDE, *angrily.*) I will never use soldiers against American citizens and that's that. Now I have to get back to my meeting.

> (AIDE *exits. Has frustrated look.*)

IKE: Do what you have to do with this Armstrong, Edgar. If he is posing a threat to national security then he has to be monitored.

HOOVER: (*Smiling.*) Thanks, General.

> (*Looks at watch.*)

Well I've got to get to the track. Don't worry, Mr. President. We'll take care of this Armstrong. By the way, how were the arrangements at the Shoreham?

> (*Winks, and smiles at* IKE *evilly.*)

IKE: A . . . fine . . . Fine, J. Edgar.

HOOVER: Good.
>   (HOOVER *exits.*)

EISENHOWER: How did he know about that, Nat? Did you tell him?

NAT: I've been working here for thirty years, Mr. President, and I've never betrayed the confidence of a president. That Hoover is a wicked man. He knows about everybody in town and is a loathsome blackmailer. And the man's own private life is degenerate. The man should be fired—

IKE: But how can I? He knows about me and Kay.

NAT: Unfortunately that's how he remains in power. Getting under peoples' bedsheets. Like a piece of lice. And now he's trying to destroy Louis Armstrong, one of the most beloved figures in the world of music.

IKE: But what about his calling me gutless?

NAT: Mr. President. Louis has done more for the image of the United States than your Secretary of State, John Foster Dulles,
>   (*Slide projection: John Foster Dulles*)
a man whose very name inspires hate and contempt around the world. This nutty thing he has about massive retaliation, for example. If somebody attacks us with A-bombs and we retaliate, it will blow up the world. It's stupid. Louis, on the other hand, is a gentle person. He's our ambassador of goodwill.
>   (*Slide projection: Armstrong in Ambassador's clothes*)

IKE: J. Edgar seems to think otherwise.

NAT: You should hear what Louis says.

IKE: What Louis says. How can I find that out?
> (NAT *goes out and brings* ARMSTRONG *in.* ARMSTRONG *enters with trumpet. Grins widely.*)

IKE: What's the meaning of this?

NAT: I brought him here, sir. He was down the hall meeting with Vice President Nixon. He wanted to see you, but your staff wouldn't hear of it. I'm sure that this misunderstanding can be worked out. You two should talk. Get acquainted. You've only spent a total of forty-five minutes talking to black leaders since you took office.
> (*Awkward silence.*)

IKE: Don't we have a black member of the administration?

NAT: Fred Morrow. The man resigned from his good job at CBS when you invited him to join the Administration and now he's living on his savings. People here won't even answer his calls. And that Alabaman, Wilton B. Persons, threatened a boycott if a Negro came to the White House in a capacity other than that of a butler, like me.

IKE: (*Embarrassed*) I didn't know. Maybe I'll invite him to sit in my box at the baseball game. Well, Armstrong, what do you have to say for yourself?
> (*Looks at watch.*)
Make it quick, Armstrong. I got to get to Burning Tree. Play some golf.

ARMSTRONG: (*Offers hand.* IKE *refuses to shake it.*) Mr. President, I'm sorry if I embarrassed you. But those little children. It just made my blood boil when I saw them treated this way. The white man spitting on that child as she tried to enter the school. It made me mad. And then you allow this man, Faubus, to defy you. You have him call up the National Guard to stop those kids from entering school. Mr. President, with all due respect, are you going to let this moonshine-guzzling barefoot redneck peckerwood do this to you?

IKE: I can understand your concern. But you know, Louis, I have to think of how history is going to treat me.
     (*Puffs up his chest. Assumes visionary gaze.*)
I've already reached the pinnacle. Why should I get into a pissing contest with some stupid southern governor? This fool Supreme Court and that Earl Warren—that liberal—they've just caused a lot of trouble for the good people of the South.

ARMSTRONG: They may be good to you, Mr. President, but my people have caught hell from these good people of the South. We can't get booked in good hotels and when my men have to go to the bathroom, they have to sneak and go do it in the bushes.

IKE: Is that so?

ARMSTRONG: That ain't all. They still have those night riders. Roaming the countryside. Foaming at the mouth. Terrorizing Negroes. A few months ago, some hillbilly exploded a bomb outside of a hall in Knoxville, Tennessee, where I was performing.

IKE: It takes time Louis. You must have patience. Your people should go slow. The good decent people of the South will come around. Your people should use moral persuasion.

ARMSTRONG: We've tried all of that. Some use oratory. I use my trumpet. But my trumpet can only do so much. Sometimes, it takes the sword, General. Sometimes it takes more than moral persuasion.

IKE: I'd never use the bayonet against Americans.

ARMSTRONG: But you already have, Mr. President. Don't you remember those Bonus Marchers?

IKE: Vaguely.

ARMSTRONG: Vaguely? You remember the unemployed veterans who came to Washington in 1932. All they wanted was the thousand dollars which they felt the government owed them by law. These poor people set up squatters' camps and vowed to remain until Congress acted on their demands. What does MacArthur do? In July, he drove them out of Washington by bayonet. Not only the men but women and children. Clubbing them and teargassing them.

IKE: That was MacArthur's doing. He thought that he was a god.

ARMSTRONG: But you were his aide. Couldn't you have said something?

IKE: It's not that simple, Armstrong.

ARMSTRONG: Mr. President, are you saying that the army can be used against hungry citizens exercising their rights, but not used against that howling bunch in Little Rock who are threatening these black children? Mr. President.
    (*Grins.*)
I'm a musician and you're a general. Both of us are leaders of men. Both of us had mentors. Yours was General Marshall, and mine was

King Oliver. Both of us have to use tactics and strategies to accomplish our goals. We both try to accomplish what people in our fields never before reached. Every time I hit those higher registers on my trumpet, I believe that I'm going someplace where nobody's ever been. That's what you must do Ike. Hit the high note of your career. Hit that C above C above high C.

IKE: I've hit the highest of notes, using your metaphor. I was the Supreme Commander of an army, which scored one of the great victories of history. The presidency is a step down for me.

ARMSTRONG: That's not what they say in Europe. They say that General Montgomery was . . . was . . .

IKE: Go on—

ARMSTRONG: They say that Montgomery could have won the war a year earlier if it hadn't been for your blunders. They say that you lost Berlin to the Russians, and that it was Montgomery who won the Battle of the Bulge while you were jazzing your driver.

IKE: (*Agitated, angry.*) God damn it, who told you that? That Montgomery was an egotistical little fart.

ARMSTRONG: (*Grins.*) Don't get excited Ike. You know that I travel. People will talk. The royal families of Europe have receptions for me which are attended by the high-army brass of different countries. They gossip about the soldiers in Korea. The ones you left behind?
(*Sound Up: The sounds of combat.*)

IKE: (*Stunned. Shaken.*) How did you know about that?

ARMSTRONG: Not much you can keep from Pops, General. My band performed at a party for one of the higher-ups in your administration. The cat had a few cups and started shooting off at the mouth. He said that the North Koreans didn't hand over all of the soldiers during the prisoner exchange at the end of the war. Said that they kept some behind and that these men were sent to Russia and were experimented upon. He said that you knew about it but kept quiet.

IKE: (*Nervous. Agitated. Lights cigarette.*) We had to do it. We had to sacrifice those men. We wanted to get the war over. It was the best that we could do.

   (*Defensive.*)

I told those clowns that we shouldn't have gotten ourselves in a land war in Asia in the first place. You can't beat those people on the ground. They came at us in human waves in Korea. Those Asians. They don't give a rat's ass about human lives. If we'd remained there would have been more casualties.

   (*Pause. Lights up a cigarette.*)

Louis. Let me level with you. I have tried my best to serve my country. I love my country more than I love my wife. And what good has it done me? Criticism throughout my career. Even Omar Bradley, who wasn't a show-off like that rich bastard Patton—always displaying his ivory handled pistols—was constantly second-guessing me. Monday-morning quarterbacking. These lily-asses up at Harvard are already rating my presidency as a failure and I haven't even finished my term in office.

ARMSTRONG: Montgomery says that after he defeated Rommel, the Desert Fox, it was only a matter of time before the Germans surrendered anyway.

IKE: That was just a lucky break. Rommel got sick and had to return to Germany and the general that he left in command got himself killed. I can't do anything right, for some people.

ARMSTRONG: You don't have to tell me, Mr. President. I've taken my lumps. Ever since I was a kid they talked about me. People would come to my gigs in Chicago and wait to see whether I would fail in hitting my high Cs. They spread such nasty rumors about me—that my mother came up from New Orleans to see whether I was all right. When I was a kid they said that I was a hoodlum.

IKE: Why would they call you that?

ARMSTRONG: It was New Year's Eve. January 1, 1913. I never will forget it. I got a hold of a gun and fired some shots into the air. I was arrested and put in the Colored Waifs Home.

IKE: That's too bad. Your parents must have taken it real hard.

ARMSTRONG: I had one parent. My mom. I got into trouble a lot when I was a kid, but I straightened up. Got myself together. Had some real mentors in the home who taught me how to play the bugle.

IKE: Is that so?

ARMSTRONG: I've been around the block, Ike. While you were living your apple-pie life in Abilene, I was gettin' arrested for stealing newspapers.

IKE: Apple pie is it? Well I'll have you know that we lived from hand to mouth. My father, a good man, was constantly in debt. He was swindled. He spent the rest of his life paying off his bills. He never complained. Never felt sorry for himself. And my mother. She held the family together through the hard times. She taught me and my brothers discipline. Perseverance. Hard work. We all have her smile. That woman. She was faithful to my father, to us. Wouldn't sit down at the table to feed herself

(*Sniffles*)

until we were fed. Sewed patches on our clothes so we wouldn't be embarrassed when we went to school. Boy did I have a bad temper when I was a kid. One Halloween night, my folks let my brothers go out trick or treatin' but because I was the youngest, they made me stay home. I went outside and banged on an apple tree until my hands were covered with blood. Well, after I went to bed, my mother came into my room and she said something that I'll never forget. She said, "He that conquereth his own soul is greater than he who taketh a city."

ARMSTRONG: My mother stood by me, too. God Bless Her. We had nothing. Nothing. When we were sick, we couldn't afford doctors. She'd go down to the railroad tracks and gather herbs. They'd work just fine.

(*Tearfully*)

My mother always said to me. She said that if you treat people nice then they will treat you nice. You express that attitude nowadays and you're accused of groveling. Of kissing the behinds of the white public.

IKE: I've heard that said about you. I thought that you were reasonable. America's uncle. A frequent guest on the Ed Sullivan Show. Not like that hothead, Roy Wilkins.

ARMSTRONG: Yes, well they may call me a Tom, but I'd never treat my people the way you did yours.

IKE: I don't follow.

ARMSTRONG: Your family came from Germany, from around the Rhine. The original spelling of your name was Eisenhauer. Your forbearers were Mennonites. They fled Germany to escape religious persecution just like my people are trying to overcome racial persecution. Yet after the war you starved hundreds of thousands of German prisoners even though you and they were of the same bloodline. The way I look at it, you had internalized your self-hatred. You felt that you had to whip on your own people in order to show your loyalty to Anglos. You're what might be called an "ersatz German." "Ersatz" is a word that those French people use.

IKE: War is a dirty business. Sometimes you have to bargain with the devil.

ARMSTRONG: Like those French Nazis you made a deal with in Tunisia. The Darden Affair. What about that, Mr. President!

IKE: Well, at least I didn't have dinner with a Nazi General like Montgomery did.

ARMSTRONG: You're a big hero now but sooner or later your mistakes will catch up with you. You have to stand by the kids down in Little Rock. That way you will be regarded as one of the great presidents. They'll say that here was a man who defended the Constitution in the face of a mob. You know, the way George Washington handled those mountain men. Shays' Rebellion. The old man put on his uniform, polished his boots and sword, mounted his horse, and began moving toward the source of the trouble. Here's a man who won the American Revolution. You didn't see him resting on his laurels. You know they always said that you were just a professional. A man who got breaks because he shined up to older men. You know how your seniors were jealous of you because you got your command only twelve months after being a Colonel. They said that your rapid rise was due to your cynicism. By standing up to these crackers, Ike, you can prove that you believe in something. That you have a heart. That you're just not one of these . . . these . . . ni-hi-lists.

IKE: What?

ARMSTRONG: Mr. President, why are you letting this Orval Faubus do to you what Mussolini and Hitler couldn't do? Defeat you. And you know, Mr. President, you may have killed Hitler's body, but you didn't kill his soul. His soul lives on in America. If you don't do something about Little Rock, his soul will grow right here in the United States. By letting this hog farmer, Faubus, off the hook, the way I see it, you're watering that evil. You're helping that evil grow. You're spreading that evil around. No wonder your people couldn't find Hitler's corpse. Hitler lives. He's laughing at you. He won. I see Hitler in the eyes of the Negro-stomping police, in the glare of the innkeeper who refuses Negroes. Hitler will have the last laugh on you and Churchill. His name will be around after both of you have gone on. It's up to you Ike to see that it doesn't happen. You let him get away and it'll encourage all of the rest of the haters. Besides, didn't Faubus go back on an agreement with you that he would maintain law and order down there?

IKE: It'll work out.
> (*Puts a cigarette in his mouth. Searches pants pocket for a match without success.*)
Louis. Do you have a match?
> (ARMSTRONG *lights his cigarette.* IKE's *hands are shaking.*)

ARMSTRONG: Ike. Why do you feel the need to smoke so much? It ain't going to help your heart condition one bit.

IKE: I don't know. It's a habit I developed along the way.
(*Smiles.*)
You think that you're the only one who could raise some hell. I was a real cut-up in my day. I almost got kicked out of West Point, I received so many demerits. Graduated sixty-fifth in my class. Why, if they had these newfangled test scores in those days, I probably would never have gotten into West Point. Most of the time, I got into trouble for smoking. I was always lighting up. During the war, I smoked three, sometimes four packs per day. Didn't eat right either. Sometimes just a chocolate bar. That's why my stomach is messed up.

ARMSTRONG: Try a cup of hot water at night.

IKE: What?
(*Gazing into the distance.*)

ARMSTRONG: A cup of hot water. Duke Ellington says that it works wonders. Mr. President, you're not even listening to me. What's bothering you?

IKE: Louis? You ever been in love?

ARMSTRONG: Of course, Ike. What man hasn't.

IKE: I mean do you think that the heart can be divided?

ARMSTRONG: I don't follow, General.

IKE: I mean, do you think that it's possible to love two women?

ARMSTRONG: Are you talking about Kay and Mamie?
(IKE *nods.*)

Any man who is in love with two women at the same time is asking for an early grave. It's better to love one. Now Ms. Summersby met you when you were already a legend

(*Mutters.*)

to those who don't know any better. She was impressed by Eisenhower the star. Or shall I say, two stars. Mamie, on the other hand, stuck by you when you were shifted back and forth from one crummy post to the other. She's the mother of your children—the one who died, and John. If I were you, Ike, I would stay with the one who was with me when I had the least.

IKE: Thanks, Louis.

ARMSTRONG: Ike you're a good man but you're getting the wrong advice. You're surrounded by evil. You know that Hoover likes black entertainment. Some of my buddies say that he sometimes comes to after-hours joints. Dressed up like a woman. Goes by the name of Mary. And that ain't all. He is in hock to the mob. Frank Costello places bets for him at the track. The mob has photos of him making love to a man. They own his ass.

IKE: Look, Louis. If you're going to spread scurrilous rumors about people in my administration we can end this interview right now.

ARMSTRONG: Suit yourself Ike. I've achieved my high C. But will you get yours? History smiles upon you right now, but history is a fickle lover. It will turn on you. The people will eventually discover the real role that you played in the war. How you lost Berlin to the Russians. Your blunders. Your abandonment of the Korean POWs. The atrocities you inflicted upon unarmed German prisoners. All of it will come out, Ike. It's not too late, Ike. It's not too late to get your C above C above high C. One last deed that will seal your place in history as a great man.

(*Begins to exit, but turns around.*)

By the way Ike, I'm sure that you know what the Russians say. They say that they were at the suburbs of Berlin when the Americans entered the war. They said if it weren't for them Hitler would be living in America and his capital would be Cicero, Illinois. The Russians lost twenty million people in the war. They say that General Zhukov won the war and that you only played a minor role.

(*Starts to leave again.*)

IKE: (*Shrugs his shoulders.*) Look, Louis. Before you leave, would you play something on your trumpet?

ARMSTRONG: Oh, first you're going to kick me out, then you want me to play something for you.

(*Pause.* IKE *pleads with his eyes.*)

You white folks is a mess. Well alright. Maybe I can say in music what I can't say with words.

(*Sound Up:* ARMSTRONG *plays "The Star Spangled Banner." At the conclusion the two men stare at each other.* ARMSTRONG's *is more of a glare. But then he breaks into a wide grin.*)

IKE: (*Wiping away tears. Moved. Shaken.*) Thank you Louis.

ARMSTRONG: (*Dramatic pause. They shake hands.*) Do the right thing, Daddy.

(ARMSTRONG *exits.*)

ACT II

SCENE 3

(ARMSTRONG, *as though he is alone on stage.* BEBOPPER *stands off to the side. Doing the junkie nod. Eyes closed. Reeling. Scratching himself. Begins to slowly wake up. Damp spot at crotch.*)

ARMSTRONG: That Eisenhower isn't such a bad joe. Just a sad melancholy man. Couldn't have the woman that he wanted. It's like a knife in his soul. Took me a long time to find mine. Daisy. I almost ended up in the cemetery with that one. Lil. Man don't like a woman talking back to him and second-guessing him. She came between Joe Oliver and me. I wouldn't have been anywhere had it not been for Papa Joe. Used to bail me out of difficult situations. He gave me my first cornet. And fixed one of my women's stomach. Irene was her name. Lil put an end to a friendship that went back to the early days. She was wearing the pants in the family. I couldn't even wear a pair of shoes without her choosing them. She was always pushing me. I was young. In those days, I liked them headstrong and highstrung. But Lucille. Lucille is different. Washes my clothes, feeds me, gives me sympathy when I'm having a bad day. She's the right one for me. She loves me from my head to my feet.

BEBOPPER: (*Waking up. Notices* ARMSTRONG.) Hey Louis. Play something for me on that corny trumpet of yours, you square little black motherfucker.

(ARMSTRONG *knocks* BEBOPPER *down. Helps him up.*)

ARMSTRONG: You okay, son?
(*Brushes* BEBOPPER *off.*)
You know you young boppers have wandered so far off that sometimes, it becomes necessary for you to come in contact with the cold fist of reality. That's why I characterized you as "poor little sheep who have lost their way." Let me share with you a proverb I learned in Africa last year. "The calves follow their mothers. The young plant grows up near the parent stem. The young antelope leaps where its mother has leaped." The melody is the mother, son. That's what you young musicians forget. Don't ever go so far out in deep water that you can't get back. And respect continuity, son. These critics have divided us. Interrupting a chain of tradition that reaches back to the rain forests of Africa. I teach you something. You pass it on to your generation. They pass it on to a future generation. I know that you boys think you're doing something new, but if it wasn't for me, and Joe Oliver, and Bunk Johnson, Baby Dodds, Kid Ory, Jelly Roll, and a whole bunch of other cats, you wouldn't have your precious bebop. Understand.

BEBOPPER: Yessir, Mr. Armstrong.

ARMSTRONG: (*Holds his nose.*) You stink. Go and get yourself cleaned up and then get back to practicing your scales.

BEBOPPER: Yessir Mr. Armstrong.
(*Blackout.*)

NEWSCASTER: We've just received the following bulletin. Fifty-two C-123s and C-130s have brought twelve hundred battle-equipped paratroopers to Little Rock to see that integration is carried out at Central High School without further violence. Planeloads of the men of the 101st Airborne Division, stationed at Fort Campbell, Kentucky, started landing at Little Rock Air Force Base at 3:30 P.M. this afternoon, at half-hour intervals. The troop convoy is entering Little Rock to take up positions at Central High School.

> (*Spotlight on* LUCILLE. *Middle-aged. Wears dance outfit worn by Cotton Club chorus line. On the video monitor we see a Cotton Club routine.* LUCILLE *imitates the dance that they are performing on the monitor.*)

LUCILLE: I still can do my kicks. Louis is always out of town. I'm lonely. Maybe I should rent a studio. Get my routines in shape. No time for that. When you marry a public man you are placing yourself in a prison. Oh, the prison is nice. Furnished well. All of the amenities. But it's still a prison. You can watch television to wile away the time. You can sew or talk to neighbors. Out here people play mah-jongg a lot. But ultimately you have a rival. This rival gives him more pleasure than what a woman can give. It's easy to compete with those whores who are always throwing their arms around Louis. It's much harder to compete with a thing. A trumpet. I know what his other wives knew. Daisy and Lil. That there's no woman who is going to come between him and that horn. These sweet-talking black musician men. They are so full of sex that they can eroticize a piece of metal. A chunk of ivory. Louis's other wives couldn't accept it. I can. Do I have regrets? Sometimes, I wonder whether I would have succeeded. How far I could have gone with my dancing. Whether I would have become another Katherine Dunham. Or a Pearl Primus, or Eartha Kitt. Ethel Waters. Sometimes I wonder whether I sacrificed my career for Louis. Should I have hovered in the shadow of a great man, just to spend some time in his company. Just to love him. Have his clothes ready. Cook his meals. Run his household. Why do I do it? No matter where he goes or with whom he does his one-night stands, he always comes back to Queens. He comes home to me. And when he does the neighbors turn out as though he were a conquering hero. Dogs barking. Children running after him. Mobbing the ice-cream truck while Louis buys. People honking their horns. Shouting, "Hey, Louis. Hey, Satchmo." It's like a holiday when Louis comes home. Those are the days that make it all worthwhile. When my man is here eating his greens and chitterlings and sweet potato pie. Recovering from the road, making love to me. Maybe one day people will look back and say that Mamie and I were wrong. That she gave it all up for a man who went to his grave loving another woman. Or maybe I will be seen as someone who abandoned a career just to become a great man's caretaker. Maybe they will dismiss us as victims, shut up in the 1950s, our opportunities stunted, condemned to carry on the tradition of our mothers, nurturing children and their husbands. But right now I look forward to those golden moments and those moments with Louis make it all worthwhile. It's me and Louis against the world. That's the way it should be.

> (LUCILLE *puts a domestic dress over her Cotton Club outfit. Somebody provides her with a birthday cake. Center Stage lights up and we see* ARMSTRONG *sitting in his dressing room, applying white cream to his face.* GLASER *enters. The three approach him.* GLASER *stands about five feet away.* ARMSTRONG *looks up.*)

LUCILLE and GLASER: Happy birthday, Louis.

ARMSTRONG: (*Grins.*) You guys are full of surprises. Really sweet of you to remember my birthday.

> (*He embraces them.* NAT *enters.*)

NAT: Happy birthday, Louis.

ARMSTRONG: Nat, what brings you here?
(*Introduces* NAT *all around.*)

NAT: General Eisenhower wanted me to deliver this telegram to you, personally.

ARMSTRONG: It's been eight years since Little Rock, how is Ike doing?

NAT: He and Mamie are enjoying the Gettysburg farm. They both seem at peace. It's the longest period of time they've ever spent with each other.
(*Slide projection:* MAMIE *and* IKE.)

GLASER: People still are puzzled about why he sent the troops into Little Rock. So unlike him.
(NAT *and* ARMSTRONG *exchange knowing glances.*)
Strange, complicated man. A product of the military, yet when he left office he warned about the military-industrial complex. Talked about nuking China, yet criticized the dropping of the A-bomb on the Japanese.

NAT: I hear that Governor Faubus is working as a teller in a bank.
(*Everybody laughs but* ARMSTRONG.)

ARMSTRONG: Cut it out people. You don't piss on a man when he's down. Read the telegram.

NAT: "Mrs. Eisenhower and I are happy to be among those wishing you a happy birthday. The date of your birth, a national holiday, would seem to insure a gala celebration. May you have many more years of good health and happiness." Signed, Dwight Eisenhower.

LUCILLE: He's got his nerve, Louis. After what that old queen J. Edgar Hoover did to you.

ARMSTRONG: Ike made mistakes. But finally, he got that *C* above *C* above high *C*. Oh Yeeeaaaaahhhhhhhhhh.

GLASER: What do you mean by that, Louis?

ARMSTRONG: (*Exchanges knowing glances with* NAT.) Just a secret between Ike and me. Nothing important.

LUCILLE: Louis. Ain't you goin' to cut the cake?
    (ARMSTRONG *rises as the three begin to sing "Happy Birthday." At the conclusion* ARMSTRONG *begins to cut the cake when* GLORIA *rushes on. The four are astonished*)

GLORIA: Mr. Armstrong. They published my book.
    (*Smiles,* ALL. *Freeze: Spotlight on* IKE *in suit.*)

IKE: (*Sound Up: In the background of this speech is Armstrong's "West End Blues." Speech should begin after opening trumpet flourish by Armstrong.*) For a few minutes this evening, I should like to speak to you about the serious situation that has arisen in Little Rock. To make this talk, I have come to the President's office in the White House. I could have spoken from Rhode Island, where I have been staying recently, but I felt that in speaking from the house of Lincoln, of Jackson, and of Wilson, my words would better convey both the sadness I feel in the action I was compelled today to take and the firmness with which I intend to pursue this course until the orders of the Federal Court at Little Rock can be executed without unlawful interference. In that city, under the leadership of demagogic extremists, disorderly mobs have deliberately prevented the carrying out of proper orders from a Federal Court. Local authorities have not eliminated that violent opposition and, under the law, I yesterday issued a Proclamation calling upon the mob to disperse. This morning the mob again gathered in front of the Central High School of Little Rock, obviously for the purpose of again preventing the carrying out of the Court's order relating to the admission of Negro children to that school.

Whenever normal agencies prove inadequate to the task and it becomes necessary for the Executive Branch of the Federal Government to use its powers and authority to uphold Federal Courts, the President's responsibility is inescapable. In accordance with that responsibility, I have today issued an Executive Order directing the use of troops under Federal authority to aid in the execution of Federal law at Little Rock, Arkansas. This became necessary when my proclamation of yesterday was not observed, and the obstruction of justice still continues.

It is important that the reasons for my action be understood by all our citizens. As you know, the Supreme Court of the United States has decided that separate public educational facilities for the races are inherently unequal and therefore compulsory school segregation laws are unconstitutional.

CURTAIN

BODY PARTS

A SERIOUS COMEDY IN TWO ACTS

Body Parts, A Serious Comedy premiered at the Nuyorican Poets Café in New York City on October 25, 2007, where it was produced and directed by Rome Neal. This was a significantly revised version of *Who's Who in the Tough Love Game*, which premiered November 12, 2004 at the Black Repertory Group, in Berkeley, California, as part of their fortieth-anniversary celebration, where it was directed by N. Bruce Williams and produced by Dr. Mona Vaughn Scott.

CAST OF CHARACTERS

JOHN FRIDAY, Distinguished black man about 60, graying temples. Blazer, cordovans, striped tie. Cufflinks. Think Duke Ellington. He is Executive Assistant to Marse Only, Jr. the son of Marse Only, the founder of Only Pharmaceuticals.

MICHAEL CHEN, Chinese American Company Manager of Only Pharmaceuticals.

MARSE ONLY, JR., Replaced his father as head of Only Pharmaceuticals. Son of the founder who runs the Tough Love Institute. Mean-spirited nasty yuppie. About 35–40. Bald white man, dark glasses, black suit, shirt, tie. Wears an earring and shiny black shoes.

WADSWORTH WYUMS, Senior Fellow of the Tough Love Institute. Also about 60. Wears a three-piece conservative pinstriped suit. In his style, he is a cross between George Kingfish Stevens of *Amos 'n' Andy* and Redd Foxx of *Sanford and Son*, and uses gestures of both.

JUANITA WYUMS, Wadsworth Wyums's wife. Black woman about 40. Constantly changes hair weaves and hair color throughout the play. Always overdressed. Speaks with heavy Jamaican accent. Is an immigrant.

WHITE CLUBSWOMAN, Tacky hat, heavily made-up, stockings, conservative shoes, calico dress.

WAMU RUDURUDU, African exchange student and houseboy to the Wyums.

KLANSMAN/DEAN ANTHONY HALL, Can be played by the same person since he will be wearing a Klansman's masked outfit when playing the Klansman. When Dean, in conservative suit. He is Chairman of the English Dept. of John Wilkes Booth Memorial University.

JOHN MCKNUTLEY, High-strung yellow black man, thin, effeminate speaks in high-pitched voice. Delicate. About 30–35. Wears Confederate uniform.

EVA STARR, Black feminist about 40. Dresses like an academic. Glasses. Dreads. Prim. Frilly blouse, black suit, black granny shoes. Studious. Serious.

BLANCHE WALLMART, President, John Wilkes Booth University.

SAN JOSE NEWSCASTER, Attractive young Hispanic woman.

AMY ALLGOOD, White woman. Plain dress. No make-up. Bohemian.

COP, Standard uniform.

CLUBSWOMAN

ACT 1

SCENE 1

ALL *characters are frozen onstage.* MICHAEL CHEN *is in the act of talking to* MARSE ONLY, JR. MICHAEL CHEN *is dressed in a business suit.* MARSE ONLY, JR. *as described above.* JOHN FRIDAY *stands near them.* WADSWORTH WYUMS, *a black portly middle-aged man, is sitting in a sofa, asleep. He is bald, with an expansive waistline, and holds* The Sacramento Bee *in his lap. Glowering at him, with hands on hips, arm folded, is* JUANITA WYUMS. EVA STARR, *a black woman in her 30s, wearing an ankle-length black dress, black shoes, braided hair, is being interviewed by a* MAN *dressed as a* KLANSMAN, *covered by white sheet with holes for eyes. A white* CLUBSWOMAN, *chairman of the Valley Forge Book Club is standing at a lectern. Church hat, white gloves that reach her elbows, fur collar.* JOHN MCKNUTLEY *sits next to her. He is waiting to be introduced. He is effete and wears a Confederate uniform.* (*The spotlight will shift from character to character, as they begin their speeches.*)

AMY ALLGOOD: Questions are being raised today about the mysterious fire that gutted the offices of Only Pharmaceuticals the day after the Attorney General of California subpoenaed all documents and materials, including, but not limited to, emails, letters, reports, and memoranda, in order to determine whether the company had knowledge of the dire side effects of their antipsychotic drug, Poxin. Marse Only, Jr., who succeeded his father as CEO, insists that the company had no knowledge of the effects of the drug on the thousand patients who've committed suicide as a result of taking these drugs. Critics charge that experiments were conducted on thousands of homeless persons, many of whom have disappeared. This comes on the heels of a study released today that condemned the double standard used by psychiatrists to give a more severe diagnoses to black mental patients than to white. The diagnosis of schizophrenia, the study reported, was given disproportionately to black mental patients. Black mental patients are labeled schizophrenic, white mental patients are given a milder diagnosis. They are more likely to be sent to a talk therapist. This cooperation between psychiatrists and drug companies makes it easier to test new drugs on poor black patients who are often forcibly assigned to dungeonlike mental hospitals. If it is determined that Only Pharmaceuticals had knowledge of the drug's effects, the company could face not only a class-action suit from those who've taken the drug but a suit by the stockholders. This would mean the company's ruin. But with the loss of the company's records, such a charge would be hard to prove. Some recall that two years ago, authorities in Nigeria accused the Eli Lilly company of conducting drug experiments in that country that led to the deaths of more than a dozen children, and those who survived were injured with brain damage, paralysis, and slurred speech. Eli Lilly recently had to pay one billion dollars in 28,000 lawsuits from individuals who contended that they developed diabetes and other diseases from taking Zyprexa. Nigerian authorities have also brought criminal charges against the top executives of Only Pharmaceuticals. Marse Only, Jr. of Only Pharmaceuticals denies the claim that their drug Poxin was used during trials in that country.

John McKnutley of the Tough Love Institute, and one of the Institute's leading brains, disputed the claim that there exists a double standard by which black and white mental patients are treated. He attributed such claims to the same victimologists—as he called them—who attributed the AIDS epidemic to some sort of diabolical smallpox experiment that originated in Philadelphia, a claim that he termed "ridiculous."

(*Spotlight on* MARSE ONLY, JR.)

MARSE ONLY, JR.: You sure that they can't trace the fire to us?

MICHAEL CHEN: Listen, there are some things that I don't need to know. Suppose they call me as a witness.

MARSE ONLY, JR.: You rat on me and I'll expose your Uncle's importing that heroin from Afghanistan and selling it in Harlem.

MICHAEL CHEN: Look, they took a plane out after the fire. Those guys are back in New Jersey by now.

MARSE ONLY, JR.: (*Ignores him.*) But I still don't understand. Those cigarette CEOs were found to have known about the dangers of smoking—nothing happened to them—why should it be different for us? Look at Paxil, Zyprexa, and that drug—Avantia. The companies that manufactured those drugs got away with class-action suits. The profits from selling those pills exceeded the costs of the class-action suit settlement. Why couldn't we get a deal like that?

MICHAEL CHEN: Our people in Washington say that with the election coming up, they can't be seen as being too close to the oil, tobacco, and pharmaceuticals industries. We have to find a way out of this jam. We're on our own. They want to make you an example. Show that they're not all that cozy with pharmaceuticals. They fired the people in the FDA who gave you a pass. If they find out that you knew about the side effects, it might mean jail time for you.

MARSE ONLY, JR.: All because a thousand or so nuts committed suicide.

MICHAEL CHEN: Not only suicide but the side effects include kidney and brain damage, weight gain, blindness, slurred speech.

MARSE ONLY, JR.: What about that lawsuit in Nigeria. Our drug trial there?

MICHAEL CHEN: That'll be in the courts over there for the next dozen years.

MARSE ONLY, JR.: Why haven't they accepted the bribes?

MICHAEL CHEN: The guy whom we usually deal with is in jail. I feel terrible about my role in this. I've gone into therapy.

MARSE ONLY, JR.: Since the fuck when have you gotten so high and mighty. Your family made their money in prostitution during the Gold Rush. That's how they were able to pay your way through Princeton and buy that mansion on Knob Hill. Anyway, how much did we contribute to the Republican Party?

MICHAEL CHEN: (*Checks figures.*) Two million.

MARSE ONLY, JR.: And we can't get these clowns to call off this investigation. The all-expense paid trips to Paris. The most exclusive golf courses in the world. French hookers.

MICHAEL CHEN: You're going to have to cut back on expenses. These lawyers are charging a thousand dollars per hour. We've laid off two hundred people, but we still need to make cuts. The Tough Love Institute's expenses for example.

MARSE ONLY, JR.: What's that?

MICHAEL CHEN: It's a think tank. We have three blacks whom we put out front to see that our viewpoint is part of the National Dialogue on Race. John McKnutley traces all of the grievances made by the civil rights leaders to victimology. And Wadsworth Wyums backs our anti-affirmative action propositions. He's part of an older generation and is lacking the intellectual power of the academic stars, McKnutley and Eva Starr. The guy barely finished high school but he's pretty effective with the old right-wing crowd. The Reagan types. He pours on the old charm and the old farts reach for their checkbooks. Starr has successfully changed the subject from attacks on the white male power structure to gender and LBGT issues.

MARSE ONLY, JR.: LBGT what?

MICHAEL CHEN: Lesbian, Bisexual, Gay, and Transgender communities.

MARSE ONLY, JR.: Oh.

MICHAEL CHEN: Eva's completely neutralized those black hotheads. She's saying that black men are the real oppressors. Not white men.

MARSE ONLY, JR.: Brilliant.

MICHAEL CHEN: We're seeing to it that the blacks are being phased out. Like Katrina. All of their issues should be handled that way. Let them drown. With Moynihan you had the doctrine of benign neglect. Now it's malevolent neglect. We set up this Tough Love Institute for that purpose. Got these black brains on the payroll so that Sharpton and Jackson can't scream racism every time they say something. Tell these blacks that their problems are self-inflicted.

Get our black brains on TV to spread this gospel. Tell them that poverty is their fault. That the cause of dislocation in the inner city is the result of a dysfunctional culture or their own behavior, not racism. Blame it on black male culture. Hip-hop. That way the free market system can thrive unhindered by the unnecessary taxes that result from a huge welfare state. Our black brains' role is to convince the blacks, Latinos, and others that discrimination is a thing of the past and that this is a post-race period. That if they'd learn Standard English and stop wallowing in victimization, they could enjoy the fruits of the American mainstream. Our black brains write op-eds, they do lectures, they get on talk shows. They've completely turned the debate around. Unlike the 1960s when radicals controlled the campuses and the organs of opinion, they've routed the left so that it's now atomized. Feminists against the blacks, gays against the feminists, immigrants against the native born, and so on. The Tough Love Institute is vitally important. They've influenced public policy with our steady stream of position papers and policy studies. Preaching individual responsibility and self-sufficiency. Outsourcing for example has become the trend, thanks to our efforts. We tell American workers that their right to a job is not God-given. They have to fend for themselves. There's a problem though. The bills for the institute are much too high. Look at this: $2000 for lunch at Sardi's. $50,000 for hotel suites, $10,000 for tickets to the theater. Lavish outings at Palm Beach. McKnutley and Eva Starr are racking up some big expenses.

MARSE ONLY, JR.: Only what about what's his name?

MICHAEL CHEN: Wadsworth Wyums?

MARSE ONLY, JR.: Yeah. I read an op-ed of his in the *Journal* that praised George Bush.

MICHAEL CHEN: We wrote it for him; he signed his name to it. He made his money in the body parts business. Now, since working for us, he's made a lot of money. But he can't hold onto it. His wife is a shopaholic. Squanders his money so that between proposition drives he's usually broke. He's always calling asking if we have some more anti-affirmative action drives that he can front. He failed in Colorado. They voted against the proposition that would outlaw affirmative action in that state. I have questions about his future effectiveness.

MARSE ONLY, JR.: He made money dealing in body parts? I don't get it.

MICHAEL CHEN: Yes, he supplied the cadavers of black indigents to medical schools.

MARSE ONLY, JR.: Ghoulish. How low can you get. Using bodies for experimentation. So this Tough Love Institute . . . What do you suggest that we do?

MICHAEL CHEN: We don't need three of them saying the same thing. We should choose one. That way we can save some money.

MARSE ONLY, JR.: I'll tell Friday to relay the message to them.

MICHAEL CHEN: We can get rid of Friday, your valet. He doesn't seem to do much.

MARSE ONLY, JR.: Executive Assistant. We don't call him a valet.
(*They both laugh.*)
He's a proud old man. My Dad trained him well. Always there with theater tickets when I need them, gets my stuff out of the laundry, drives my car, instructs me on etiquette, takes some of my women

to dinner when I need an excuse to get out of a date. The guy is indispensable.

MICHAEL CHEN: Didn't know that he was that important.

MARSE ONLY, JR.: Couldn't do without him.

MICHAEL CHEN: Marse.

MARSE ONLY, JR.: Yes Chen.

MICHAEL CHEN: I've been working here for ten years. Some of the white men I've trained have moved up to vice presidency, while I'm still a company manager. When we go to trade conventions, they stay on the VIP floors and get a key to the elevator while I have to stay on the economy floors. They fly first class. I fly coach. They get club memberships, I—

MARSE ONLY, JR.: You're not getting angry, are you?

MICHAEL CHEN: No I was just pointing out—

MARSE ONLY, JR.: Look, anger won't get you anywhere. It didn't get blacks anywhere. You see them pushing grocery carts and sleeping in doorways? That's because of their anger.

MICHAEL CHEN: Yessir, Mr. Marse, I was only—

MARSE ONLY, JR.: You were only?

MICHAEL CHEN: Skip it.
(MICHAEL CHEN *exits, annoyed.*)

MARSE ONLY, JR.: (*Presses button.*) Send in Friday.
>(JOHN FRIDAY *enters. Carries clothes on a hanger.*)

JOHN FRIDAY: I brought your suit for tonight.

MARSE ONLY, JR.: Suit for tonight?

JOHN FRIDAY: You have to present a plaque at the Rock and Roll Hall of Fame.

MARSE ONLY, JR.: (*Goes behind screen and begins changing.*) Forgot all about it.
>(*Continues talking while hanging up clothes behind a screen.*)

Look, Friday, I've made up my mind about the Tough Love Institute. We don't need three people saying the same thing. Redundancy is costly. Call a meeting and give them the news. Tell them that we'll choose one by next week. Let the other two go.
>(JOHN FRIDAY *from his gestures and expressions throughout this dialogue indicates that he doesn't think highly of* MARSE ONLY, JR.)

Chen says they're running up big bills. That Eva Starr. Must she always take a limousine from Santa Cruz to Sacramento?

JOHN FRIDAY: I don't see why. There's public transportation. BART.

MARSE ONLY, JR.: And McKnutley. He was on CNN last week. Chen says that he checked in at the Waldorf Astoria. Took all of his friends to Sardi's for lunch. Get him back here. Where is he anyway?

JOHN FRIDAY: He's taking part in a Civil War reenactment.

MARSE ONLY, JR.: Which side?

JOHN FRIDAY: (*Sarcastically*) Your side.

MARSE ONLY, JR.: Good.

JOHN FRIDAY: He's appearing before the Valley Forge Book Club tonight. He's promoting that new book of his.

MARSE ONLY, JR.: Yes. About blacks taking personal responsibility. Did you read it? What did you think of it?

JOHN FRIDAY: I haven't gotten around to it yet.

MARSE ONLY, JR.: Read it. I think that you will like it. I never was much of a reader. But this McKnutley is very lucid. He's not bopping you on the head with a lot of angry rhetoric.

JOHN FRIDAY: (*Pauses and stares at the partition.*) Right.

MARSE ONLY, JR.: You know. I used to be a radical. But when the blacks turned to violence and ripped apart the consensus that was about to welcome them into full citizenship and equal rights under the law, they left me.

JOHN FRIDAY: (*Mumbles*) Wonder did that consensus include those screaming mobs and the ugly welcome they gave to those kids trying to integrate those schools?

MARSE ONLY, JR.: (*Emerges from behind partition.*) How do I look?

JOHN FRIDAY: You look fine Mr. Only.
    (MARSE ONLY, JR. *turns around, models.*)

MARSE ONLY, JR.: Thanks for covering for me last night with that blonde. Was she disappointed because I didn't show up?

JOHN FRIDAY: At first. But after dinner and about five martinis she forgot all about the date, Mr. Only. I had to send her home in a cab.

MARSE ONLY, JR.: Good work, Friday.

JOHN FRIDAY: Mr. Marse . . .

MARSE ONLY, JR.: Yes Friday.

JOHN FRIDAY: Mr. Chen seemed awful mad. He brushed passed me without saying hello—

MARSE ONLY, JR.: Oh, he feels that he's being overlooked for a vice presidency. He's okay where he is. We have to watch these Chinese. We're in an arms race with the little suckers. Plus they're holding our money. If they were to call in our debt, the U.S. would collapse. Why if we ever had to fight them we'd first have to borrow money from them.

JOHN FRIDAY: But Mr. Marse. Chen isn't from China. He was born here.

MARSE ONLY, JR.: I know. But haven't you noticed. They stick to-gether wherever they are or wherever they come from. I'm think-ing of replacing him with a South Asian Indian. Maybe Dr. Sanjay Gupta. Look, I'd better get going.

    (MARSE ONLY, JR. *exits.*)

JOHN FRIDAY: How am I going to break the news? Eva Starr. John McKnutley and Wadsworth Wyums. I hate being the bearer of bad news. Wadsworth and those propositions. All we'd have to do would be to write those propositions and there he'd be on the television promoting them. Didn't even understand them. He made hundreds of thousands of dollars bad-mouthing black people before white right-wing audiences.

He became rich because his white backers suspended their belief in a color-blind society long enough to realize that a black face fronting for Proposition 209, the measure that ended affirmative action in California, would mean its success. But he failed on that last one. The one about eliminating racial classifications on state forms. But then, with the endorsement of the Klan, he got rid of affirmative action in Michigan. The old guy is losing his touch, though. He's an old school Negro. Clawed his way up. Never went to college. Earned a living by providing the body parts of black people to medical schools. Paid bribes to morticians. Not as polished as McKnutley, Eva Starr, both Ph.D.s. He's always waiting for his sponsors to come up with a new proposition so that the right wing groups on campuses and elsewhere will once again pay for his expensive lecture fees. He doesn't come cheap. If he were a prostitute he wouldn't have to do the stroll. He'd entertain his clients in a suite at the Ritz-Carlton. And there's his charming

(*sarcastic*)

wife, Juanita. Daughter of Jamaican immigrants. Always on the mainland brothers and sisters about their backwardness. Always comparing hardworking immigrants with dependent African Americans. She used to be part of the Republican dirty tricks operation. Oppositional Research division. As a matter of fact, the two met at a cocktail party sponsored by the American Enterprise Institute. She was in much demand on college campuses, comparing hardworking Caribbean immigrants with American blacks whom she described as being dependent upon government handouts. Like many immigrants, she got all of her notions about the United States from movies and television. If she knew anything about America, she'd know that millions of white Americans didn't have a pot to piss in before Roosevelt. His deal with the Southern Dixiecrats made it impossible for blacks to benefit from the New Deal, and since there was segregation in the Armed Forces, blacks were denied the G.I. Bill, the measure that brought millions of underclass whites into the middle class. The Federal Housing Administration, which denied blacks loans, financed white flight to the suburbs with freeways subsidized by the taxpayers. White Americans are perhaps the most government-subsidized class in the history of the world. Now, with the money Wadsworth has made on the lecture circuit and from ghostwritten books stressing right-wing values, Juanita spends all of her time at the mall, while Wamu Wamu Rudurudu, their African exchange student, who lives with them, does all of the housework. Juanita used to be a take down take no prisoners firebrand right-wing intellectual. Now her life is all about hair, skin, and nails.

> (*Spotlight on* WADSWORTH *sitting in the chair, snoring. From time to time the newspaper nearly falls from his hands and he jerks it back to its position. His wife* JUANITA *enters. Arms loaded down with packages. Stares at* WADSWORTH *angrily.*)

JUANITA: I should never have listened to those people at the American Enterprise Institute.

(*Mimics*)

"Why don't you meet Wadsworth Wyums; he's a real star of the conservative movement. He's going somewhere." Now they're saying the same thing about McKnutley and Starr. They represent new leadership, they say. They're more attuned to the post-race generation, one that places issues about race in the background. Wad is not as successful as he used to be. They're telling me. Now he sits next to the phone. Waiting for someone to call him. He hasn't heard from the Only Institute since his proposition to eliminate affirmative action in Colorado failed. McKnutley and Starr are getting all of the lectures and television appearances. He's dependent upon these propositions. Though he says that his brothers and sisters are dependent, he's an African American like them. Dependent. Why did I ever leave Jamaica? America isn't like those movies we used to see back home. We thought everybody was either Meryl Streep or Sidney Poitier.

(*Puts her hands on her hips. Walks over and kicks* WADSWORTH's *foot. Startles him. She shakes him.*)

WADSWORTH: (*Annoyed that his sleep has been interrupted.*) Wha the—

JUANITA: Wad Wyums, you been sittin' in that chair all day. It's been months since your proposition failed in Colorado. The men who wrote it haven't called you during all that time. Nobody wants you to lecture. Give keynote speeches or nothin'. How am I going to go shopping and get my hair done if the cash flow around here continues to dwindle?

WADSWORTH: Those white men needs me more than I needs them. Besides, that preposition failed in Colorado failed because those people up there is suffering from altitude sickness. Every time I go up there I get a nosebleed. You just watch. Who is going to be the Negro to front for them as they create what we all desire? A color-blind society where there ain't no racial classification and nobody getting ahead of the next fella because of the quantity of his pigmentation. As Martin Luther King, Jr. said, "It's the content of our character that counts."

JUANITA: You may sell that rhetoric to those white people, Wad, but you can't fool me. You wouldn't have that job if it wasn't for race.

WADSWORTH: That is true. But look at all of the money we was bringing in, dear. Have patience, dear. They'll call. They'll come up with some new affirmative reaction prepositions. They'll realize that the Colorado vote was just a fluke. Harvesting those body parts didn't pay half as much as speaking before these rich right-wing white folks. Plus my car always had a foul odor. Couldn't get rid of it. Boy those banquets and things. I done gained twenty pounds since I got this job. All that French food and those sugar drinks with pineapples with them little bitty flags sticking out of them. Heady stuff for an old Louisiana boy like me.

 (*Cell phone rings.*)

WADSWORTH: Hello.
 (*Unctuous, with a wide grin:*)
Why Mr. Friday. What a pleasure to hear from you.
 (*Puts hand on phone, as speaks to wife:*)
See, I told you they needed me. This is Friday on the phone. That's the Negro who is always trying to talk so proper.
 (*Mimics. Back to caller:*)
A meeting. Tomorrow. Yes. Of course. Of course. I'll be there. You can count on me. You can always count on me.
 (*Hangs up.*)
See that what I tells you. They wants to see me. Bet they got another one of them prepositions for me. They done forgot all about Colorado.

JUANITA: I knew that I should have patience, Wad. You always come through.

(*Young black man, about 25, enters.* WAMU *is dark skinned and smiling. Wears a janitorial outfit. Brown workman's shirt and pants, like a UPS delivery man. Has rags hanging from his back pocket.* JUANITA *jumps up from her husband's lap.*)

WADSWORTH: Here comes Wamu Wamu. Hey, Wamu.

JUANITA: Hello Wamu—

WAMU: Mr. and Mrs. Wadsworth. My wonderful sponsors. I must express my appreciation to you each day that I live on earth. Ten years ago, I was a gang boy in Nigeria, a street urchin, But now, because of you, I enjoy the fruits of the free market system.
    (*Bows.*)

WADSWORTH: Glad to help you, Wamu. You are like the son that we never had. Unlike these African-American youths, always cutting up, rioting at hip-hop concerts and spending all of their money on sneakers and unable to speak Standard English, and going around with names like Jamal and Omar, you are a hard worker. And you are taking advantage of the opportunities that a free society has made available to you. You ain't asking for no handout like some of our African-American brothers and sisters.

WAMU: You have taught me well. You will not find me wallowing in victimization. And Ms. Juanita, the garden is coming along well. Are there any other tasks that you need done today? I am eager to please both of you. Both of you are like my parents—

JUANITA: You don't have to talk about it, Wamu.

WAMU: They—

JUANITA: (*With much exaggerated effort, rises, approaches Wamu. Embraces him.*) Wamu, son, I can't imagine all of the horrors that you have had to put up with. Forced to fight in the streets of Lagos. Beaten, starved, humiliated when you disobeyed orders from the older boys, found shivering and near death by those Christian missionaries.

WADSWORTH: Now you is a candidate for a master's degree at one of our finest colleges. Sacramento State. Why you is like that Obama fella.
(*Frowns*)
Only that fella is a socialist.

WAMU: I despise socialism. It ruined Africa. It sapped our people of their incentive to improve themselves. There is nothing like the competitive spirit. The older African intellectuals were always blaming every thing on colonialism. This was a waste of time. Everybody knows that we are entering a post-race post-colonial period. If you were to ask me, sir, I would say that African independence was a big mistake. The irresponsible black leaders have driven the nations of Africa to ruin while our former colonial masters stand by helplessly with their hands-off policies, watching the beloved continent which they nurtured and civilized go up in flames. Mr. Wadsworth, my mentor, you have taught me well.

JUANITA: Wamu, you have worked so hard. You even do all of the plumbing and electrical work around here. No job is too small for you.

WAMU: (*Bows again.*) How else would I show my gratitude?

JUANITA: You may have the rest of the day off, Wamu.

WAMU: Oh, Ms. Juanita. How can I ever thank you?

WADSWORTH: It's the least we can do. What do you plan to do with your free time?

WAMU: Free time. There's never free time for me, sir. I am always trying to improve myself in case opportunity knocks at my door. Today, I plan to go to the library and study free market values. Memorize some more Adam Smith and Edmund Burke and Horatio Alger.

JUANITA: (*Concerned*) It must be cold in your little apartment above the garage.

WAMU: Thank you Ms. Wyums. And that apartment may be little to you, but in comparison to my life in Nigeria, it is like a suite in the Four Seasons.
  (WAMU *exits, bowing.*)

WADSWORTH: A real enterprising young man. Won't he be surprised when we tell him that the adoption papers have almost been processed. That he will be our son for real.

JUANITA: We'll throw a party for him. I'm already in contact with a caterer. African cuisine will be served.

WADSWORTH: African cuisine. Don't you think that's dangerous? Those people be stickin' they hands in they food. I might catch typhoid or something.

JUANITA: Wad. Don't be so provincial.
　　(*Looks at watch.*)
Oh, I have to run. I'm gettin' my hair done.

WADSWORTH: Yeah, and I have to go to the Regents' meeting. Make my behind sick. It's boring. Ever since Governor Balco appointed me to the Board of Regents, I have to go to these meetings. All they do is talk talk talk when the issue is simple. These black and Latino kids ain't hittun' the books like the whites and the Asians. Everything is excuses to them. They should turn off the TV and turn on the books. Hey that's catchy. Maybe Governor Balco can use that in his anti-affirmative reaction speech—turn off the TV and turn on the books.

JUANITA: Wad, since when have you been interested in books? I have to go.
　　(WADSWORTH *remains on stage. Smiling, pleased with his idea.*)

CURTAIN

INTERMISSION

ACT II

SCENE I

(Spotlight on ring being interviewed by KLANSMAN *covered in a white sheet on public access television. Sign above says "The KKK Hour.")*

EVA STARR: And it's the domination of black patriarchal households that deprived black women of agency. Why black women in prison are better off than those in the households. I was married to one and so I know. He wanted to be a writer, too. Ha. That was a joke . . .

KLANSMAN: I know how you feel, sister. We've had issues with the brothers for a long time. A very long time.

EVA STARR: So you know. I try to reach them. With my bookstore appearances and of course my many television and talk-show spots, I try to tell them how a modern feminized man should behave. That they should soften up. Cry. Be vulnerable. Be girlie men.

KLANSMAN: Sister, you are doing the Lord's work.

EVA STARR: It's up to white men like you to deliver your black sisters from . . . from . . . the clutches of evil, just as Christopher Columbus liberated Indian women from cruel misogynistic Indian men. These

Indian men believed that they were the ones who were disempowered and colonized when, in fact, they were the colonizers. As for these patriarchal black men, their sexual performance doesn't measure up to their macho boasts. Why, making love to a black man is like having a root canal.

KLANSMAN: (*Pauses.*) Is that so?

EVA STARR: Now, many would criticize me for coming on this show, given your attitudes about the brothers. All I can say is that the enemy of my enemy is my friend.
(*They shake hands. Lights fade on* STARR *and* KLANSMAN.)

ACT II

SCENE 2

(*Spotlight on white* CLUBWOMAN, *chubby, church hat, white gloves, white high heels, stockings, corny dress,* JOHN MCKNUTLEY *sits next to her. Conservatively dressed, bow tie, clean-cut look, shoes shined.*)

CLUBWOMAN: Ladies of the Valley Forge Book Club. Our guest tonight needs no introduction. You have read his columns and you have watched him in his numerous television appearances. His analysis of the problems confronting black Americans is lucid and brave. He comes down hard on the failures of such leaders as Jesse Jackson and Al Sharpton. He criticizes black youth for their self-sabotaging attitudes toward learning—their belief that intellectual activity is a white thing. And this awful hip-hop. As Bob Herbert of *The New York Times* said, if whites were doing to blacks what blacks are doing to blacks there'd be riots all over the country. And now, McKnutley has dared to redeem one of the most misunderstood and vilified characters in our country's history, Simon Legree, in his new book, *Simon Legree, Merciful Slave Master*. As you know, Simon Legree belonged to a small number of southern planters who were white, the overwhelming majority of slave masters being black. The blacks not only sold themselves into slavery but were the slave masters who were there to greet the slave ships when they arrived. We have to thank McKnutley for setting the record straight. And now without further adieu I give you our guest for this evening. Mr. John McKnutley, author of *Simon Legree, Merciful Slave Master.*

(*Applause.*)

JOHN MCKNUTLEY: Thank you. Thank you very much. My black brothers have said mean, unprintable things about me. Called me a rent-a-Negro and other wicked names. But they are ignorant and blinded by bitterness. So desperate they are in their victimization that they criticize our brave men in blue, members of the thin line that separates civilization from barbarity. The police. The police have always greeted me with a friendly nod and a smile. So demented are my critics that they call the police who beat Rodney King and shot Amadu Diallo racists, a ridiculous proposition if there ever was one. Put yourself in their places, ladies and gentlemen. You're in a one-hundred-miles-per-hour chase with this man who has evaded arrest. Your adrenaline is pouring into your arteries. You're angry. Maybe you haven't had much sleep and have gone on an espresso binge. You have what I call an autistic moment. Your senses are scrambled so to speak, and before you know it, you have this man who has caused you so much trouble, lying prostrate before you. For all you know, this powerfully built man might be on PCP or something. What do you know? And so you and your fellow officers use the tried and true method for quelling the behavior of a riotous individual. Nightsticks. Nightsticks to calm him down. And suppose you're in New York. The streets are inhabited by dangerous criminals. It's dark. It's an urban jungle. You're on a dark street in an unfriendly neighborhood. You tell a man to halt. He doesn't heed your warning. He flees. You corner him in a dark hallway. He reaches for his wallet and some-one says, "He's got a gun." You shoot and the others follow. And one of these white policemen, realizing that a mistake has been made, cries, ladies and gentlemen. Sinks to the curb and cries like a baby. Does that sound like racism to you? I argue that it is not racism, but compassion. To say that the police treat black people differently from the way they treat white people is to play the race card. Is to engage in those awful identity politics. And did you ever consider that this might have been a case of suicide by cop. That Diallo actually invited this disaster upon himself. How do we know that perhaps his peddler business was in trouble. That he'd broken up with his girlfriend or gotten some terrifying diagnosis. But we are not here to discuss the fabrications and delusions of my misguided brothers and sisters. We are here to honor one of the most misunderstood figures in American History. Simon Legree, the subject of my book, *Simon Legree, Merciful Slave Master*. Odd you say. No, not odd, say I. For over one hundred years, he has been maligned as a result of the abolitionist propaganda. Especially from that most PC writer of all PC writers, Harriet Beecher Stowe. All because he disciplined that plantation militant, Uncle Tom. I know, I know. We are all fed the idea that Uncle Tom was some sort of obsequious shuffling Negro, but I maintain that Uncle Tom was a danger to the stability of the Southern Way of Life. In those days in the southern Camelot, a place of knights and ladies, black folk did not stand around idling on the corner, or wasting time listening to those awful rap records, they worked from sunup to sundown, 24/7, ladies and gentlemen, under the merciful supervision of Simon Legree, one of those Southern gentlemen who built the South. But Tom was an endless source of disruption for Simon Legree, his master. Stubborn and defiant, insolent and rebellious. We should ignore the appeal of those who apply the outmoded philosophy of presentism. That one should apply the values of today to those of the nineteenth century. Slavery was the law at the time. And when he refused to reveal the whereabouts of Cassy and Emmeline, women who challenged the most chivalrous society America has ever known, Uncle Tom was breaking the law and Simon Legree punished him. This was not a racist gesture ladies and gentlemen, it had nothing to do with race—it was the act of a law-abiding citizen, disciplining a slave that had become unruly.

(*Sound Up: applause, murmurs.*)

ACT II

SCENE 3

(JOHN FRIDAY *stands in the center of the stage. He is taking notes and holding a clipboard.* EVA STARR *enters.*)

EVA STARR: What's the meaning of your asking me to come up on Bay Area Transit instead of sending a limousine?

JOHN FRIDAY: (*To audience*) She doesn't know it, but if the cutbacks continue here, she might be walking before it's all . . .
(WADSWORTH *enters.*)

WADSWORTH: (*To* JOHN FRIDAY) I figured you'd come to your senses. I was always the one who delivered. Why I'm the senior fellow of this whole mess.
(JOHN MCKNUTLEY *enters.* WADSWORTH *and* EVA STARR *glare at him.*)

JOHN MCKNUTLEY: Sorry I'm late but I decided to spend an extra day at the gravesite of Stonewall Jackson's arm. You know when he was buried his arm was separated from his torso. It was a very moving experience. Had that great Confederate General Stonewall Jackson not been killed by one of his own men, the Civil War would have come to a more beneficial outcome.
(JOHN FRIDAY *gets a phone call and* WADSWORTH *and* EVA STARR *begin to gesture as though they are arguing, ignoring*

JOHN MCKNUTLEY's *monologue*)

The knightly way of life that existed before the invasion of the beloved Southern land would have been sustained. A land of ladies' recitals and afternoon teas. But tragically, barbarians from the North, people who didn't know the first thing about where to place a soupspoon, prevailed. We will never forget his heroic exploits on the battlefield, his defeat of the Union troops at McDowell, Front Royal, Cross Keys, Port Republic, Cedar Mountain. So there I was, with my fellow tourists, the only black person in the bunch. Some of them had seen me on C-Span and they congratulated me for breaking the silence. You know, saying the unsayable—about how the brothers and sisters are losing the race. Are engaging in self-sabotage.

> (*Becomes almost tearful. Recovers and turns to* JOHN FRIDAY, *whose phone conversation is over.* WADSWORTH *and* EVA STARR *turn to him.*)

Maybe someone can explain to me why I was flown back economy instead of first class. And what is the meaning of—

JOHN FRIDAY: All of you were late. Try to be on time next time.

EVA STARR: On time. Since when has time been such a big deal around here?

JOHN FRIDAY: Since now. Mr. Only's son wants to get more bang for his buck, in fact, he's decided that there should only be one person should to carry forth the message that African Americans are prone to victimization and are their own worst enemies.

EVA STARR: Should be me. I have a Ph.D. from Yale; I have French theory down pat—

JOHN MCKNUTLEY: Well it has to be me, I have Ph.D. from Harvard.

WADSWORTH: I is the one who is the most regressive. I got through all of those prepositions. I was here fo' all of these other folks.

JOHN MCKNUTLEY: Propositions, you idiot. If you ask me, he should be the first one to go. Every time he opens his mouth, it's an embarrassment to the Tough Love Institute. He treats the English language the way a hit-and-run driver treats a victim.

WADSWORTH: (*Lunges for* JOHN MCKNUTLEY.) Why you—I have a good mind to bust you in the mouth with a fist sandwich—

JOHN FRIDAY: You're out of line Wyums, we'll have none of that language.

EVA STARR: He's right. Not only is he a homophobe, but a sexist as well. He's nothing but a lowly grave robber selling medical colleges body parts. And we know how he treated some of the female interns. There are dozens of sexual harassment complaints that have been filed against him. He told one that she could have a cadaver under the table if she'd have sex with him.

WADSWORTH: (*Defensive*) Those women is a lie. Besides, a chicken hawk like you got the nerve talking about my relationships with women. You done scored more women than Barry Bonds hit home runs. I heard all about what happened at that international short story conference—
    (EVA STARR *lunges for* WADSWORTH. *They have to be separated.*)

JOHN MCKNUTLEY & EVA STARR: HOMOPHOBE!!

JOHN FRIDAY: Okay. Lady and gentlemen, calm down. The two who aren't picked will receive a very generous severance pay from the Institute. Now I have a meeting with Mr. Only. You may leave now.
    (*They exit, grumbling.*)

ACT II

SCENE 4

(JOHN MCKNUTLEY *enters, and a* COP, *head covered with a white sheet with holes, policeman's cap, and carrying a nightstick. They cross each other.*)

JOHN MCKNUTLEY: Why hello, Officer.
    (COP *turns and studies him.*)

COP: What did you say, nigger? You trying to be smart?

JOHN MCKNUTLEY: Why no, sir. I was just offering a greeting as any law-abiding citizen would to an approaching Constable.

COP: What did you call me, nigger?

JOHN MCKNUTLEY: A . . . a Constable . . .

COP: I thought so. Let me see some ID you black bastard.

JOHN MCKNUTLEY: No use becoming offensive, sir, I was—
    (*Reaches into his pocket.* COP *examines his ID.*)

COP: Call me that name one more time.

JOHN MCKNUTLEY: A . . . a Constable?
> (COP *shoots* JOHN MCKNUTLEY.)

JOHN MCKNUTLEY: (*While dying*) This is no way to treat a person who might become a Pulitzer Prize finalist.
> (JOHN MCKNUTLEY *dies.* COP *takes gun and places it in* JOHN MCKNUTLEY's *hand. Flees.*)

ACT II

SCENE 5

(WADSWORTH *is seated in the chair, snoring. Newspaper in hands.* JUANITA *enters loaded down with bags of clothes from expensive stores.*)

JUANITA: Wad it's 5:00 in the afternoon. You still asleep. You should tell those doctors to take you off of Prozac—

WADSWORTH: This Prozac keeps my mind off the hurtful criticism that is made by my black brothers and sisters, who don't realize that there is no free handout and—

JUANITA: Save that speech for the American Enterprise Institute. They use to wine and dine you in Washington, but ever since Eva Starr and McKnutley were brought on—they don't even return your calls. All because of that Colorado debacle. Say they the new breed. They introduced you to lecture opportunities that were worth thousands of dollars—

WADSWORTH: (*Mutters*) Which you commenced to spend on clothes and makeup.

JUANITA: What did you say, Wad?

WADSWORTH: Nothing dear—

JUANITA: So what did they decide at the meeting? They have some more propositions for you to back?

WADSWORTH: They say that they cutting back because of some stock market reverses. The stockholders are nervous about the investigations that are going on about the drugs that they givin' out. They say that they only need one person to promulgate the proposition that black people is they own worse enemy. Guess I have to return to robbing body parts. But now that the body parts business done gone high-tech, what am I going to do? It would take millions to compete with these newfangled operations. They done taken to shipping heads, ears, arms, legs, and eyes through UPS. Since the prices for these parts has gone up there's more competition. Hell, they paying a thousand dollars now for heads with brains.

JUANITA: You won't have to hang around charity hospitals waiting for some poor fool to croak anymore. If they are going to pick one spokesperson for the Tough Love Institute, you're going to be that one. None of those others have done as much for the Tough Love Institute as you.

WADSWORTH: That's true.

JUANITA: You have to be sure that none of those people take the job that you have earned. You were the old man Only's favorite. Remember those times when the old man would have those conferences? He'd fly in executives from all over the world and for entertainment he'd bring you in to sing for them. You'd put on quite a show. That song you used to sing—

WADSWORTH: (*Begins to sing "My Way."*)

JUANITA: (*Interrupts him.*) Wadsworth, please.

WADSWORTH: His son is different. All he knows or cares about is the bottom line. He ain't interested in no show tunes. So how we going to make me the one that's the Tough Love Institute's spokesperson about how black people don't have it together?

JUANITA: By exposing the weaknesses of the others.

WADSWORTH: But won't that be unmoral?

JUANITA: Immoral? What about sending those black homeless people to carry signs opposing affirmative action in the state of Washington? They didn't even know what the issue was and couldn't read the signs. They did it for food. Then you stranded some of them. Wouldn't pay for their trips home. What about them immorals, Wad?

WADSWORTH: Well the people who is doing all of the thinking about this mess said that our ends of making this a society built on merit requires that we use whatever tactics that is available to us.

JUANITA: You leave it up to me.
    (*To audience:*)
These African Americans have no drive at all. Lethargic and tepid. I have to do all the thinking in this household. Orlando Patterson was right. How did he put it? These black Americans are caught in an "atavistic cocoon."

WADSWORTH: What do you have in mind, dear?

JUANITA: Don't you remember? My oppositional research experience? We'll dig up dirt on those with whom you are competing for the job. I'm sure that there's something in their backgrounds that we can use against them.

(*Blackout on* WADSWORTH *and* JUANITA. *Spotlight on* AMY ALLGOOD.)

AMY ALLGOOD: This is Amy Allgood, from Atlantic Listener Sponsored Radio. Questions are still being raised about the shooting of an unarmed black man, John McKnutley. The officer says that the young black man pulled a gun, but nobody believes it. Thousands of citizens are expected to march through the streets of San Francisco behind the funeral procession of this young martyr and some of the biggest names in folk music and hip-hop will assemble to sing his praises. People have left flowers at the spot where the young man was shot by the police. Activists are especially incensed that the right-wing Tough Love Institute hired a lawyer for the officer and, while the policeman is under suspension, has paid for a one-month all-expense-paid trip to Bermuda for him and his family. The policeman said that the young man called him a cussword, and proceeded to give the black power salute. His lawyer is saying that his client, the officer, shot the revolutionary during an autistic moment. We'll see if that theory flies at his trial.

In other news, Marse Only, Jr. of Only Pharmaceuticals has said that he will survive the investigation launched by the State Attorney General into the distribution of the antipsychotic drug, Poxin, found to be a factor in the suicide of hundreds of individuals. The U.S. Attorney maintains that Only, Jr. and the company knew about the harmful effects of the drug before it was distributed. Only, Jr. says that the drug was developed by his late father and that he had no knowledge that it was being distributed by the company. U.S. Marshals are still combing the ruins for e-mails and other documents that might have survived the mysterious fire that gutted the offices of Only Pharmaceuticals, but so far haven't found any evidence that Only, Jr. had foreknowledge of the drug's harmful side effects.

ACT II
SCENE 6

(BLANCHE WALLMART *is a middle-aged white woman. She is dressed in a business suit and is heavily made-up. She is resting comfortably in a chair. She has removed her shoes and is sipping from a drink.* ANTHONY HALL *is sitting next to her. He is a middle-aged white man. Dressed impeccably, with cuff links, etc.*)

BLANCHE WALLMART: We should have gotten rid of her a long time ago. A surly Negress. The only reason we hired her was to avoid one of their men. The kind who are always flirting with white women at faculty parties. We also have to fulfill these affirmative-action demands. Now that Justice John Roberts is running the court that'll be done away with soon. These black academics are always replaceable. Now we have an excuse to get rid of her.

ANTHONY HALL: She writes the same book over and over again, repeating the same arguments. I never had much use for her. You sure that there won't be riots? The students might come into your office at the President's Mansion and stage a sit-in.

BLANCHE WALLMART: When's the last time there was a sit-in around here. There are only a handful of black students on campus. Thanks to Wadsworth Wyums and that affirmative-action drive. Do I admire that man. For him to defy these crazy black militants and white haters. Life must be really hard for him. All of that hate mail. Death threats. The prank that was pulled. Someone putting urine in his drinking glass. He thought it was ice tea. And then remember he was run out of town on two occasions. Tarred and feathered. What courage. He's made it so that only black football players remain on campus.

ANTHONY HALL: Wadsworth Wyums is a hero of mine. To take all of that abuse for the sake of merit. How did he say it, "We should be judged by the content of our skin not the content of our character."

BLANCHE WALLMART: You got it wrong. It's the content of our character. Besides it was Martin Luther King, Jr. who said it. Just think. If Ronald Reagan hadn't instituted tuition costs as a way of keeping out "black troublemakers," as he put it, we'd have more of these nappy-headed bastards to contend with.

ANTHONY HALL: His face should be on Mount Rushmore with all of the other great presidents. Would you like another drink?
> (*Goes to the cabinet. Comes back with a bottle. Pours a drink. She knocks it backs and pushes the glass for a refill.*)

What about Women's Studies? Aren't they going to start some trouble at the sight of one of their black sisters being let go?

BLANCHE WALLMART: I'm bringing in a young scholar from Kenya to take her place. You don't keep tabs on the changes in radical chic as I do. Even that Women's Studies crowd is weary of these traditional African Americans, as they like to call themselves nowadays. *Vanity Fair* devoted a whole issue to Africa. Unlike these disgruntled black Americans, this Kenyan scholar is glad to be here. Thinks that America is a Utopia.
> (*They laugh.*)

She has this phony British accent. Has a framed photo of Queen Elizabeth hanging over the fireplace of her campus apartment. And if she doesn't work out we'll get an Indian South Asian. Among these colored groups, they're the most assimilable. Like household pets.

ANTHONY HALL: Well why shouldn't she be glad to be here? The African continent is a basket case. Wars. Famine. Those people are never going to get it together. Lawrence Summers was right. We should turn the Sub-Sahara into a dumping ground for our wastes.

BLANCHE WALLMART: She was educated by nuns—

ANTHONY HALL: Perfect. By the way, who informed you of the plagiarism in Starr's book, *Brothers, Atone!*

BLANCHE WALLMART: It was an anonymous package. It cited all of the passages that had been borrowed from some French writer. I need another drink.
>   (ANTHONY HALL *accommodates.*)
George is going away to some scientific convention in Switzerland. He'll be gone for three weeks.

ANTHONY HALL: We can go up to the cabin in Tahoe.

BLANCHE WALLMART: What about Anne?

ANTHONY HALL: I'll tell her that I need some privacy. Work on my book about the pagan influences on the works of John Donne. She always falls for that one. This weekend?

BLANCHE WALLMART: I'll meet you there. You know. You've been working on that book for thirty years. It's become increasingly difficult for me to cover for you. There is already gossip about why I led the fight for your tenure and appointed you Dean and you haven't produced a single article or a book.

ANTHONY HALL: I won't disappoint you.
> (ANTHONY HALL *rises and attempts to embrace* BLANCHE WALLMART. *She pushes him away.*)

BLANCHE WALLMART: Are you mad? If anyone finds out about our relationship, it will ruin both of us.
> (BLANCHE WALLMART *exits.* ANTHONY HALL'*s phone rings.*)

ANTHONY HALL: Send her in.
> (EVA STARR *enters.*)

EVA STARR: You wanted to see me Dean?

ANTHONY HALL: Yes, Professor Starr. Sit down.
> (EVA STARR *sits in a chair next to* ANTHONY HALL.)

EVA STARR: Wasn't that the President of the College who just came out of your office? I haven't seen her since the luncheon they threw for me when I was hired. She was gushing all over me then. Just now, she didn't even say hello.

ANTHONY HALL: (*Clears throat.*) Yes, that was she, Ms. Starr. As you know, some years ago, we gave in to the demands that we create the Department of Ethnic Studies here at John Wilkes. Some of my colleagues were against it, believing with me that the great achievements of mankind have been created by Europeans and also the brightest of thoughts and writings, but, as you know, I am much more progressive than my more backward-thinking colleagues. I buy my white sheets at Bloomingdales. Mail order. But even I, a liberal, have become weary of the constant demands. The leveling of our academic standards. Women's Studies and now Queer Studies. Where it will end nobody knows.

EVA STARR: Women's Studies were necessary to challenge the dominant patriarchal discourse.

ANTHONY HALL: Yes. Right.

EVA STARR: So is that the only reason you called me? To complain about Women's Studies?

ANTHONY HALL: No Professor Starr. I've called you in to ask for your resignation.

EVA STARR: (*Rises.*) Resignation?

ANTHONY HALL: Yes. Ms. Starr, it has come to our attention that whole portions of your book, *Brothers, Atone!*, was lifted from the work of the French transvestite scholar, Charlene LaFreaque.
    (*Pause.*)

EVA STARR: (*Slowly sits down.*) Who told you?

ANTHONY HALL: It was an anonymous tip.

EVA STARR: (*Pause.*) I have an explanation. While I was writing the book, her open book was lying on the desk next to my laptop. I might have inadvertently transferred a few passages from her book to mine, Dean.

ANTHONY HALL: Inadvertently! My dear Ms. Starr. We found fifty lines from her book showing up in yours. Here is a page-by-page computer analysis complied by my staff.

(*Hands* EVA STARR *a sheet of paper. She examines it.*)

EVA STARR: (*Pause.*) How many people know about this?

ANTHONY HALL: We had to protect ourselves, Professor Starr. The newspapers are running the stories in tomorrow's editions.

(*She jumps up.*)

EVA STARR: What!!

ANTHONY HALL: The *San Francisco Chronicle*, the *Oakland Tribune*, *The Montclarion*, the *Contra Costa Times*, and the *San Jose Mercury News*.

EVA STARR: But my reputation—

ANTHONY HALL: We also felt obligated to inform the Tough Love Institute of your indiscretions. After all, the late Mr. Only was one of our most generous contributors.

EVA STARR: You didn't. How could you?

ANTHONY HALL: We had no choice, Ms. Starr.

EVA STARR: (*Standing, hands on hips.*) Well how am I going to become famous if I don't plagiarize? That's how to get ahead these days. This guy at the *New Republic*, Stephen Glass—nobody thought of giving him a book contract until he was caught plagiarizing. Stephen Glass's story was even made into a movie. And what about you and the rest of this faculty. The only difference between you, them, and me is that they give their sources credit. Footnote plagiarism. There hasn't been a single original theory that has arisen from this faculty since the school was founded one hundred years ago. And what about you, you been on the faculty for thirty years and you haven't published an article or a book. Why does publish or perish apply to everybody but you? I think I know why.

ANTHONY HALL: I'm sorry Ms. Starr. But the school is not going to change its mind. You will receive a nice severance package and the tipster who informed us of your intellectual transgressions will also be rewarded. Now, if you will excuse me. I have a luncheon engagement.

     (*Exits, hurriedly.*)

EVA STARR: Who could the anonymous tipster be? My ex-husband I'll bet. Jealousy. Here I am, my name in the newspapers, and where is he? Teaching at a community college in Texas. Or could it be my sister? All I'd hear about when growing up was Jadine. Jadine this. Jadine that. They all said that she'd succeed. Talented. Pretty. She was the one with all of the dates. Now she's in and out of the Betty Ford Clinic. Or maybe it's one of those horrid nationalists, the one who was made an honorary chieftain while on a trip to Africa. Now he sits at home all day, attired in a robe. He won't come out of the house unless one of his followers comes to his home and kisses his ring every morning. I know one thing. I'm not going to take this lying down. Most of my colleagues are parroting theories that did not originate with them. French. German. Attend any MLA convention and every paper includes the same jargon. So what is the difference between parroting and borrowing? One could say that parroting is cowardliness while borrowing without attribution takes boldness. Daring. And so what if they call it plagiarism. Look at all of the white people who have been caught plagiarizing from other authors over the last few years. Doris Kearns Goodwin. That fellow who worked for *The Boston Globe*, Mike Barnicle. He's on cable all day. Got his own show. David McCullough. An honored guest at the White House Literary Festival. What happened to them? Nothing. In fact, they received more fame and money than ever before. The words infamous and notorious no longer exist in the American dictionary. Janet Cooke and Jayson Blair continue to be criticized by the media. They neither borrowed nor plagiarized. They made up stories. They should be recognized for inventing fiction, instead of being disgraced. And what about Judith Miller? Who wasn't a reporter but a stenographer for members of the Bush Administration. She's going to make a million from her book deal. At least nobody died as a result of Jayson Blair's fibs. Judith Miller should be writing letters to the soldiers at Walter Reed Hospital for becoming little more than a journalistic shill for the Bush White House. Channeling their lies about Saddam having weapons of mass destruction. And oh yeah, what about James Frey. Author of *A Million Little Pieces*, a memoir that was largely made up of fibs. He even fooled Oprah. And how is he doing? A millionaire. Just got a new book contract. And what about Shakespeare? One of the greatest plagiarists of all time. And what about Bobby Dylan. And even the late Susan Sontag. A saint of the New York intellectual world. Plagiarizing Barthes and Laura Miller. And so whites who plagiarize are rewarded while we black plagiarists are ostracized and condemned. An injustice if there ever was one. I know what I'm going to do. I will see to it that black plagiarists have all the rights and privileges of white plagiarists. This will be my Rosa Parks moment.

(*Blackout.*)

ACT II

SCENE 7

(WADSWORTH *is asleep. His wife enters.*)

JUANITA: Wad, good news. Good news.
(WADSWORTH *wakes up.*)

WADSWORTH: Whaaaa. What?

JUANITA: One down and one to go.

WADSWORTH: What happened?

JUANITA: McKnutley was killed by a policeman, he—

WADSWORTH: (*Shocked*) McKnutley? That boy was killed? Hell, we had our disagreements—but—I mean he had his good points—

JUANITA: Get real, Wad. Don't you see, this narrows the field. You're on the short short list, now. Think of all of the money. The think tanks, the institutes, the lecture fees. You'll make millions. All we have to do is make one more disappear.

WADSWORTH: Yeah, you mean, there will be some more of those prepositions and things? I can go on C-Span and debate Jesse Jackson, Jr. and that Maxine Waters. She ain't got a bit of integrity. I'll show those two a thing or two.

JUANITA: You can bet on it, Wad. And I can go shopping again. They're having a great sale at Neiman Marcus.

WADSWORTH: Yes dear. But what about Eva Starr. How am I going to handle that competition?

WADSWORTH: Already taken care of. Read tomorrow's newspapers.
    (*Blackout.*)

ACT II

SCENE 8

(MARSE ONLY, JR. *and* JOHN FRIDAY *on stage.* WADSWORTH *enters.*)

WADSWORTH: I guess you called me here to tell me that I done won out. That I is the man who will now represent the Institute. That the Colorado thing is all but forgotten. Let bygones be bygones. What state we going to do now. Hope that it's on sea level.

JOHN FRIDAY: No more affirmative action prepositions, as you put it, for you.
(JOHN FRIDAY *and* MARSE ONLY, JR. *laugh.*)

WADSWORTH: What do you mean?

MARSE ONLY, JR.: We've decided to outsource the job.

WADSWORTH: (WADSWORTH *collars the white boy.*) Outsource. You mean somebody else gets the job after all I've done for you white folks? All the abuse I took, the name-calling, people calling me an Uncle Tom, mashing pies into my face, why I have a good mind to smack you—and you!
(WADSWORTH *gives a threatening look to* JOHN FRIDAY.)

JOHN FRIDAY: Don't look at me, I retire tomorrow.

(WAMU *enters.*)

MARSE ONLY, JR.: We've chosen Wamu.
(WADSWORTH *is shocked, angry. Starts pacing up and down.*)
He's young. He has humility. He speaks Standard English. And he
doesn't show up for receptions and drink all the whiskey and eat all
of the free food. Unlike you African Americans, these immigrants
are hardworking and devoted to American values.

WAMU: You have trained me well Mr. Wadsworth. I will always be
grateful to you.

WADSWORTH: Don't try to butter me up, you tree shrew. I put you
up in my house and fed you and you betray me like that. If it wasn't
for me, one of them African fellas would be having yo' ass for
breakfast.
(WADSWORTH *goes for a knife and starts toward* WAMU.)
Why immona cut—
(JOHN FRIDAY *and* MARSE ONLY, JR. *restrain him.*)

WADSWORTH: And to think I was thinking about adopting you—
what I fool I is.

WAMU: But we can become relatives in a way. We will have Juanita
in common. We can be . . . well . . . husbands-in-law. We can be
advocates of
(*Pause*)
same wife marriage.

WADSWORTH: (*Starts for* WAMU. WAMU *retreats.*) What you mean by
that, sucker?
(JUANITA *enters. She and* WAMU *embrace and kiss.* WADS-
WORTH *lunges for them, is restrained.*)

JUANITA: While you were out campaigning against affirmative action I was getting some action at home, and it was indeed so affirmative that I would say "yes, oh yes—"

> (*She and* WAMU *embrace again.* WADSWORTH *lunges again and has to be restrained with difficulty.*)

That's right. It's me and Wamu. He's a winner. You're a loser. Nobody wants you around anymore. You can go back to robbing graves.

> (*They laugh.* JUANITA *to others:*)

The only reason I married this reject was to get a green card. These African Americans, so nineteenth century. Still talking about the Middle Passage. The chains. The whips. The many thousand gone. Boring.

> (*They all laugh except* WADSWORTH *and* JOHN FRIDAY.)

WAMU: The only reason they were captured was because they were docile. Cowardly.

> (JUANITA, JOHN FRIDAY, *and* WADSWORTH *glare at* WAMU.)

I mean—

> (*changing the subject*)

Look! I taught your wife a dance we do in Africa. It's called the Mukulumuke. It goes like this—

> *Does brief snakelike motion.* JUANITA *imitates him.* WADSWORTH *lunges at the two again and has to be restrained. Finally calms down.*)

JOHN FRIDAY: Here are the plane tickets for you both.

> (*Hands plane tickets to* JUANITA *and* WAMU.)

MARSE ONLY, JR.: You will have a tough schedule in New York. Fox News, a luncheon at the Manhattan Institute. A debate with Cornel West at Town Hall, and a call-in with Rush Limbaugh.

JUANITA: I can't wait to get to Saks Fifth Avenue.

> (WAMU *and* JUANITA *exit arm-in-arm followed by* MARSE ONLY, JR. WADSWORTH *stands at stage center. A hangdog expression on his face.* JOHN FRIDAY *approaches him and puts an arm around him.*)

JOHN FRIDAY: You should have quit while you were ahead, Wadsworth. After 209 passed, you were at the top. But then you kept going back for more glory. Washington State, Michigan, Florida. Colorado was your Waterloo. The irony was that somebody like you—someone in the body parts business—didn't detect the irony.

WADSWORTH: What irony is you talking about?

JOHN FRIDAY: You, McKnutley, and Starr. Your brains were for hire. While you were formerly making money selling body parts. Marse was selling your own body part. Yours and McKnutley and Eva's. You pressed your luck by going back to the well too many times. Finally, the well just dried up. But knowing you, you'll connive yourself into some new kind of action.

WADSWORTH: Dried up, huh. Look to me like you is the one who is dried-up. For me, it was strictly cash. Reciting some old BS lines about personal responsibility was an easy way of making money for me and keeping my wife in jewelry and fast cars. All I wanted for those white audiences I spoke before to do for me was to open they checkbooks. You think I cared anything about those prepositions? I was perfectly willing to back any preposition those white folks put before me as long as it meant that a good living was to be had. Senators and Congressmen respecting me. Five-thousand-dollar lunches with some of the most powerful white folks in the country. The delectable juices of filet mignon dripping down my lips.

> (*Smacks his lips.*)

Whiskey flowing like Niagara. On a first-name basis with people like Newt Gingrich. He and I are alike. He criticized Clinton for getting down with Monica, yet he had a skeezer on the side himself. He's making a comeback and so will I. But you—you fetching his cologne, polishing his boots, and making his dinner reservations. You wasn't nothing but a flunky for both the father and the son. Executive Assistant. That's a laugh.

JOHN FRIDAY: I still have some surprises up my sleeve. Stay tuned.
> (JOHN FRIDAY *exits.* WADSWORTH *is left on the stage.*)

WADSWORTH: (*Muttering*) Corny Negro.
> (EVA STARR *enters.*)

EVA STARR: Where's everybody?

WADSWORTH: Wamu and my wife have gone to New York.

EVA STARR: Wamu, that houseboy of yours?

WADSWORTH: They chose him to represent the Tough Love Institute.

EVA STARR: What!

WADSWORTH: Yes. Wamu Rudurudu. And I'm the one who taught him the right-wing values that qualified him as a candidate. Oh, I could kick myself. Not only did he steal my ideas, but he stole my wife.

EVA STARR: (*Ignores this last comment.*) They chose a houseboy over me? One of the handful of academics to understand deconstructionism?

WADSWORTH: But you were convicted of plai—plai—of copying folks? It was in the newspapers.

EVA STARR: What, you haven't heard? I won my case. Now it's possible for blacks to plagiarize as much as white folks. Why I'm going to become as famous as all of the white plagiarists. Maybe I'll get my own daytime show. Get invited to the White House.

WADSWORTH: I have a confession to make—

EVA STARR: What's that?

WADSWORTH: Juanita was the one who tipped the Dean off about you stealing that Frenchwoman's work.

EVA STARR: Forget about it. We have work to do. But first, let's take care of Wamu.

WADSWORTH: How we going to do that?

EVA STARR: You'll see. Just so happens that I have some connections in Nigeria.
   (*Blackout.*)

ACT II

SCENE 9

NEWSCASTER: Welcome back to *The Eye*, from San Jose. Our guest is a man who has been in the news this week. John Friday. As you all may have read, Mr. Friday was instrumental in the Attorney General's indictment of Michael Chen and Marse Only, Jr. of Only Pharmaceuticals for obstruction of justice, extortion, racketeering, and arson. Friday, who posed as Mr. Only's valet, began cooperating with the Government, which was investigating Only Pharmaceuticals' testing drugs in Africa, Haiti, and among the nation's homeless. The Attorney General has also charged the company with arson in its attempt to cover up its crimes. Mr. Friday, welcome to *The Eye*, from San Jose.

JOHN FRIDAY: Glad to be here. But one thing. I wasn't Marse Only, Jr.'s valet. My real title was Executive Assistant.

NEWSCASTER: Sorry. Mr. Friday, when did the government ask your cooperation in bringing down Only Pharmaceuticals?

JOHN FRIDAY: The government didn't contact me. I contacted them. I was about to retire but after I told them that I overheard Marse and Michael—

NEWSCASTER: The company manager—

JOHN FRIDAY: They were discussing the government's investigation of Poxin. Scores of blacks in Africa and Haiti had died as a result of taking these pills. Others were stricken with slurred speech and brain damage. They talked about shredding the papers and getting rid of the hard drives and e-mails that would implicate them. I gave this information to the Attorney General. The Attorney General asked me to stay on and work for them so that the state could compile evidence. When they hired some out-of-towners to burn the evidence, thinking that they were in the clear, they didn't count on my backing up the files. Sometimes they would speak as though I weren't even in the room.

NEWSCASTER: Where did you learn the skills to retrieve the files?

JOHN FRIDAY: My kid is studying computer science at Hampton University. He hipped me to some things. So when they burned the evidence, I was able to turn what I had saved over to the Attorney General's office.

NEWSCASTER: Marse Only, Jr.'s father had the reputation for being a member of the far right. People have asked, how could a black man like you work for such a person?

JOHN FRIDAY: Only was much more complicated than that. He grew up the hard way. An orphan. Worked his way through schools by doing janitorial jobs. Got a degree in chemistry and gained a foothold in the biochemical industry. Made billions, until the stockholders forced him out and the corporation was subjected to a hostile takeover by his own son. Marse Only, Jr. That broke the old man's health. A generous soul if there ever was one, despite his kook side. Like Goldwater, his views weren't always predictable. He was full of contradictions, unlike these neocons for whom everything is black or white.

He felt that there was some kind of Jewish conspiracy ruining the West, yet the CEO of his corporation and all of his accountants were Jewish. He was a creationist, but established chairs at universities for the study of evolution. Homophobic, but when it was revealed that one of his top executives was gay, he kept him on. Believed that blacks were inferior to whites, but would always talk about my smarts. "John, that's a brilliant idea. Why didn't I think of that?" he'd say. He used to entertain us with those ribald jokes of his. Would have us in stitches. Though he was devoted to a bunch of Grassy Knoll-type theories, he was a good boss. Built the Tough Love Foundation, dedicated to ending what he felt was the country's slide toward socialism. But after Mr. Only died his son took over. The old man would never have put drugs on the market that hadn't undergone rigorous testing in trials. The son didn't give a damn. For him there wasn't a difference between a black and a test rat. He was all out for profit. Plus, he brought in all of these advisors—psychiatrists who played along with the deal for profits. As you saw in the newspapers, a number of psychiatrists were also indicted along with Only and others. The psychiatrists were charged with receiving kickbacks from the drug companies. Some as much as forty five thousand per year for steering blacks into dangerous antidepressant drugs manufactured by Only Pharmaceuticals while recommending talk therapy for white middle-class people. They did this by diagnosing blacks with schizophrenia while delivering a milder diagnosis to whites. I think that we should begin a watchdog group—one that would keep tabs on how blacks and Hispanics are treated by the psychiatric industry. I've done a little research. Dig this. Have you ever heard of a man named Benjamin Rush?

NEWSCASTER: No.

JOHN FRIDAY: Well Rush was a psychiatrist who said that the color of blacks was caused by an inherited disease called "negritude." He said that it was derived from leprosy. In 1918, an advocate of eugenics—that's the pseudoscience that divides races into stocks like animals with blacks and others regarded as a lower stock—Dr. Paul Popenoe said that the IQ of blacks was determined by the amount of "white blood" they possessed. The lighter-skinned the black was the higher the IQ. In the 1950s, psychologist Lewis Terman said that poor children can never be educated and should never be allowed to reproduce. In 1994, Charles Murray and Richard Herrnstein's book, *The Bell Curve*, a book that has influenced public attitudes towards blacks, argued that blacks were "genetically disabled." That's why Katrina was treated with indifference by the Bush Administration. Instead of burning the "genetically damaged," which was the policy of the Nazis, we let them drown. Let natural disasters happen to them without coming to their rescue. But you can't blame everything on the Republicans, who have put an embargo on the subsistence needs of the poor. Black infant mortality has risen as a result of Clinton's welfare reform bill.

NEWSCASTER: You mean to tell me that those attitudes of nineteenth century psychologists and psychiatrists persist to this day?

JOHN FRIDAY: Yes. Not only are psychiatrists cooperating with the drug companies, psychologists are designing the torture techniques for prisoners at Guantánamo. Prisoners who haven't been charged with anything. I'm beginning to think that the AIDS virus originated in a Philadelphia smallpox experiment that went horrendously wrong.

NEWSCASTER: Isn't that a conspiracy theory?

JOHN FRIDAY: Given the treatment of blacks and Hispanics by the medical profession I wouldn't put it past them. Ever heard of James Marion Sims?

NEWSCASTER: No.

JOHN FRIDAY: He is called the "Father of American Gynecology." He sought to improve the health of white women by conducting dangerous experiments on slave women during surgeries for which they received no anesthetic. These surgeries were excruciatingly painful.

NEWSCASTER: You've received an award from a foundation that sponsors whistle-blowers. What do you plan to do with it?

JOHN FRIDAY: With my gift from the anonymous donors, I plan to begin a watchdog group. People who will keep an eye on this far right agenda dressed up in a lab coat and Brooks Brothers suit. Look at it this way. If the caretakers of the American soul are corrupt, what hope is there for us?

NEWSCASTER: I thought that you were one of these black conservatives. You sound like a populist.

JOHN FRIDAY: I may be a black conservative but I ain't no Nazi. Why do you think that these right-wing people and their colored stooges insist upon a color-blind school system and not a color-blind police force, a color-blind medical and psychiatric profession, a color-blind mortgage-lending industry? It's because they perceive the commingling of white and black students as a genetic threat to those whom they deem to be members of a master race.

Look at that last Supreme Court decision on school integration. The Louisville and Seattle cases. Arguing on behalf of the plaintiffs was a member of the Pacific Legal Foundation. Where does the Pacific Legal Foundation get its money from? The Bradley Foundation, which finances studies purporting to show the blacks as a genetically damaged people. Sure I'm all for a color-blind society but color blindness shouldn't just end at the schoolhouse door.

NEWSCASTER: Thank you very much Mr. Friday. Our next guests are Wadsworth Wyums and Eva Starr, former members of the right-wing Tough Love Institute.

> (*As* JOHN FRIDAY *exits,* EVA STARR *and* WADSWORTH *enter to be interviewed. They exchange greetings.*)
> (WADSWORTH *and* EVASTARR'*s attire should change here to indicate that they have moved to the left. They both wear berets and leather jackets.* WADSWORTH'*s jacket is open and so we see a T-shirt with Che Guevara's picture.*)

NEWSCASTER: Our next guests have co-authored a book that's climbing to the top of the Bestseller's list. They have received an advance of $500,000

> (*Both grin widely.*)

to write about their horrid experiences as unwitting captives of the far-right Tough Love Institute, which was financed by Only Enterprises, the global conglomerate.

> (*To pair of interviewees*)

Congratulations on your success.

EVA STARR & WADSWORTH: Thank you!

NEWSCASTER: How is the movie adaptation going?

WADSWORTH: They trying to get Denzel to play me. But all the leading black male actors want the role so Denzel is going to have a lot of competition.

NEWSCASTER: And Eva, who will play you?

EVA STARR: I think that Angela Bassett will play me.

NEWSCASTER: You just received some more good news.

EVA STARR: That's right, John Wilkes Booth College has agreed to settle my lawsuit. Now, black plagiarists have as much rights as white plagiarists. A victory for equal protection under the law. I got some extra money from the Dean. He addressed me as "dear," a clear reflection of his sexist nature. And I wasn't surprised that the Dean and the President of the college were found drunk and driving under the influence last night on the way to their little hideaway. Everybody knew they were lovers except her husband.

NEWSCASTER: Mr. Wyums, what has been the reaction of your former conservative allies to your conversion to the left?

WADSWORTH: Well, they is very unhappy with me of course, but I had to follow my conscience. I got tired of being the black front man for those affirmative reaction prepositions. I had Eva read them prepositions to me while we was waiting in the green room. Those things was bad. Hell, the black kids have to go to schools that is underfunded, where they have teachers who don't have credentials and where the teachers who take an interest in them have to buy the textbooks, and where the kids have to take turns learning. How is they expected to compete with the suburban schools which is much more richer? Some of these kids go to college through affirmative reaction and they catch up. You wouldn't have no Willie Brown and Colin Powell or Condoleezza Rice if it wasn't for affirmative reaction. Now let me ask these conservationists one thing.
(*Turning to the camera*)
Why do you all praise Colin Powell and the other officers who rose through the ranks because of affirmative reaction but oppose affir-

mative reaction for these kids? Is you only for affirmative reaction when the black man is protecting you by putting his behind in the line of fire? Also, I'll let you and your audience in on a little secret. You know that body parts operation that I had? I was gettin' a little affirmative reaction on the side myself. The medical schools had to take organs and limbs from me exclusive. But now, I is seen the light. Like Comrade Lenin said, capitalism will provide the rope with which to hang itself, and me and Eva is the ones who is tightening that rope. Ain't that right, Eva.

EVA STARR: That's right, Comrade Wyums. Here I was thinking that my brother was the enemy when the monster that threatens us all is international global imperialism.

> (WADSWORTH *laughs.* NEWSCASTER *and* EVA STARR *glare at him.*)

NEWSCASTER: Mr. Wadsworth, now that you've switched sides, do you see any difference between the right and the left?

EVA STARR: Well, I—

WADSWORTH: I'll answer that one Eva if you don't mind.
> (EVA STARR *glares at him.*)

WADSWORTH: Though I don't regret leaving the right, the receptions that the right had was much more better. At these left-wing receptions you lucky to get some cheese and crackers and they always have these grapes. You rarely get something to drink. You have to settle for this boring mineral water. At these right-wing millionaires' functions you get some sumptuous something to eat. Sometimes you get a steak
> (*Gestures*)
this big. And the whiskey be just a flowing. Sometimes I'd drink

so much that I'd leave these receptions on unsteady feet. My wife would have to help me home.

NEWSCASTER: Speaking of your wife, have you heard from her since your houseboy Wamu Rudurudu was taken to the Hague?

WADSWORTH: Well she returned to Jamaica, I guess.

NEWSCASTER: How did you find out that he wasn't a street urchin from Nigeria, but wanted for war crimes in Sierra Leone?

WADSWORTH: Eva can answer that one

EVA STARR: His story didn't add up. We did a little checking and found out that he was a fugitive and came into the country illegally. They're going to begin trying him in The Hague. Let's hope that he receives a fair trial. The poor brother was confused. He wasn't a rebel. He was financed by the imperialists who are raising mercenary armies in order to exploit African countries for their resources.

NEWSCASTER: Thank you Wadsworth Wyums and Eva Starr, two former members of the Tough Love Institute, who have written a book about their exploitation by that organization and the far right.

WADSWORTH: Wait . . . wait . . .

NEWSCASTER: Mr. Wyums, you have something else to say?
> (WADSWORTH *rises and begins singing, "My Way."* NEWS-CASTER *and* EVA STARR *exit while he's singing. After he ends the song and takes a bow, the stage goes dark.*)

CURTAIN

ISHMAEL REED is the author of over twenty-five books—including *Mumbo Jumbo*, *The Last Days of Louisiana Red*, and *Yellow Back Radio Broke-Down*. He is also a publisher, television producer, songwriter, radio and television commentator, lecturer, and has long been devoted to exploring an alternative black aesthetic: the trickster tradition, or "Neo-Hoodooism" as he calls it. Founder of the Before Columbus Foundation, he taught at the University of California, Berkeley for over thirty years, retiring in 2005. In 2003, he received the coveted Otto Award for Political Theatre.